China's Reforms
and Reformers

ALFRED K. HO

Westport, Connecticut
London

Library of Congress Cataloging-in-Publication Data

Ho, Alfred Kuo-liang, 1919–
   China's reforms and reformers / Alfred K. Ho.
      p. cm.
   Includes bibliographical references and index.
   ISBN 0–275–96080–3 (hardcover : alk. paper)
   1. China—Politics and government—1949–
2. Communists—China—Biography. I. Title.
   DS777.75.H62 2004
   951.05′092′2—dc22   2003027469

British Library Cataloguing in Publication Data is available.

Library of Congress Catalog Card Number: 2003027469
ISBN: 0–275–96080–3

First published in 2004

Praeger Publishers, 88 Post Road West, Westport, CT 06881
An imprint of Greenwood Publishing Group, Inc.
www.praeger.com

Printed in the United States of America

The paper used in this book complies with the
Permanent Paper Standard issued by the National
Information Standards Organization (Z39.48–1984).

10 9 8 7 6 5 4 3 2 1

Contents

Acknowledgments

The author is grateful to Laura Fineman, his daughter, and Mrs. Ethel Snow for editing the manuscript. Their patience, effort and expertise are greatly appreciated. The author is also indebted to Mr. Carl Snow, her husband, for his input to the editing. The author thanks Marjorie, his wife, for her part in typing and proofreading.

This book is dedicated to the author's teachers and mentors: President John Leighton Stuart, Dean Gideon Chen, Michael Lord Lindsey, and Professor Ralph Lapwood of Yenching University at Beijing; Professor George Taylor and Professor Frank Schultheis of the University of Washington, Seattle; Professor William S. Carpenter of Princeton University; Professor David N. Rowe of Yale University; Professor Soren Frankian of Los Angeles City College; Professor H. M. Somers and Professor William R. Allen of the University of California at Los Angeles; and Professor Robert S. Bowers of Western Michigan University, Kalamazoo. The author is indebted to them for giving him guidance, training, and assistance.

Introduction

From 1920 to now, there has been in China a struggle involving hundreds of millions of people and touching on every corner of the country. It was a struggle between China and Japan and, within China, between farmers and landlords, between the Communists and the local militia supporting the landlords, between the Nationalists and the warlords, between the Communists and the Nationalists, and, within the Communists, between the reformers and the fundamentalists. These struggles were fought to the finish with no holds barred, thus making this period one of the bloodiest episodes in Chinese history.

It took the utmost determination, devotion, and courage and the willingness to make sacrifices to make it possible for the reformers to win at last, as many had lost their loved ones or suffered bodily injuries or lost their own lives in the process. They had literally gone through hell.

The reformers were able to put through a program of reforms involving various aspects of activities in the country: agriculture, industries, technology, military affairs, the rule of law, and foreign relations. The book is intended to examine these reforms.

To bring to the reader the reality of the human endeavors in this period of struggle, this book tells the life stories of some of the reformers in the course of historical events. These stories show who the reformers were, what they did, how they conducted themselves, and what prices they paid in these struggles. From the combined life stories of these people, a broad picture can be pieced together to illustrate the social change of China in this period and to give the historical events a human touch.

There have been scanty accounts of the life stories of these reformers in Western literature, so the author used mainly Chinese sources to bring the stories to light in the West for the first time.

It is lucky for China that the reformers have won. Now China is militarily prepared, economically prosperous, politically stable, and secure in foreign relations.

This book contains chapters on the revolution, the wars, and the various aspects of development and reforms.

Western readers are sometimes confused by Chinese names. A guide to personal names is provided at the end of this book as an aid.

Notes are given at the end of each chapter, and there is a selected bibliography at the end of the book.

CHAPTER 1

The Revolution

Before Communist rule, five classes of people existed in the traditional society: from the top down, the gentry, farmers, workers, merchants, and soldiers. The gentry were the intellectuals from whom officials were recruited to help the rulers manage the affairs of the government at the central and local levels. The lower classes of people might advance into the gentry by getting educated by private instructors and by passing the civil service examinations operated by the government. Therefore, some interclass mobility existed. Landlords dominated farmers, collecting rents from farmers and paying taxes to the government.

Income was unevenly distributed among society. In hard times, the poor would starve or be driven by poverty into crimes and illegal activities. They would become bandits or start local uprisings. To suppress the poor, the government maintained a military force and local militia. Soldiers were recruited from the poor and were used against the poor. Local uprisings by the poor usually would not last long because it was difficult to organize the poor to obtain the necessary resources and manpower to sustain the struggle against government troops.

The revolution led by the Communists brought about a complete turnover of the traditional society, in Chinese terms, *fan shen*. The working class of farmers, workers, merchants, and soldiers became the ruling class, and the intellectuals were degraded.

To eliminate extreme wealth, people working for the government received pay commensurate with their jobs, which were carefully classified. The military had ranks, and the civilians had grades. People with equal ranks or grades would be paid the same with some consideration of the location of work and the working conditions. The gap between the pays of the highest rank and the lowest rank was fixed large enough to provide incentive but not too large to cause a severely uneven distribution of income. The guiding principle was egalitarianism.

To make the new society work, individuals were to go through reeducation for a fundamental change of their life purposes to replace selfish gains with a devotion to serve the common good of the community. The process was like a revival meeting of some churches and was referred to as "brainwashing," or *xi nau* in Chinese. So-called May 7 schools were used for reeducation.

College professors and students were no longer of a privileged class. They were sent to farms a few months a year to work with farmers.

The first stage of the Communist revolution lasted from 1920 to 1934 and the second from 1935 to 1976.

In the first stage, the party was led by Zhou Enlai and agents sent over by the Communist International (the Comintern) from the Soviet Union and was supported by the Soviet government. The headquarters of the party was in Shanghai. When conflicts started between the Communists and the Nationalists, Shanghai was no longer safe, so the headquarters moved to Ruijin in Jiangxi Province. The strategy was to raise armies to stage urban uprisings with the hope of gaining nationwide support from the workers following the pattern of the revolution in the Soviet Union.

In the second stage, Mao Zedong replaced the Comintern agents as the leader of the party. He led the party in agrarian reform in rural areas.

THE REVOLUTION UNDER ZHOU ENLAI

Ever since 1911, when the Manchu dynasty was overthrown, to now, China has gone through difficult periods of political development. A statesman was needed who enjoyed the confidence and respect of the people and could keep a strong hand on the helm of the nation to guide it to its destiny. That man was found in Zhou Enlai, a leader of the Communist Party from its beginning.

Zhou Enlai was a sophisticated, educated man, friendly to all and making no enemies. He had a keen mind and was a good listener. He had his beliefs and ideas, but he was broad-minded enough to appreciate the opinions of others. He was polite, and he managed to establish contacts with many groups. This helped him search for consensus on controversial subjects and to find a way to maintain unity by bringing together different factions. To keep his leadership, he had to be on the winning side.

Zhou Enlai's family originated in Shaoxing District in Zhejiang Province, which is south of Jiangsu Province, where the Yangtze River flows into the sea. Shaoxiang, located on the coast of the East Sea and in the Chiantang River delta near Hangzhou on the railway trunk line, is an important commercial center and is famous for its enterprising business-people and establishments.

Zhou is from a prominent family in the district. Members of the family pursued careers as either gentry scholars or businessmen. Zhou Enlai's branch consisted of scholars. Traditionally, students were taught by tutors. They studied the classics and were trained in the legal and literary styles of writing and the art of calligraphy. They would then qualify as masters by passing the government-operated nationwide examinations at the lo-cal, provincial, and national levels. They would then join the bureaucracy, working for the government, or the gentry, working for private concerns as secretaries, consultants, accountants, or assistants.

Zhou Enlai was born on March 5, 1898, in Shaoxing. The family moved to Shanyang District, Huaian Prefecture, Jiangsu Province, when Zhou Enlai's grandfather was appointed the district magistrate. The family was well-to-do and prominent.

Zhou Enlai's father was a nonachiever and had a number of odd jobs, and the family was in poverty. Zhou Enlai's mother (née Wan) had three sons, and he was the eldest. One of his uncles was ill and about to die without producing any offspring, a predicament considered a major sin. Zhou Enlai was adopted by this uncle. After the uncle's death, Zhou Enlai went with his aunt (née Chen), now his foster mother, to live with her wealthy family in Chinghe District. Zhou Enlai was miserable, as he was mistreated by his cousins as a poor relative. Luckily, his foster mother was devoted to him. She supervised his studies and taught him how to deal with people.

Misfortunes hit Zhou Enlai again. In 1907, his natural mother died, and in 1908, his foster mother died. His father left him and the two younger brothers and went to Hubei to look for work. At age 10, Zhou Enlai took on the responsibilities as the head of the household. He did not feel wel-come to stay on with the foster mother's family, so he took his two broth-ers and returned to his home in Huaian. They lived by borrowing money or by selling or pawning family belongings, but they still put up a front to maintain the family's social status. On the whole, Zhou Enlai had a miserable boyhood.[1]

In 1910, when Zhou Enlai was 12 years old, a prosperous uncle in Liao-ning in northeastern China sent for him and put him in a modern grade school. Here his formal education started. This was in the tradition of the extended family system in China. Under the head of the household, all brothers lived together even after they were married unless their jobs required them to move out. After the head of the household had died, the brothers families might stay together or move away, but they were still held responsible for one another. They were obligated to look after any nephews or nieces in times of need. If a promising youngster needed support, relatives would support him in his training and education, even in going abroad if need be. That is how many Chinese immigrants and students have come to the United States. China does not have developed unemployment insurance or social security systems; rather, the extended family is the social system that provide private resources to fill such needs.

Modern schools started in the 1910s in China and were modeled after those of the West in their curricula but with emphasis on Chinese history and literature. Special attention was paid to the training of students for their physical well-being and moral character. Students attended classes six hours a day, six days a week.

Zhou Enlai, similar to the majority of students, was nationalistic, and he assumed as his responsibility the bringing about of a modern, prosperous, and strong China.

At school, Zhou Enlai was small with a southern accent, and he was often bullied by bigger boys. He made friends with schoolmates more his stature, and they formed a gang to defend themselves. He was a natural leader. By doing this, he felt he was righting a wrong. This strategy emerged later as a characteristic of his foreign policy. China would not bully other nations but instead would side with the developing nations, binding together to face the superpowers.

Politically, the faculty consisted of two groups: one was for revolution, believing that China needed a basic change in social structure and that China had to start from scratch if planning to modernize; the other was for gradual change that would keep the basic culture and social structure intact.

In 1913, at the age of 15, Zhou Enlai's uncle found a job in Tianjin and brought Zhou Enlai to the city with him. This is the first time that Zhou Enlai was exposed to the urban environment of a metropolis. He was enrolled in Nankai High School, one of the best in the country. For four years he stayed in the dormitory, and these were the best four years in his life. He not only became physically strong but also received an excellent education. English was taught as a second language. Most textbooks were translations of books in English. Toward the end of the four-year program, textbooks in English were used, as the students had learned enough of that language to get along.

In order not to cause a financial burden to his uncle, Zhou Enlai lived a frugal life. His clothing included a long white gown for the summer and a black cotton quilted gown topped by a blue outer gown for the winter.

In school, he excelled in Chinese literature and mathematics. He was good in the literary style of writing and composed Chinese poems well. He was a model student and was befriended by the president of the school, Dr. Zhang Polin, on whom he often called to have long chats.

By the time Zhou Enlai graduated, he had the preliminary makings of a great man. He was said to be modest, honest, friendly, and mild in temperament and always did his best in school and community affairs.

An interesting incident in his high school life occurred when he played the female lead in a student play. He was not a transvestite; rather, in the 1910s, China was puritanical, such that actors and actresses were not allowed to appear on stage together. Stage performances were done by either all-male troupes or all-female troupes, In each troupe, some performers would have to take the opposite-sex parts. Zhou Enlai performed in an all-male troupe and because of his good looks was assigned a female role. Eventually, this ban was removed, and now in China actors and actresses perform together. In Japan, however, all-female troupes still perform, with actresses taking the male roles.[2]

In 1917, Zhou Enlai graduated from Nankai High School. Many of his friends had gone to Japan for college because at that time China had not developed any top-notch colleges. After some 50 years of modernization that started in 1860 with the restoration, Japan could boast a few fine colleges. In September 1917, Zhou Enlai borrowed money from friends to make his journey to Japan to join some of his schoolmates. His plan was to learn Japanese and prepare for the college entrance examination in half a year with the hope that he could pass the examination in March. If he could do so, then scholarships from the Chinese government would be available to support him in his studies. The examination had oral and written parts. It turned out that half a year was not enough time to learn the Japanese language, and he failed the examination. After another four months of study at more than 13 hours a day, he tried again in July, this time at another college. Again he failed. With his funds exhausted, he returned to China in August 1918. Personally, this was a big blow for him, but it was not bad for China, as he could later turn his attention to a political career playing a role in China's revolution and reforms.[3]

At that time, Japan was a budding capitalistic country. Zhou Enlai's disappointment in Japan somehow turned him against capitalism.

After Zhou Enlai returned to China, an earthshaking event took place on May 4, 1919: the May 4 movement. At the end of World War I, China emerged as a country among the victors, but the Paris Convention did not award China with any favorable treatment; rather, it allowed Japan to take over the naval base at Qingdao and other concessions that Germany had acquired from China. This started a protest involving some 20,000 people. The protestors burned down the home of one official and beat up another official who was involved in the negotiation. The government arrested some 30 students. Hundreds of student gathered and marched to the president's house demanding the release of students arrested and requesting that the government not sign the Paris Convention. Troops were dispatched to put down the uprising. Many students were beaten up, and some were arrested. This movement spread throughout the country and gained wide support from the general public. This marked the beginning of a nationwide nationalistic movement in China. At that time, students were organized in two groups—one for boys and the other for girls—as it was still the custom that boys and girls were not to associate with one another in public. Zhou Enlai was among the leaders of the boys' group and a Miss Deng Yingchao of the girls' group. Eventually the two groups merged into one, and the tradition of sexual segregation began to break down, and boys and girls met in public with increasing frequency.

During one of the protests, Miss Deng Yingchao was wounded and Zhou Enlai arrested. The arrested students staged a hunger strike and demanded a public trial. They were tried and given various terms of imprisonment. After serving his term, Zhou Enlai was released. Up to that time, he had been considering two approaches to modernize China—revolution or gradual reform—and this experience pushed him to the position of revolutionary.

In September 1919, Nankai High School was converted to Nankai University. Zhou Enlai enrolled in the university as a first-class student. He was widely recognized as a promising young leader for the new China. The university sponsored him and another student to participate in the work–study program in France. The lawyer who defended Zhou Enlai in court did not charge him any fees but instead gave him $500 for his trip. The leading newspaper in Tianjin signed him up as a correspondent and would pay him for his articles sent back from France. He was much better prepared this time than he was on his trip to Japan. In October 1920, he left China for France.[4]

Zhou Enlai traveled in France and in 1921 made a trip to England. He wanted to compare the system in the West with that in China, hoping to discover the strengths and weaknesses of the two and to discover Western policies or institutions that China could borrow to use to modernize the country. He was rather disappointed. World War I crippled Europe, where the economy was in a poor shape and unemployment rampant. The England he saw in 1921 was in the midst of a long strike by coal miners.

Some 2,000 Chinese students had been sent to France by the Sino-France Education Association to participate in the work–study program. The program, however, was not well planned. The association assumed that France was prosperous and that the students could find work easily and would need only a small stipend to tide them over for a brief period; eventually, the students would become financially self-sufficient. In reality, most of them could not find work. Some who found jobs in factories were doing heavy work for half the pay of French workers or took odd jobs in the city, such as shining shoes on street corners, peeling potatoes in restaurants, or collecting garbage. Before long, their small stipends stopped, and the students became despondent. A group of students marched to the Chinese legation demanding help. Chinese officials sought help from the French government but were not successful, as many French workers were out of work. A scuffle ensued between Chinese students and the local police. Many Chinese students were detained for a while, and some were deported back to China.

After World War I, the revolution led by the Communist Party succeeded in Russia by overthrowing the imperial government, and the Soviet Union was born. This event, together with Marxist ideology, had a tremendous influence on a group of intellectuals in China. In 1920, the Chinese Communist Party was formed under the leadership of Li Dazhao, a professor at Peking University. In 1921, the Youth Corps of the Chinese Communist Party was formed in Europe, and many of the poverty-stricken Chinese students joined, including Zhou Enlai. They became the first generation of party members, and many of them later became prime ministers, ministers, and generals in the People's Republic of China.[5]

In 1911, a revolution began in China under the leadership of Dr. Sun Yatsen advocating a "doctrine of three peoples": of the people, by the people, and for the people—in other words nationalism, democracy, and socialism. At this time, the Manchu, a minority group from the northeastern region, ruled China over the majority Han, who wanted to overthrow the Manchu to regain control of the country. The Manchu army had degenerated, and the forces of the central government fell to the Han, Governors of the various provinces declared independence and became the warlords of their regions. The Manchu dynasty ended when the emperor was forced to abdicate. In 1912, the Republic of China was formed and a parliament elected. That year, the Nationalist Party was formed under the leadership of Sun Yatsen and gained the majority of the seats in the newly elected parliament. But the warlords disbanded the parliament, and China suffered through a period of chaos in which the warlords constantly fought among themselves. Sun Yatsen, with the support of the warlords of Yunnan and Guangxi provinces gained a foothold in the Pearl River delta in Guangdung Province. He wanted to reunite China, and for that he needed a central army. He obtained assistance from the Soviet Union to establish the Whampoa Military Academy for the training of army officers. The Chinese Communist Party in Europe was ordered by the Soviet Union to return to China to collaborate with the Nationalists. In 1924, one group that included Zhou Enlai returned, and another group went to the Soviet Union for a period of training and then returned as well. Zhou Enlai was made a political instructor at the academy. An officer, Chiang Kaishek, who had been training in Japan and the Soviet Union, was made president of the academy.

A long friendship developed between Zhou Enlai and Miss Deng Yingchao, as they were student leaders collaborating in the May 4 movement in 1919. At that time, Zhou was 21 years old and Deng was 15. For years they had been corresponding with each other. In 1924, they were united in Guangzhou when Miss Deng was assigned there from Beijing. They fell in love and soon discovered that both were Communist Party members. The Nationalist Party had an open party membership, but the Communist Party had always been an underground organization; party membership was kept in secret and was known only to members of the same cell. In 1924, Zhou Enlai and Miss Deng were married. This was ideal because Zhou Enlai would not want to marry anyone but a Communist Party member for fear that family life would hinder his work. Now this marriage would give him support, making it possible for him to be totally devoted to his work.

Miss Deng's family originated in Zinyang District in Henan Province. She was born in 1904 in Nanning in Guangxi Province. Her father died when she was young, and her mother supported the family working as a tutor for a family. Miss Deng went to Beijing to study in 1913 and met Zhou Enlai in 1919.

This marriage, like many others at that time, marked a drastic break from the tradition. In the traditional puritanical society, to prevent premarital sex, young people were not allowed to mingle with one another. Young ladies seldom appeared in public. For public gatherings, such as attending temple services or going to the theater, the audience was divided into two sections: the males on the left and the females on the right. Young boys and girls could only eye one another but were not allowed to meet. Families, with the consent of the young couple (who were allowed to meet only briefly), would arrange the marriages. On the wedding night, the couple were almost strangers. If love could develop between them, it would have to do so after marriage. The traditional system did not ensure love or happiness in the family. By the 1920s, the old system broke down, most schools became coeducational. Boys and girls developed friendships, fell in love, and got married following the system in the West.[6]

The Zhou household was happy and harmonious, but Zhou Enlai was seldom at home. As a member of the Politburo, he was required to travel throughout Shanghai (where the headquarters was), to travel to Hong Kong (where he could meet overseas contingents), and to keep an eye on certain activities, such as strikes by workers, local uprisings, and battles against the Nationalists. The Nationalists had secret service agents assigned to capture, detain, or execute Communists. In taking these trips, Zhou was constantly in danger. He would disguise himself as a worker or a merchant. Each time on departure, he would say good-bye to his wife, not knowing whether he would return. His wife would not ask him why he had to go, where he was going, or how long he would be away for fear that she could be arrested and have the information extracted from her. This precarious way of life put tremendous stress on her, a heavy cross to bear her entire life.

In 1925, the Peasant Movement Training Institute was organized in

Guangzhou. Mao Zedong chaired some sessions teaching guerrilla warfare and agrarian reforms.

In 1925, Sun Yatsen died. The Nationalist government was established in Nanjing in 1926, and Chiang Kaishek began to consolidate his military command. Four armies were established. Chiang Kaishek gained the control of the First, Second, and Third Armies by expelling the Communist agents from the ranks, thus leaving only the Fourth Army, under Yeh Ting, controlled by the Communists.

In order to establish a military base to form a Communist government, attempts were made to stage uprisings in a number of cities. One of these attempts took place in Nanchang in Jiangxi Province in 1927 and was led by Zhou Enlai and several military men: Zhu De, Yeh Ting, Liu Bocheng, He Long, Pin Biao, and Nye Rungzhen.

These military men were officers of the Nationalist army, but really they were Communist Party members. The group held a meeting at the Grand Hotel, a prestigious establishment, instead of a secret hiding place. They succeeded in gaining control of the city but had to give it up to the superior Nationalist forces. There in Nanchang, the Red Army was born with the military commanders and Zhou Enlai as its founders. The Communist forces pushed south. Zhu De led his troops to Zinggangshan to join Mao Zedung, and the rest went farther south. They traveled through Jiangxi and Guangdong provinces and reached Shantou on the coast of the South Sea, hoping to establish a base with possible overseas support. But when the Nationalist forces arrived, they had to flee again. A local Communist agent, Yang Shihun, found a small sailboat, and the five of them—Zhou Enlai, Ye Ting, Nye Rungzhen, Yang, and the boatman—pushed out to the sea. Zhou was suffering from malaria and had a high fever. They put him in the bottom of the boat, which was enough to accommodate only one person, and the rest would have to stay on the deck. A strong gale and heaving sea caused the boat to rock violently. The four had to rope themselves tightly to the mast to prevent being washed into the ocean. They sailed westward along the coast. After two nights and a day of tossing and rocking, they finally arrived at Kowloon, a town on the coast separated by a strait from Hong Kong. Yang carried Zhou on his back to a friend's house where Zhou received medical treatment and recuperated.[7]

In 1927, Chiang Kaishek, after having gained military control of the major part of China, turned his attention to fighting the Communists and started several expeditions against the Communist strongholds.

To combat the Nationalists, the Communists developed some 13 armies spread over several provinces: Hubei, Hunan, Jiangxi, Anhui, Fujian, and Zechiang. Among others, the three major forces were the First Red Army under Xu Jishen in Hubei, the Second Red Army under He Lung in Hubei and Hunan, and the Fourth Red Army under Mao Zedung and Zhu De in Zinggangshan in Jiangxi.

In 1933, many officers at the Communist headquarters in Shanghai were arrested and then executed by the Nationalists. Shanghai was no longer a safe base. The headquarters was moved to Juijin in Jiangxi Province. In the same year, Chiang Kaishek went to Nanchang to direct the fourth expedition against the Communists in northern Jiangxi. Zhu De was assigned the commander to defend the area, and Zhou Enlai was the commissar.

At the front, Zhou's office was a small room. There was a square table, a student's desk, and a door taken from a farmer's house propped up on two benches for a bed. Military maps captured from the enemy were posted on the walls. A kerosene lamp was seldom used because of the shortage of kerosene. Instead, vegetable oil in a dish lit with a wick was used as a lamp by which Zhou could study the maps. Straw was spread on the bed in lieu of a mattress and a piece of a brick used for a pillow. At nighttime, Zhou covered himself with a thin blanket. A piece of rag was used for washing, as no towels were available. These were his normal living conditions both at the front or on field trips.[8]

After repeated defeats, the Communist forces greatly dissipated and had to pull back to Jinggangshan in Jiangxi, a hilly and heavily forested area under Mao Zedong and Zhu De. A fundamental mistake in the Communist strategy was revealed in that the Chinese Communist Party took orders from the Comintern in Moscow. Agents were dispatched to China to take command and direct operations. In 1934, the agents sent over were Bogu, in charge of political affairs, and Li De, in charge of military affairs. Zhou Enlai worked with both of them. The strategy was to stage urban uprisings with factory workers as the driving force and to hold cities as bases for the revolution following the Soviet Union's pattern. But China is different from the Soviet Union in that China is agrarian, and factory workers amount to a few percent of the population—not a dominant force for social change. Holding cities would be difficult considering the superior military force of the Nationalists. The Nationalists had a large infantry that was fully equipped with armaments and munitions and supported by an air force, a tank force, and mechanical units for the transportation of supplies; the Communist infantry had none of this. There were many defeats, including the loss of many lives and supplies.

In 1934, Chiang Kaishek started the fifth expedition, attacking Jinggangshan, the last stronghold of the Communists. He had met with some success in surrounding the area and began to move in, threatening to wipe out the Communist forces. The Communist Party decided to give up the base and break out from the encirclement to move west and eventually northwest to the border regions. This meant a fatal blow to the Comintern's strategy, as no large cities existed in the border regions from which to carry out the operation. The retreat to the west is referred to as the Long March, which eventually took 86,000 people on a long journey of 8,000 miles, going west through Jiangxi, Hunan, Guizhou, Yunnan, and Sichuwan provinces and north to Shaanxi Province.

Zhou's wife, Deng Yingchao, suffering from tuberculosis; she wanted to stay behind but was ordered by the party to join the journey.

On the Long March, Zhu De was the commanding general in the field, and a committee of three at the headquarters was directing the operations. This committee included Mao Zedong, Zhou Enlai, and Zhang Zhiaxiang. During the march, Zhou Enlai suffered from hepatitis and had to be carried on a litter (a hammock carried between two bearers).

In 1935, at a conference in Zunyi, a change in the party structure transferred authority from the Comintern to Mao Zedong, making him the leader of the party, a position that he maintained throughout his life. Mao had a different strategy. He wanted to start the revolution in the rural area using farmers as the driving force, as farmers formed the majority (80 percent) of the population and were exploited by the upper classes. Moreover, the task force of the Long March consisted of the armies under Mao and Zhu De. At the conference, people spoke up against the Comintern and especially against the agents Bogu and Li De. Zhou Enlai spoke at the conference in support of Mao and criticized himself for his part in working with the Comintern. Zhou realized that Mao's strategy was the only one to follow and that Mao was the leader of the party. Zhou pledged his support and loyalty to Mao, a dedication that never faltered throughout his life.[9]

THE REVOLUTION UNDER MAO ZEDONG

Mao Zedong was the leader of the Communist Party from 1935 to 1976 and was the president of the Republic of China from 1949 to 1959. His life was a continuous struggle against pressure from abroad and domestic problems at home.

Mao Zedong brought about a comprehensive revolution in China that would build a socialist state, provide the country with the ability to maintain peace and order at home and security in the world, begin making progress in agriculture with the maximum use of the land, and improve the infrastructure base for further economic progress.

In Chinese, the family name comes first, and the given name follows in an order different from that of names in the West. In the name Mao Zedong, Mao is the family name, meaning "feather," and Zedong is the given name, meaning "the one from the east side of the river." Mao led the life of a rebel. He wanted to break away from traditional China and start a new society. Mao was born December 26, 1893, in Shaoshan, Hunan Province. His father was a middle-income farmer with two years of schooling, and his mother was illiterate. At the age of eight, he started school. When he was 15, his father selected a girl, much older than Mao, for him to marry. The custom was that an older wife would be more able to take care of the husband and to raise the children, thus adding manpower to the farm. Mao could not refuse, so he married her, but later, after a long separation, the marriage was dissolved. In 1911, at age 18, Mao witnessed the revolution in Changsha, the capital of Hunan. This incident was one of the local uprisings that resulted in the overthrow of the Manchu dynasty and the ushering in of the Republic of China under the leadership of Sun Yatsen.

In his youth, Mao read extensively. His life was greatly influenced by three books: *Water Margin, The Maxims of Sunzi,* and *The Romance of the Three Kingdoms. Water Margin* was translated into English by Pearl Buck under the title *All Men Are Brothers.* It tells the story of a group of outlaws occupying the stronghold of Mount Liang, where they were out of the reach of government troops. They robbed the rich and helped the poor in the manner of Robin Hood in Sherwood Forest. *The Maxims of Sunzi,* written in 500 B.C., provides the tactics for a war of movement. Instead of fighting a positional war, the troops would retreat, zigzag, and circle back to confuse the enemy and attack only when the odds of victory were favorable. *The Romance of the Three Kingdoms* described the wars fought among these kingdoms, which partitioned China into one area in the north, one in the center, and one in the west. It was a story of heroes and their loyalty and bravery. Eventually, the north, with its geographical superiority, was triumphant.[10]

In 1915, when Yuan Shikai, a warlord, gained control of northern China, he proclaimed himself emperor. Sun Yatsen declared war on him, and Mao joined the army. Shortly after, Yuan was overthrown without a war. Mao resigned from the army and returned to his studies.

In 1918, Mao graduated from high school. The next year the revolution in Russia succeeded. The Comintern was organized and began its activities in China, preaching Marxism–Leninism in the country.

In Beijing, Mao obtained a position as an assistant to the head of the Peking University Library, Li Dazhao, and studied under Professor Yang Changqi, professor of ethics. The dean of the Faculty of Letters was Chen Duxiu. The three scholars wrote articles in a magazine titled *The New Youth,* which introduced Western ideas as well as Marxism–Leninism. Mao was greatly influenced by the three scholars.[11]

In 1919, Mao went to Shanghai to help set up a work–study program for Chinese students to go to France. Zhou Enlai and Deng Xiaoping were among those who went. Mao did not go because it was difficult for him to learn the French language.[12]

Within the year, Professor Yang died, and Mao returned to Beijing for the funeral. There he fell in love with Professor Yang's daughter, Yang Kaihui, and they were married in 1921, the year the Chinese Communist Party was born. Dean Chen Duxiu of Peking University, Mao Zedong, and Zhang Guotao were among the founders of the party.[13]

The two parties in China were the Communist Party and the Nationalist Party under Sun Yatsen and Chiang Kaishek. From 1922 to 1928, the two parties cooperated with each other.

In 1927, Mao organized an uprising in Hunan and attacked Changsha. It was hoped that the workers would rise in support following the pattern of revolution in Russia. The uprising failed. Because China had not yet been industrialized, workers constituted a very small fraction of the Chinese population and could not act as the driving force to revolutionize China. According to the Chinese tradition, workers were treated as members of the business family. Employers tended to be paternalistic, and the worker was loyal to the employer. Workers were given lifetime jobs. They seldom went on strikes, to say nothing of revolt. Mao left Changsha with about 1,000 men and went to Jinggangshan, a mountain area in Wenjiashi at the border of Hunan and Jiangxi. It was a refuge for outlaws. Here Mao realized his boyhood dream to lead the life of the heroes in the novel *Water Margin*. He did not bring his wife with him, believing that she would be safer hiding in the countryside.[14] When the Nationalist forces captured Changsha, Mao's wife and a younger sister were caught and executed.[15]

By this time, the Communist Party had two factions: the Moscow faction and the Mao faction. Chinese students who were trained in Russia and supported by advisers of the Comintern led the Moscow faction. They wanted to concentrate on urban uprisings even when the results were not encouraging. The Mao faction was led by Mao and Chinese students trained in the Whampoa Military Academy and several provincial military institutions and Chinese students trained in Europe. This faction wanted to concentrate on peasant uprisings in the countryside. An age-old hostility existed between peasants and landlords, and rural uprisings gained popular support from farmers. Severe infighting took place between the two factions, and before 1935, the Moscow faction had the upper hand.

Mao was physically strong and had a will of his own. He often wanted to challenge himself. One stormy night at Baidaihe, a summer resort on the coast north of Beijing, the ocean was black with thunder and lightning overhead. Mao decided to go swimming to see whether he could conquer the violent sea. Several bodyguards tried to stop him, but he kicked and fought and managed to jump into the ocean. Eventually, the guards had to jump in to rescue him.

During a battle, Mao gave commands through telephones connected to the various field officers, his room strewn with maps of the battlefields. Too excited to sleep, he worked throughout the course of the battle, which sometimes lasted several days. He chain-smoked, drank cups of tea continuously, and sipped brandy. Interruptions annoyed him. He could not stop for regular meals, existing on a bowl of oatmeal or a few roasted taro roots. He had the mental concentration of Sherlock Holmes when "the game was afoot." After the battle was over, he would order a bowl of stewed pork, his favorite food. "Its protein," he said, "would replenish my brain power."

As a socialist leader, Mao insisted that everyone should live the life of a farmer. All through the revolutionary days, he wore no new clothes. He wanted his clothing to be clean, but his suit would be patched and his socks mended. His first new suit was tailor-made for him for the celebration of the founding of the People's Republic of China. He appeared in that suit on the platform at Tiananmen Square. Later, when he outgrew the suit, it was given to the commander of the bodyguards, Li Yinchiao. The government searched all over the country for Li's suit to display it in a museum, but unfortunately Li had the suit cut short and altered for his own use.

The Long March

After 1935, the Long March proceeded west under the leadership of Mao, with the Nationalists in pursuit. The Nationalists depended on supplies to be brought to the front from the rear, and this sometimes caused delays. The Communist forces had no supply lines from the rear and had to live off the land and keep moving. After defeating the Nationalists and militia forces of a village, the Red Army would call a public meeting at which the propaganda group would stage a show, singing folk songs and presenting a short play for farmers. The weapons, horses, and supplies of the landlords' militia would be confiscated. The Red Army would recruit young men from the farm families, sometimes paying a few dollars to compensate them for the loss of manpower and to pay for food and supplies. The wealth of the landlords, such as gold, silver, coins, and the Nationalist currency, would be confiscated. The Red Army would find foster homes to care for both the wounded soldiers who could no longer travel and the babies born during the march. After some rest, the Red Army would move on. The land reform pleased the peasants and gained their support for the Red Army. With the peasants on their side, the Red Army was able to live off the land.

Life for the Red Army on the Long March was harsh. A soldier would be given a ration of rice and would have to carry his rifle or machine gun, his munitions, and his bedding. He wore a straw hat and a pair of straw or cloth shoes. In daytime, he would march on foot, the only means of transportation. If he were wounded, he would be carried on a litter. The litter bearers could move rapidly; they could walk or run, swinging the person in the hammock right and left. At night, unless a soldier could find shelter under a tree or in a cave, he would sleep in the open on straws. His best protection against wind and rain was a piece of oil cloth to wrap around himself. The second best was the bark of a birch tree of shoulder width, as it is wind- and rainproof and durable enough for one night. The drawback was that the stripped trees would reveal the location of the troops to the pursuing enemy. When the enemy was close behind, the troops would not sleep through the night but rather would wake up in the middle of the night and move to a new location to avoid being overtaken by the enemy. For that reason, the troops would sleep with their clothes and shoes on. The officers did not fare much better. They were given horses to ride, but they slept and ate alongside the troops. Sometimes the doors of farmhouses were removed to make beds for the officers.

Women joined the Long March. Most of them were part the propaganda unit, singing and performing plays for the peasants and soldiers. Members of the secret service often went to the Japanese occupied territories to organize and maintain underground units. It was their job to recruit young girl students and actresses for the propaganda units. The head of the secret service, Kang Sheng, often went as far as Beijing or Shanghai to find such girls. There were, of course, battlefield romances and marriages. Husbands and wives did not travel together. Women traveled as a group in the rear. It was only on weekends or during a few days of rest that the wives could join their husbands. One exception was Kang Keqing, the wife of Zhu De, who fought by the side of her husband every day on the Long March. She was a combat soldier, a markswoman, and a troop leader and was armed with two pistols and a rifle. A robust peasant woman, the daughter of a fisherman, she was given away when she was one month old and worked as a slave girl until the age of 15, when she ran away and joined the Red Army. Zhu De and Kang Keqing were married in 1929, when she was 17 and Zhu De was 43. Zhu De's first wife, Wu Ruolin, a revolutionary, had been arrested and executed by the Nationalists in 1928. It was a romantic picture: General Zhu De, later the commander-in-chief of the Red Army, with his warrior wife by his side, riding in the front and directing the battle.

There are also sad stories about the wives. After Mao went to Jinggangshan in 1927, he met a girl, He Zizhen, a slim, energetic young woman with a heart of gold. She joined the revolution in 1926 at the age of 16. She had fought shoulder to shoulder with the troops in many of the early engagements in Jinggangshan. Mao and He Zizhen lived together. They did not marry until 1930, when Mao was informed of the death of his wife, Yang Kaihui. In 1934, when the Long March began, He Zizhen was 24 years old and was pregnant. She did not march by the side of Mao but was assigned to the convalescent unit. On the March, she gave birth to a girl. The baby was wrapped in a blanket and given to a peasant family with a few silver dollars. The peasant family promised to take care of the baby. After the war, attempts were made to locate the baby, but no trace was ever found. One day in Yanan, a Nationalist fighter plane strafed a group of wounded soldiers. He Ziuzhen jumped on top of a commissar to cover him with her body. She was wounded in 17 places, including the head. She remained unconscious for several days. She recovered but was in poor health. In 1937, she went to Russia for medical treatment with the approval of Mao and did not return until 1948. Meanwhile, Mao had divorced her and married Jiangqing. He Zishen went to Shanghai and lived there. After Mao died in 1976, He Zizhen was permitted to go to Beijing to view Mao's body in the glass sarcophagus for the first time. After Jiangqing and the Gang of Four were arrested, He Zizhen was elected to the National Committee of the People's Political Consultative Conference. She died in Shanghai in 1984.[16]

During the Long March, heavy casualties were sustained, but medical facilities were scarce. Chen Yi suffered a hip wound when the Long March started. He was born in 1901 in Lezhi, Sichuan, where his father was the magistrate. Short and stocky, he was soft spoken and outgoing and had a sense of humor. At school in Chengdu, he learned to play basketball at the local YMCA, where Jack Service's father was the head. He went to France as a work–study student and joined the Communist Party in 1923, working as an assistant political instructor at the Wuhan Military Academy. A veteran of military operations at Nanchang, Jinggangshan, and South Jiangxi, he was ordered by Zhou Enlai to fight a delaying battle against the Nationalists and not to join the Long March. For six weeks, he did not receive any medical treatment for his wound. The x-ray machine, which would have revealed the bone splinter in his wound, did not work for lack of batteries. He was carried around in a litter. By September 1935, the hip pain was excruciating, and his legs began to swell. He ordered a guard to squeeze the pus out. Without anesthesia, Chen went white with pain, and his body shook all over. When the guard stopped, Chen ordered himself tied to a tree. Thus, the guard was able to continue until all the pus was forced out together with the bone splinter. No antibiotics were available, so the guard packed the wound with Tiger Balm ointment (a camphor product), the famous Hong Kong cure-all. Miraculously, the wound healed.

When the Long March started, Chen had 25,000 men, of whom 10,000 were wounded. By 1936, when Chen joined Mao at Yanan, his troops had almost been wiped out.[17]

The War of Movement

In 1934, the Long March started with Mao in command. The forces were grouped into a few armies among which was the First Army, led by Lin

Biao, and the Third Army, led by Peng Dehuai.[18] In the fight between the Comintern and Mao, Deng Xiaoping was dismissed because of his support for Mao. After a period of study of Marxism and self-criticism, he was appointed as a foot soldier and joined the Long March. This process of study, self-criticism, and reassignment is called rehabilitation. The fighting was most severe at the beginning. In the first 10 weeks, the Red Army lost about 50,000 men.[19]

From 1935 to 1949, the history of China was shaped by the contest between two individuals: Chiang Kaishek of the Nationalist Party and Mao Zedong of the Communist Party. The two became locked in a conflict to the finish.

By 1935, after the battles in Guizhou, the Long March headed west and entered Sichuan. At Jiaopingdu, the troops crossed the Yangtze River and moved north. A short rest was taken at Huili, and Mao called a Politburo meeting. The authority of Mao was established, but not always without challenge. Lin Biao, the commander of the First Army, found Mao's orders to send the troops in all directions difficult to understand, but he always carried them out. He knew that Mao did not have any formal military training. At the meeting, Lin Biao proposed that Mao turn the military authority over to Pend Dehuai, the commander of the Third Army. Meanwhile, Liu Shaoqi and General Yang Shangkun sent a telegram to Mao suggesting that the forces on the Long March join He Long's Second Army to confront the Nationalists.[20] A feeling existed that Mao's strategy of a war of movement had made the march too long and the troops exhausted. Here *The Maxims of Suntzi*, one of Mao's favorite books, came to his assistance. The challenge was serious, as it came from the generals who were in command of most of the Red Army. Mao explained that the Red Army was facing a formidable enemy and that it would be difficult to win a positional war. The war of movement allowed the Red Army to use its knowledge of the terrain because the war was fought in familiar areas. Mao used a bow to demonstrate his point. The shortest distance from one end of the bow to the other was to follow the bowstring. But the enemy knew that, and it could set up a trap in the middle. It would be best to go left, away from the destination, and follow the bow. The enemy would then lose you and would have to search for you. Meanwhile, you could turn around toward the destination. The next time, you followed the bow again, but by turning right, away from the destination in. Thus, you moved in a zigzag fashion. The technique was often used in naval battles to avoid gunfire and torpedoes. When the pursuing enemy was very close, it might be best to circle back, causing the enemy to stop and search for you. In addition, the air force used this technique in dogfights. The idea was to confuse the enemy. The war of movement made the journey longer and the troops tired but would keep the Red Army forces intact and reduce casualties. They did not always run away from the enemy but would attack on their terms when the odds were in their favor. The decision was for Mao to keep his command, and the generals began to learn from him the basics of guerrilla warfare. This meeting caused Mao to hold some reservations about the men who challenged his authority, including Lin Biao, Peng Dehaui, and Liu Shaoqi. Zhou Enlai never challenged Mao. Zhou was Mao's coequal before 1935, but after 1935, Zhou remained always the second man, producing whatever plays Mao wanted to put on stage.

As Mao led the Long March north, he was approaching the area occupied by General Zhang Guotao, the Communist commander of the 30th Army, which did not join Mao in the Long March but was operating in Sichuan area.

Zhang was born into a rich farmer family. He studied at Peking University when Mao worked in the University Library. The two became acquainted then. They were among the founders of the Communist Party in Shanghai. Zhang participated in the Nanchang uprising. He went to Russia and spent three years there. In 1931, he was sent to Shanghai. He fought many battles against the Nationalists in Jiangxi and moved from there to Hunan, Hubei, and Anhui. In 1932, he settled down in the area of Sichuan and Shaanxi.

Mao's and Zhang's armies joined forces at Lianghekou, Sichuan, and a conference was held. Mao's forces were about 10,000 strong, while Zhang's were about 80,000 strong. There followed a number of institutional reorganizations. While Mao remained the chairman of the Military Commission, Zhang was named a vice chairman. Zhou Enlai relinquished the post of general political commissar to Zhang, and Zhu De was named the commander-in-chief of the combined forces, which were divided into two columns. Mao led the right column and Zhang the left column. The generals were reassigned to integrate the two armies. Generals Li Xiannian and Xu Xiangqian from Zhang's forces were assigned to Mao's column, and Generals Zhu De and Liu Bocheng of Mao's forces were assigned to Zhang's column. A debate ensued over where to proceed from Sichuan. Mao wanted to go north, but Zhang did not. Mao remembered what he had learned from *The Romance of the Three Kingdoms*. In the wars of the three kingdoms, when the force in central China was defeated, it had no hinterland to which it could retreat and recuperate. The force in the west, once it lost Sichuan and retreated to the mountains, could be bottled up there, never to come out again. The force in the north had the hinterlands of Manchuria and Xinjiang to serve as a refuge, a secure retreat and staging area for future attacks. Mao led his right column north and eventually reached Yanan. Zhang refused to go north (in which case he would be in a subordinate position in relation to Mao), considering that he had the much larger force. Zhang moved south and attacked Chengdu. There he met 200,000 Nationalist forces with their powerful air force and heavy artillery. Zhang suffered a resounding defeat and retreated to Xikang, his forces reduced to 40,000. Eventually, Zhang went to Yanan, but he never felt at home. In 1938, he slipped away and went to Canada by way of Hong Kong.[21]

After a stronghold at Yanan was established under Mao, all the Communist forces that had not joined the Long March but scattered throughout the country gradually arrived, including the Second Army, led by He Long, and the forces led by Chen Yi. At Yanan, officers and men of the Red Army began to relax. Their favorite pastimes were playing contract bridge and social dancing. Journalists from all over the world came to get to know the new emerging power of the Communists in China. Among them were Edger Snow and Agnes Smedley. Many articles were written about Mao, Zhu De, and Zhou Enlai and their spectacular experience on the Long March. Smedley was attracted to Zhu De, the commander-in-chief. Zhu was dark and strong, every inch the image of a guerrilla commander. Smedley had a portable phonograph and records of popular dance music. She invited Zhu to dance with her, and she taught the general how to dance. They were seen dancing together for hours.[22]

The Long March stretched from Jinggangshan in Jiangxi to Huili in Sichuan and to Yanan in Shaanxi. Twenty-four rivers had to be crossed. It took the army two years to complete. Thousands of casualties were sustained, the official number of which is difficult to estimate. The Long March was a heroic demonstration of collective determination, bravery, and resourcefulness. The Red Army had gone through a test of fire and come out seasoned warriors. The experience boosted their self-confidence. They knew that once they had gone through hell and survived, they could never be put down.

NOTES

1. Jin Chungji, *A Biography of Zhou Enlai*, 1898–1949 (in Chinese, *Zhou Enlai Zhuan*, 1898–1949) (Beijing: People's Publishing Co., 1993), pp. 1–10.

2. Ibid., pp. 11–21.

3. Ibid., pp. 22–37.

4. Ibid., pp. 38–52.

5. Ibid., p. 53.

6. Ibid., pp. 79–114.

7. Ibid., p. 155.

8. Ibid., p. 263.

9. Ibid., pp. 291–292.

10. Stephen Uhalley, Jr., *Mao Tse-tung* (New York: New Viewpoints, 1975), pp. 21, 156; *The Biographical Literature* (in Chinese, *Zhuanzhi Wenxue*) (Taipei: Biographical Literature Co.), vol. 40, no. 2, pp. 132–134.

11. Uhalley, *Mao Tse-tung*, pp. 19–22.

12. Immanuel C. Y. Hsu, *The Rise of Modern China* (New York: Oxford University Press, 1983), p. 776.

13. Uhalley, *Mao Tse-tung*, pp. 62–65.

14. Ibid., pp. 106–120.

15. Ibid., pp. 138–143.

16. Harrison E. Salisbury, *The Long March* (New York: Harper & Row, 1985), pp. 79–86, 151, 173–175.

17. Ross Terrill, *China in Our Time* (New York: Simon & Schuster, 1992), p. 71; Salisbury: *The Long March*, pp. 5, 211–212, 215.

18. Salisbury, *The Long March*, pp. 31–33.

19. Ibid., p. 103.

20. Ibid., pp. 193–194.

21. Ibid., pp. 145–325.

22. Ibid., p. 4.

CHAPTER 2

The Wars

Wars were fought between the Communists and the Japanese in northern China from 1937 to 1945 and between the Nationalists and the Japanese from 1931 to 1945. The Japanese surrendered in 1945, then a civil war broke out between the Communists and the Nationalists from 1945 to 1949, ending with a Communist victory. Four generals emerged from the wars as national heroes: Zhu De, the commander-in-chief; Peng Dehuai, the commander in northern and northwestern China; Lin Biao, the commander in Manchuria; and Liu Bocheng, the commander in central and southern China.

THE SINO–JAPANESE WAR

In 1931, Japan invaded Manchuria, the northeastern corner of China that borders Russia to the north and Korea to the east. It is rich farming country, producing soybeans and sorghum and being well endowed in mineral resources, such as oil and iron ores. Its wealth supported a strong army and helped develop an industrial complex. Japan's desire to obtain Manchuria brought it into conflict with Russia, which was looking for ice-free seaports in Port Arthur and Darien in order to reach the Pacific. The Japanese victory in a war with Russia in 1905 made it possible for Japan to extend its influence in southern Manchuria.

Japan marched into Manchuria in 1931. The Manchurian army, under the command of the young marshal Zhang Xueliang, moved south. Chiang Kaishek did not want Zhang to occupy northern China, so he ordered him to move his troops to Shaanxi, a much poorer region compared to Manchuria. The troops were unhappy and waited for a chance to fight their way back to their home base.

In 1935, the Communist International (Comintern) in Russia, facing the rise of Germany, Italy, and Japan, adopted a resolution urging the Communists to form alliances with all anti-Fascist groups and armies to fight the dictatorships. Chinese Communists adopted a "united front" policy to fight Japan and the Nationalists. Underground Communist agents began to infiltrate the Japanese-occupied territories and carry out land reform to support the peasants. They extended their activities to the outskirts of Beijing, Nanjing, and Shanghai and infiltrated the Nationalist armies.

In 1936, the Communists persuaded the Manchurian army under Zhang to join the united front against Japan.

On December 3, 1936, Chiang Kaishek, on hearing this development, went to Xian, the headquarters of the Manchurian army, to prevent an imminent revolt. A mutiny broke out. To avoid capture, Chiang climbed over a courtyard wall and was injured. He managed to run to a nearby hill and hide in a cave but was eventually captured by the Manchurian army. The author visited the site in 1980, tracing the footsteps of Chiang from the wall to the cave. This involved a half an hour of steep climbing. Chiang's escape must have been a terribly painful ordeal.

The news shocked the country and the world. People in major cities all over China demonstrated and paraded, demanding the release of Chiang, the leader in the war against Japan. Zhou Enlai went to mediate. Finally, on Christmas Day 1936, Chiang was released on the condition that the Nationalists, the Communists, and other forces in China form a united front against the Japanese. From 1937 to 1945, a united China engaged in a battle against Japan. Chiang was flown back to Nanjing, accompanied by Marshall Zhang for security reasons. Zhang offered himself for punishment and was under house arrest for the rest of his life.

From 1937 to 1945, the Japanese army was confronted by two armies: the Communists in northern China and the Nationalists in central and southern China. The war in central and southern China went badly for the Nationalists. Just as Chiang had pushed the Communists to move west on the Long March, the Japanese army pushed Chiang west all the way to Chongqing, Sichuan Province. Millions of civilians and soldiers made the move, carrying their luggage, belongings, and supplies and the industrial equipment they stripped from the factories. They burned their homes, buildings, bridges, and warehouses as they left, leaving only ashes for the Japanese.

In 1944, the Japanese army started an offensive and captured the cities of Wuhan, Changsha, Liuzhou, and Guiyang, delivering a serious blow to the Nationalist forces. By 1945, Chiang's army stood at 2.7 million strong. The numbers gap between the Communists and the Nationalists began to close.

In northern China, the Communist army conducted guerrilla warfare against the Japanese army and was successful in fighting it to a draw. The Communist army occupied the countryside, leaving the Japanese army to hold the cities and transportation lines. Out of the war, two Communist generals emerged as heroes: Zhu De, the commander-in-chief, and Peng Dehuai, the commander at the front.

Zhu was dedicated to the modernization and reform of China. As a military leader, his goals were to fight the warlords who disintegrated China, the landlords who exploited the farmers, and the foreign powers who encroached on China's sovereignty and territorial integrity. He was successful in achieving these goals in his lifetime and has helped bring about a new China with the capability of maintaining domestic peace and guarding the country against foreign threats.

Zhu had a healthy boyhood and grew up a strong young man who was well prepared for his military career. He was born on December 1, 1886, to a tenant farmer family in Yilong District in Sichuan Province in southern China. Yilong is 170 miles north of Chongqing, the capital of China during World War II, and 150 miles east of Chengdu. His father was a tenant farmer, and both parents were uneducated. His mother gave birth to 13 children. As the family was too poor to raise all the children, the parents kept the first eight and took the last five to the river to be drowned. Of the eight children, two were girls and six were boys. Luckily, Zhu was the fourth child and was not drowned.[1]

At the beginning of the nineteenth century, Sichuan Province was depopulated by famine, disease, and fighting among clans. A large number of people migrated to Sichuan from neighboring Guangdong and Hunan provinces. Zhu's ancestors were among the immigrants, coming from Shaoguan District in Guangdong Province. In Zhu's grandfather's time, the family owned one acre of land. When the family had grown too large for the farm to support, the grandfather sold the land and became a tenant farmer.

Zhu remembers that he was hungry throughout his childhood. He did not have any rice, and meals consisted of coarse grains and vegetables. The few meals with meat were served during the Chinese New Year, when the family would slaughter a pig for the holiday celebration. Birthday parties for the children were unheard of.

The family, like all tenant families, was constantly harassed by tax and rent collectors who were uneducated roughnecks. The only way to gain the respect of these agents was to have the children educated, creating a fear in the agents' minds that the children may someday become government officials by passing the civil service examinations. For this purpose, arrangements were made for Zhu and his two elder brothers to go to the home of a relative about a mile away to study under a private tutor. Every day, the brothers had to make two round-trips on foot: one in the morning and, after eating lunch at home, another in the afternoon, totaling four miles a day. They kept this routine for 10 years. This period of study continued for Zhu from age 10 to 18. Meanwhile, he did a great deal of swimming and mountain climbing. By age 19, he was a strong, healthy young man and well prepared for his later military career.[2]

Under the private instructor, Zhu received a thorough training in Chinese classics, including four books containing the teachings of Confucius and his disciples, the historical records of 24 dynasties, and important poems and essays. The material on Confucius contained two parts: political and social philosophy, which Zhu later repudiated, and personal ethics, which he accepted as his rule of conduct. He was a perfect Chinese gentleman, a contrast to General Peng Dehuaai. While Peng was emotional, hot tempered, impatient, and outspoken, Zhu was calm, even in temperament, deliberate in speech and action, trustworthy, and cautious not to antagonize people. All these traits made him a natural commander and later earned the respect and confidence of his officers and soldiers. He was an excellent poet and essay writer and a competent calligrapher using the Chinese brush pen.

In 1905, at the age of 19, Zhu was ready for the civil service examinations, but there was an education reform in the country. New public schools, modeled after Japan and the West, were established throughout the country, replacing the private instruction by tutors in the civil service examination system.

In 1906, Zhu was enrolled in a primary school and graduated half a year later. He then went to the city of Chunqing and enrolled in a high school. He was most interested in modern sciences and physical education. He graduated from that school in one year.

In 1907, Zhu went to Chengdu, the capital of the province. This was his first experience in a major city in his life. He enrolled in the School of Physical Education of the Normal University, again graduating in one year. He was very good in sciences and especially in mathematics. In 1908, he returned to his hometown and accepted a job as the physical education teacher in a grade school, resigning from this position in 1909. He wanted to study at the Military Academy of Yunnan, a neighboring province, but his family did not want him to go into the military, so he left his family and started out on his own. He and a friend walked all the way to the city of Kunming in Yunnan Province, a journey that lasted 70 days. He took the admission examination at the academy but failed. After enlisting in the provincial army of Sichuan Province and serving for a while, he retook the admission examination. This time he passed. The academy had an excellent curriculum and a demanding field-training program modeled after the military schools in Japan. Many instructors were graduates of those Japanese schools. A model student at the academy, Zhu was exposed to the ideas of Dr. Sun Yatsen, whose followers had infiltrated into various military establishments. Like many of his fellow students, Zhu joined the Kuomintang.

In 1911, Zhu graduated from the academy. He was among the best-educated young officer of the day in China. He was commissioned an officer with the rank of company commander in the Yunnan army.[3]

That year, the revolution against the Manchu imperial government started under the leadership of Sun Yatsen. The new armies of various provinces declared independence. The Wuchang uprising, staged by the Hubei army, led the way and was followed by uprisings in several provinces. The uprising of Kunming, led by the Yunnan army, was the fifth of such revolts. The Yunnan army was under the command of Cai E, a brilliant brigade commander who graduated from a military academy in Japan. Zhu regarded Cai E not only as his commander but also as his mentor.

The revolution succeeded in overthrowing the Manchu dynasty and ushering in the Republic of China. Sun Yatsen was made the first president of the republic.

In 1912, Zhu and a Miss Xiao Zhufang, a graduate of the teachers college, were married. A son was born, but in 1915, Zhu's wife died.[4]

A warlord, Yuan Shrkai, forced out Sun Yatsen and took over the government. Shortly thereafter, Yuan restored the monarchy and declared him the emperor of China. In 1916, Cai E led the Yunnan army and declared war on Yuan to reestablish the republic. Fierce battles ensued between the Yunnan army and the army from the north. Zhu was a regiment commander in charge of a column, and here he gained valuable experience in a major battle. When the Yunnan army gained the upper hand in battle, several other provinces joined forces with Yunnan and declared independence. Yuan died that year, and the republic was restored. General Cai E became a national hero.

In 1916, Zhu and a Miss Chen Yuzhen were married. Miss Chen was a graduate from a teachers college.[5] In the same year, his mentor and commander, Cai E, contracted tuberculosis, went to Japan for treatment, and died there. Without Cai E, the Yunnan army fell into the hands of a warlord. This dealt Zhu a great blow. A period of confusion and turmoil followed in China as the nation was divided up by a number of warlords fighting among themselves for the control of the government. One warlord would hold power for a few years, only to be defeated and replaced by another. These warlords were greedy, corrupt, and decadent: one warlord collected a large number of purebred racing horses and gambled heavily at racetracks; another kept a harem of some 30 concubines and boasted of taking several to bed each night. Wine, women, gambling, and drugs seduced the military men. Zhu disliked working for a warlord and lost all hopes for the future, becoming an opium addict. This was the darkest period of his life.

In 1922, Zhu finally decided to break away from the warlord's army, knowing that working for the warlord would not give him the future he wanted. He sent his wife and son to stay with a friend and then went to Shanghai. Years later, in 1935, he learned that his wife and son were assassinated by agents of a warlord. In Shanghai, he entered a hospital in the French concession to receive treatment to cure him of his opium addiction.

At that time, Soviet Russia had been making progress after the revolution in establishing a new order that would work for the welfare of the poor. Communist ideas began to gain popularity among the intellectuals in China. In 1921, Professor Chen Duxiou, who taught at Peking University, organized a Communist party. Zhu went to Peking to see Chen but was told that Chen had gone to Shanghai. Zhu then turned back to Shanghai. He was finally able to meet Chen and professed that he saw in Communism a hope for bringing about a new China, expressing his desire to join the party. Chen, somewhat dubious about Zhu's warlord background, refused to admit him, saying that he should spend some time studying Communism and demonstrate his devotion to the cause of farmers and workers. This was a great disappointment. Zhu was looking for a way to start a new life, hoping that Communism would give him that lead. In Shanghai, he saw Sun Yatsen, who suggested that Zhu go back to Yunnan to raise an army to support Sun's cause. Zhu refused and advised Sun not to rely on the support of warlords who eventually would betray him. Zhu decided to go to Europe to study socialism.

In 1922, at the age of 36, Zhu sailed for France, which did not impress him, as the country was still recovering from the war. The socialists in France had big ideas but not much to show for their social reforms. Zhu found out that Zhou Enlai was organizing a branch of the Communist Party in Germany, so he went to Berlin to see Zhou. When the two met, they immediately struck up a friendship. Zhou was 11 years younger. Zhu again restated his desire to join the party and was admitted. Zhu's membership in the Kuomintang was publicly known, but his membership in the Communist Party was kept secret.[6]

Zhu settled down in Germany and began his studies of the German language. He enrolled at Göttingen University to study sociology in 1923. Zhu was active in the labor movement and because of this involvement, he was arrested. After a short stay in jail, Zhu left Germany and went to the Soviet Union to study military affairs. He enrolled in the Eastern Laborer University and underwent military training.

In 1926, the Communist Party called Zhu back to China. He was assigned to be an instructor at the Officer Training Institute at the city of Nanchang in Jiangxi Province. His colleagues described him as an earnest officer leading a very simple life. His living quarters consisted of a bed of wood boards, a square table, and a few wood benches. He wore a cotton uniform, a pair of leather shoes, and leggings. He always went to office on foot and carried with him teaching materials or documents wrapped in a piece of cloth. He was not a pretentious person.[7]

Zhu participated in the uprising at Nanchang in 1927. When the Kuomintang retook Nanchang, Zhu led the army into Hunan and Guangdong and eventually joined forces with Mao at Jinggangshan. Mao was 32 years old and Zhu 42. A working relationship between Mao and Zhu was established from the beginning. Mao was the party leader and Zhu the army commander. The army was to take orders from the party, and this did not cause any problem for Zhu because he had no political ambition and was a great admirer of Mao. For his part, Mao usually gave Zhu a free hand in military operations, as he recognized Zhu's great ability as a commander.

In 1928, Zhu and Wu Yulan, a writer and a member of an intellectual family, were married in Leiyang. Her two brothers joined the Red Army, and she worked in the political department. Shortly after their marriage, she was captured by Kuomintang agents and beheaded in the city of Changsha in Hunan Province, where she was born.[8]

Some 10 months later, in 1929, Zhu married his fourth wife, Kang Keqing, an illiterate peasant girl in her late teens. Zhu was 43 years old. They did not mind the great discrepancy in their ages because they were in good health. Kang fought the landlords in the peasant units and joined the Red Army. As a soldier in uniform, she followed Zhu all the time, including on the Long March in 1934–36. In 1937, Kang was studying at the Anti-Japanese University at Yannan, where Zhu sometimes went to lecture. She stayed in a dormitory at the university and went home to visit her husband on weekends.[9]

In 1934, during the Long March, Zhu was the commander, Liu Bocheng was the chief of staff, and Mao Zedong was the commissar.

By 1935, the Red Army had reached Sichuan Province and joined forces with the army of Zhang Guotao, who had earlier established a base there. After reorganizing, the Red Army started to push north in two columns— one led by Mao and the other by Zhang. Zhu's army was incorporated into Zhang's column.

On the way north, Zhang revolted. He arrested Zhu, then turned south and settled down in Sikang Province.

On October 1935, Mao's column arrived at Shaanxi, the final destination.

In 1936, Ho Long led his army from Jiangxi in a march westward and eventually fought his way to Sikang to join forces with Zhang Guotao. Ho was able to persuade Zhang to restore the command to Zhu. The group finally went to Shaanxi.

Other Red Army units arrived. Finally, in December 1936, the Long March was completed. Zhang Guotao was put on trial. He was deprived of his position in the Red Army and made to undergo reeducation. In 1938, he escaped and went to Canada by way of Hong Kong.

Agnes Smedley was a reporter and a writer who was born in Missouri of a poor family and raised in Colorado. She went to China in 1928. After her health deteriorated in 1933, she went to Xian to convalesce. In 1937, she traveled to Yannan to report on Communist activities. Her meeting with Zhu was a great surprise to her. She had imagined that the commander of the Red Army and the hero of endless battles must be a giant, fierce-looking man with a hot temper, what she saw was the opposite. She described Zhu as a common man, like a peasant. He was five feet eight inches tall. At the age of 51, he looked much older, with his dark face deeply lined. He was undernourished and had sunken cheeks. He wore a sloppy blue-gray cotton uniform. He often appeared in shorts on the battlefield. He was soft spoken but very masculine in his movements and gestures. His black hair was stubble, and a touch of gray covered his round head. He had a broad forehead and a strong jaw, a short and broad nose, piercing eyes, and white teeth. He was never sick and had never been wounded. Wherever he went, he was received with total respect. On the battlefield, he could boost the morale of the troops by his appearance alone. When talking to the men, he stood with his feet apart and placed his hands on his hips. In his talks, he seldom mentioned Communism; rather, he always concentrated on the problems that China had, stressing loyalty to country and the duty of every man to bring about a strong modern China. He was fundamentally a nationalist.[10]

Smedley interviewed Zhu over a period of time. The two often danced in the evenings to phonograph music that she brought with her. When Zhu went to the front in the Taihang Mountains, she followed him to observe him in action. The notes of the interviews were compiled into a book, *The Great Road: The Life and Times of Chu Teh.* Smedley died in England in 1950. The book was not published in the United States until 1956, and it became a classic on Chinese Communism.

In 1937, the Kuomintang and the Communists formed a united front to fight the Japanese. Two Red Armies were incorporated into the Kuomintang forces: the Eighth Route Army and the Fourth Route Army. The Eighth Route Army operated in northern China around Shanxi, and the Fourth Route Army operated in central China around Anhui. For the Eighth Route Army, Zhu was the commander, Peng Dehuai the deputy commander, and Lin Biao and Ho Long were division commanders. For the Fourth Route Army, Ye Ting was the commander, Xiang Ying deputy commander, and Chen Yi a division commander.

The Eighth Route Army carried on guerrilla warfare against the Japanese forces and was able to control the countryside in northern China, leaving the Japanese holding on to some major cities, railways, and highways. In 1937, the Eighth Route Army started with 80,000 men. It was able to recruit 920,000 more but suffered some 400,000 casualties. By 1944, it had about 600,000 men.

Until 1940, the Kuomintang supported the two Red Armies with money and supplies. Then the two armies were left to fend for themselves. During the period of the Kuomintang's support, Zhu's pay was three dollars a month, but he did not receive even that, as the pay of all officers and men was pooled together to buy food.[11] Zhu was not concerned with material wealth. He was content to lead his troops to fight for the country. When he was working for a warlord at a salary of $1,000 and an expense account of $500 a month, he had found life worthless and without purpose.[12]

In 1940, Chiang Kaishek wanted to consolidate his control of central and southern China, so he ordered the Fourth Route Army to move to north of the Yangtze River. Ye Ting led 40,000 across the river. At the crossing, however, they were ambushed by Kuomintang forces. Ye Ting was wounded and captured. Only 1,000 men made the crossing, and Chen Yi assumed the command of the Fourth Route Army. Five years later, Ye Ting was released, but in 1946, he, his wife, and two children were murdered by the Kuomintang's secret police.

Farmers in China had repeatedly been victims of looting, rape, and murder at the hands of the troops of the warlords. Zhu grew up in a poor farmer family and thus was familiar with these atrocities. He laid down the rule that Red Army troops must not engage in looting, raping, and killing; they must pay for what they took from the farmers and return what they borrowed.

The Red Army wanted to recruit farmers into its ranks, and for this Zhu ordered the troops to make friends with the farmers. They would be polite to farmers and address the older generation as uncles or aunts and the younger generation as elder brothers and sisters. The troops were asked to give the farmers a helping hand in the field.

Whenever the Red Army gained control of a village, the farm's rent would be abolished and the land distributed to the farmers. The army would also confiscate the landlord's assets in cash, food, and supplies. The local militia maintained by the landlords would be disarmed and military supplies confiscated.

Farmers had never seen such a disciplined army, and they considered it an army for their liberation. Thus, the Red Army was able to operate in the countryside and become self-sufficient with the support of farmers.

As he rose through the ranks, Zhu became familiar with the abuse of soldiers at the hands of unfriendly officers. He ruled that officers be kind to the troops. Officers were not allowed to scold or hit soldiers, and junior officers were asked to eat and live with the soldiers.

Captured Chinese officers and soldiers of the Kuomintang army were not to be abused, as they were Chinese but just happened to be fighting on the other side. They were given two options: to join the Red Army or go home. If they wanted to join up, they would be incorporated into the ranks after a period of reeducation and training. If they chose to go home, a few dollars would be given to each for travel expenses.

Zhu wanted the Red Army to be different from the armies of the warlords in that the Red Army should be used by individuals not for political gain but rather for the promotion of national interests. The Red Army should not be involved in politics and should take orders only from the civilian authority of the national government.

Modern warfare depends a great deal on advanced technology. Zhu wanted to modernize the Red Army by improving the level of technology in officer training and in military equipment. Under his direction, some 100 war institutes and colleges were established by 1957. Zhu was keen in promoting the development of high-tech equipment, including space weapons such as missiles, satellites, and atomic bombs.

The Red Army started out mainly as an infantry force. Zhu began to develop other services, such as the navy, the marines, the air force, and the coast guard, to provide China with a comprehensive defense system. This task would require decades of continuing effort.

The Red Army was composed largely of foot soldiers with limited fighting power. Zhu began to establish various technical supporting units, such as mechanized units, artillery units, transportation and communications units, civil engineering units for road construction and bridge building, ordnance units, and the medical corps. These would help the infantry operate more efficiently and give it more firepower.

From his training in a Chinese military academy modeled after Japanese institutions, his training in Germany and Russia, and his experience in fighting the warlords, the Japanese army, and the Kuomintang forces, Zhu developed a sense what it would take for China to become a world military power. He was the undisputed military leader of China and had the respect in the country to push his program of military reform and development. The country is indebted to him for his lifetime work in raising China to its current status.

Zhu found in General Peng Dehuai a comrade in arms, and the two collaborated well through the years. Peng Dehuai had a hard life of constant struggles, making him sometimes impatient and short tempered. Peng was born October 24, 1898, in the Brown Mud hillside, Huangnipe, by the Black Stone Peak, Wushrfeng, in Xiangtan District of Hunan Province, the same province where Chairman Mao Zedong was born.

A tea merchant, Peng discovered this beautiful, sparsely inhabited hillside, then bought the place and started his farm. Peng was his sixth-generation grandson. The family was poor in his father's generation. The farm had been reduced to one and a half acres. His father was disabled, so the family depended on his mother to do the farming to support the household of six: his grandmother, his father, his mother, two younger brothers, and himself.

When Peng was six years old, he was sent to his uncle's house to study under a tutor. His mother died when he was eight years old. He discontinued his studies and took on the responsibility of caring for the family. Eventually, the farm and the house had to be sold, leaving only two rooms for the family.

One day, Peng's grandmother gave him and one of his brothers a basket and a club and sent them to go begging for food. They walked throughout the neighborhood, knocking on doors, but were chased away all day, until, in the evening, a gatekeeper opened the door and asked, "Are you the fortune angels?" Peng said no, and the door began to close. However, Peng's brother, knowing the superstition, quickly said yes. The door reopened, and they were allowed to go in and were given half a bowl of rice with a small slice of meat. The tradition was that fortune angels, disguised as beggars, would bring good luck to the household if they were treated well. The gatekeeper pretended that the boys were fortune angels. The boys brought back the food to be shared by the family. On getting back to the house, Peng fainted because of hunger and despair. The next day, his grandmother asked them to go begging again. He refused. Finally, the 80-year-old grandmother trudged out, bringing one brother with her— a picture that left a keen imprint in Peng's mind. He swore that he would work hard to make the family well off and would do his best to save the poor if at all possible.[13]

At age 13, Peng worked in a coal mine. It was cold, dark, and dirty and smelled bad. The workers were naked. They worked on water pumps or carried coal out. The second year, the mine was closed down, and the owner left without paying the workers.

A famine occurred when Peng was 15 years old. The tradition was for the rich landlords to take turns selling rice to the poor at reduced prices. When one landlord refused to do so, a group of young men broke down the door of the granary and distributed rice to the poor, following the swordsmen's tradition to rob the rich to save the poor. Peng was among the group of men, and orders were issued for his arrest. In tears, he said good-bye to the family and fled, leaving them unprovided for.

Peng found a job as a construction worker and part-time cook for a dam construction project at Dongting Lake. Most of the time, workers were waist deep in water, and the pay was low. In 1916, when Peng was 18 years old, workers called a strike demanding higher wages. Peng was among the leaders of the strike and was dismissed.

Peng enlisted in the provincial army of Hunan after a long period of unemployment. Soldiers were the lowest class in society, and their life span was short, as they fought for the warlords, who were fighting one another all the time. His army pay was better than what he earned as a manual laborer, and he could save money and send half of it home to support his family. He tried to keep supporting his family whenever he could.

Peng did well in the army and advanced to platoon leader at the age of 22. He made friends with a few young officers who came from poor families. They organized a Save the Poor Association and swore that they would work for the country and the people. They would not exploit the poor, take concubines, or gamble. They wanted to be heroes of the people and lead a simple life of high moral standards.[14]

Peng was a company commander at the age of 23, the highest rank for a military officer in a district. The custom was for community leaders to periodically wine and dine him, give him money, and provide women for him. He refused all these, earning for himself the reputation of a model soldier.

In 1922, at age 24, Peng left the army and went home to stay with his family. His grandmother wanted to get him married. A 12-year-old sister of his friend, Liu Ximai, was suggested as the bride. Peng met with the girl and agreed to the marriage. After being married, Peng renamed his bride Liu Kunme. He taught her how to read and encouraged her to go to school.

In 1922, it was recommended that Peng enroll at the Military Academy of Hunan Province. The teachers at the academy (mostly graduates from the Army University and the Officers Academy of Japan) taught him about warfare strategy, armaments, and operations. Here Peng received first-class training that prepared him for a military career. This training and his broad battlefield experience groomed him into a promising officer.

In 1926, at the age of 28, Peng rose to the rank of battalion commander. In 1928, through the recommendation of a party member (his friend at the Save the Poor Association), Peng joined the Communist Party. The same year, Peng led his battalion in an uprising in Pingjiang in Hunan Province. He invaded the city, dispatched the Nationalist garrison forces, and established a Soviet-style government. However, the Nationalists retook the city. Peng and his Fifth Red Army retreated to Xiushui in Jiangxi Province. Eventually, Peng fought his way to Jinggangshan to unite with the forces of Mao Zedong and Zhu De.

In 1935, Peng was at Yanan after the Long March. Peng had not seen his wife since 1928, when he started the Pingjiang uprising against the Nationalists. Now that the conflicts were over, his wife Liu and one of his brothers, Peng Jinhua, went to Yanan to look for Peng. On seeing him, Liu immediately burst in tears. Peng started to console her, saying, "You must have suffered a great deal during these years." She recalled that for years she had to flee from the Nationalist agents, that finally she remarried to escape their pursuit, and that she now had a one-year-old baby girl. She did not blame Peng, knowing that he had to do what he did for the country and the people, nor would Peng blame her, considering all the years of suffering she had gone through. Peng asked her to continue with her studies. In tears, they went their own ways. Peng Jinhua wanted to follow in the footsteps of his brother Peng, so he joined the Communist Party and, after returning home, began organizing local party units. Soon Peng's other brother joined the party as well.[15]

In 1938, Peng attended a meeting at the Department of Organization at Yanan. A beautiful, well-mannered young lady, Pu Anxiu, was at the meeting. Peng was immediately attracted to her. She studied at the Normal University in Beijing. At the age of 18, she joined the Communist Party and did underground work. At the age of 21, she went to Yanan to work in the Department of Organization. Peng and Pu were soon married. Li Fuchun, the vice minister of the organization, presided over the wedding. A fine dinner followed, being attended by a few close friends. A few days later, the couple left together to go to the front at Taihang Mountain, where Peng would share command with General Zhu De. Pu would work at the headquarters.

In 1940, when conflicts started between the Nationalists and the Communists competing for areas of control, agents of the Nationalists went to the home of the two brothers and then arrested and executed them. On hearing this, Peng wrote a letter to Chiang Kaishek asking for an explanation and requesting the arrest and trial of these agents, but he received no reply. Now at his home in Hunan, Peng had lost all those he loved, leaving in the family only the widows of his brothers with their children. Could there be a heavier cross to bear? However, there is a saying in Chinese: *Chrde kujungku, fangwei renshangren*, meaning "One cannot rise above others, without suffering the utmost setbacks."

In 1940, the Japanese army repaired railways and built highways to strengthen the transportation network between the major cities of northern China (including Beijing, Tianjin, Datong, and Jinan) and to facilitate troop movement to fight the Communist forces. Peng decided to attack the transportation network to slow down Japanese operations. On August 20, 1940, about 105 regiments went into action simultaneously, destroying about 3,000 Japanese strongholds and damaging 1,000 miles of railway and 3,000 miles of highway. They also demolished tunnels, bridges, water towers, and telecommunications posts. This was referred to as the Battle of 100 Regiments.[16]

The Japanese army in northern China regrouped under a new commander. After two years of preparation, the Japanese launched an offensive. A Japanese detachment disguised in Chinese uniforms surrounded the headquarters. Peng was able to break through the Japanese lines, galloping on his favorite red stallion. Later Peng was able to recover the base and carried out guerrilla warfare against the Japanese.

In 1943, Peng and a General Liu Bocheng were ordered to go back to Yanan to report on their operations and assist in the defense of the Red Capital. They and their wives had to go through the Japanese lines on foot. They put on farmers' clothing, wearing black shirts and pants and tying white handkerchiefs over their heads. They arrived at Yanan without any problems.[17]

In 1945, when Japan surrendered, Peng, at the age of 47, advanced to become a member of the Central Committee of the Communist Party and a member of the Politburo. He was also made vice chairman of the Military Affairs Committee and the chief of staff. That made him a military leader second only to Zhu De. Peng made great contributions to the army in his humane treatment of soldiers to gain their loyalty and his establishment of discipline.

The warlords and the Nationalist officers tended to abuse the soldiers and were unable to maintain discipline among them, sometimes resulting in looting and the killing of civilians. Peng, on assuming command, would immediately issue orders to maintain strict discipline for officers and soldiers.

A commissars system was established in the army. Commissars helped commanders maintain discipline and carry out land reforms in dividing the land of landlords among the farmers. As a result, the people strongly supported the army. They had never seen such a finely disciplined and kind army.

In a gathering with the troops, Peng often would ask the soldiers, "Who has given you your food?" and the soldiers would reply, "The farmers." He then would ask, "Who has given you your clothing?" and the soldiers would reply, "The workers." Peng wanted the soldiers, the farmers, and the workers to cooperate.

THE CIVIL WAR

The civil war between the Communists and the Nationalists lasted from April 1946 to October 1949. In the first stage, from April 1946 to early 1947, the Nationalists were winning, but the turning point came in July 1947, when the Communists started their offensive and eventually gained victory in 1949. At the end of World War II, the Nationalists and the Communists competed for the control of China. The army that received the Japanese surrender would obtain their weapons and ammunition. The Communists had no problems in the mopping-up operations in northern China, as they already controlled the countryside, and the Nationalists had no problems regaining the major cities in southern China. The race was for control of Manchuria was between the Nationalists and the Communists.

American military advisers, considering that Manchuria was too far away, suggested that Chiang consolidate his forces in southern China. Chiang was not content with a stalemate situation, leaving the Communist in place in the north and himself in the south. That situation could give the Communists the upper hand later. Chiang considered Manchuria crucial. He wanted all or nothing, so he sent his best troops into Manchuria by sea and by airdrops.

Shortly before the end of World War II, Russian troops moved into Manchuria and accepted the Japanese surrender. When the Communists reached Manchuria, the Russians gave most of the captured Japanese weapons and ammunition to them. The Communists incorporated the Manchurian army and the local militia into the Red Army. With the food supplies acquired from the peasants, the Communists had a solid hold on the entire countryside of Manchuria.

Through airdrops, the Nationalists gained the control of the major cities in Manchuria. The troops coming by sea were delayed. The Russians controlled Port Arthur and Darien and denied the Nationalist troops the right to land there. Finally, the Nationalist troops had to turn south and landed at Qinhuangdao.

American military advisers again urged Chiang to pull out of Manchuria, knowing that the odds were against him and that he needed the best regiments for the defense of southern China. Chiang insisted on staying, and fighting broke out.

In 1945, U.S. President Harry Truman had the naive notion that the Communists and the Nationalists were two amiable parties that differed only in policies and that they could work together in a coalition government. He first sent General Patrick Hurley and then General George C. Marshall to China to mediate from 1944 to 1947. The two sides politely met. Mao Zedong even managed to put on a conciliatory front. However, both Mao and Zhu De viewed Chiang as the killer of hundreds of thousands of their men and, moreover, as the executioner of their wives. The negotiations ran into difficulties, and eventually the mediation broke off.[18]

In 1945, at the end of World War II, Chiang's forces stood at 3.6 million and included an air force, mechanized units, and artillery support. The Communist forces stood at 1.2 million, consisting largely of infantry. From 1946 to the early part of 1947, Chiang's forces were successful in capturing Communist positions in the provinces of Jiangsu, Hebei, Shandong, and Henan, reaching as far as the Yanan area.[19]

The Manchurian battles turned badly for Chiang. It was difficult for him to bring supplies to his troops in the cities of Manchuria. Lin Biao's forces controlling the countryside had sealed off the cities from food and other supplies. Soldiers, no matter how well mechanized, could not fight on empty stomachs. The urban areas held by the Nationalists began to shrink and eventually capitulated in October 1948, all their fine weapons and ammunition falling into the hands of Communists. Lin Biao, after the victory in Manchuria, rebuilt his army to 400,000 men and acquired state-of-the-art equipment. The army was now much stronger than in the past. By 1948, Chiang's forces dwindled to 2.1 million, while the Communist forces grew to 1.5 million.[20]

Chiang pulled back his forces and regrouped at Xuzhou with 600,000 men ready for the battle of central China. The Communists, under the command of Liu Bocheng and Chen Yi, were of about equal strength. The two engaged in a fierce battle for 65 days at the end of 1948, and the Communists won. Deng Xiaoping made his contribution in directing two million peasants from four provinces to provide logistical support for the army.[21]

Chiang conceded defeat. He salvaged 300,000 troops and sent them to Taiwan. In January 1949, he resigned from the presidency and retreated to Taiwan. Vice President Li Zongren took over but could not mount any effective defense.

Lin Biao's forces started the mopping-up operations from the northern tip of China to Manchuria and moved through northern central, and southern China, ending at Guangzhuou and Xiamen at the southern tip of China, covering the entire length of the country. Peng's forces started the mopping-up operation from east to west, started in Xuzhou and ending in Xian and Lanzhou.

The victory of the Communist forces in China in 1949 shocked the world. The West was alarmed at the outcome of the event, as the future of Asia was at stake. Analysts and commentators began to search for the cause of China's defeat. Mao put his finger on the cause, as he pointed out to Edger Snow in 1936 that the support of the peasants was crucial to the control of China. Chiang lost the support of the peasants and consequently lost China. By withholding food and supplies from the cities, the peasants were able to starve the military forces and civilians in the cities, causing runaway inflation there. For example, in Shanghai, prices would rise 50 times per year from 1946 to 1947. Officials on fixed salaries could not support their families, so corruption became widespread. The morale of the soldiers broke down because of starvation. Eventually, the regime collapsed.

After 28 years of struggle, from the founding of the Communist Party in 1921 to the defeat of the Nationalists in 1949, the Communists finally won China. On October 1, 1949, the People's Republic of China was founded by the Communist Party in consultation with all the other major parties in the country.

Two generals emerged from the civil war as national heroes: Lin Biao and Liu Bocheng. Lin Biao was born in 1907 in Hubei Province to the family of a landlord and proprietor of a handicraft factory. He was the second son of four boys. He was trained at Whompoa Military Academy, which was headed by Chiang Kaishek. Lin joined the Communist Party at its founding. When the Red Army was founded in 1927, Lin was a junior officer under General He Long. In 1931, at the age of 24, Lin rose to be the commander of the First Army. He was slight of build with a high-pitched voice, a private person not inclined to socialize with his colleagues.

Liu Bocheng was born on December 4, 1892, to a poor farmer's family in Zhangjia Ba, Zhaojia Chang, Puli Section, Kai District, in Sichuan Province. The family originated in Jiangling District of Jinchou Prefecture, Hubei Province, and went to Sichuan as the government was encouraging people from the neighboring provinces to migrate to Sichuan when that province was depopulated by famine. He would lead the life of a successful military man, being well trained and educated.

Liu's grandfather started farming in the wildness and worked as an ironworker. In his spare time and to make a living for the family, he was a musician (a trumpeter) for hire for occasions such as funerals, weddings, and birthday parties.

Liu's father continued farming. The family lived in a three-room house. His father participated in the village civil service examination but was expelled because he was a musician at that time and was classified as an outcast.

From age 6 to 12, Liu studied with a tutor, learning the classics and calligraphy. In his spare time, he read popular novels such as *The Romance of the Three Kingdoms* and *All Men Are Brothers*, both of which exalt chivalry and loyalty—the code of the swordsmen. As a boy, Liu was trained in boxing and was well versed in the techniques of fighting with Chinese weapons.

In 1905, when Liu was 13, modern schools were developed to replace the old system of civil service examinations. Liu went to the city to enroll in the primary school. That year, his father died, so he had to quit school and go home to take care of the family. This was a difficult period. In times of famine, the family lived on wild vegetables or the lining of tree bark. Liu would gather firewood or mine coal to take to the city to sell. At this time, he was married to a Miss Cheng.

In 1911, the Nationalist Party organized an officers school in Chungqing. Liu enrolled in the school to begin his life as a soldier, his last chance to escape starvation. The school was modeled after the schools in Japan. Many of the instructors were graduates from Japanese schools, and the textbooks that were used were translated from Japanese. In his spare time, Liu read Chinese military books, including the *Strategies of Sunzi*. In 1912, he graduated in and became an officer. Shortly thereafter, he rose to the position of battalion commander in the service of the local warlord. All this time, he sent his pay, after expenses, to his mother to support the family.

The Nationalists were engaged in a war with the local warlord. The fighting was fierce. As a junior officer who had to fight at the front with the men, life was hard for Liu. He suffered several wounds, and, in 1912, was wounded in the left foot. In 1916, he was wounded in the head and lost the sight in his right eye, earning him the nickname "one-eyed dragon." In 1923, he was wounded in the right thigh. Because he had been away from home for years, his wife did not know his whereabouts or whether he was alive. The marriage was dissolved.

When the Nationalists defeated the local warlord, Liu escaped and went to Shanghai. In this period, he felt that his life was being wasted in senseless turmoil. He wanted to dedicate his life to build a new China to help the poor. But he knew that neither the warlords nor the Nationalists cared for the poor. Both wanted power to control China, serving the interests of landlords and businessmen. In 1923, Liu traveled to Beijing and Hong Kong and met the leaders of the Communist Party, which he joined in 1926.[22]

In 1927, Liu participated in the Nanchang uprising, serving in the 20th Army under Ho Long. After the failed coup attempt, Liu was sent to Russia in November 1927 for military training, enrolling in the Advanced Infantry Academy. At that time, he was 36 years old. In 1930, he returned to China as one of the best-trained officers in the Red Army. In Shanghai, he married Miss Wo Jingchun. In 1932, he was appointed the president of the Military Academy at Juijin. There were some 700 trainees and 15 instructors.

During the period of Nationalist expeditions to attack the Communists, Liu was the general chief of staff of the Red Army. During the Long March in 1935, he disagreed with the policies of the international agents who had the control of the party and was demoted to the chief of staff of the Fifth Army Corps.[23]

In 1937, a truce was negotiated between the Communists and the Nationalists, and a united front was formed to fight the Japanese invaders. The Red Army was incorporated into the Nationalist forces as the Eighth Route Army. General Zhu De was the supreme commander, and Liu was the commander of the 129th Division.

Liu was sent to the Taihang Mountain region in Shanxi Province to establish a base. He was successful in carrying out guerrilla warfare against the Japanese forces across five provinces in northern China. In 1938, Deng Xiaoping joined Liu as the division's commissar. This started a collaboration between the two that would last several decades.

In 1942, Liu and General Peng Dehuai were called to Yanan for a conference. What followed was a gathering of all the high-ranking officers celebrating Liu's 50th birthday and the 30th anniversary of his military service for the country.

The Red Army was organized into five field army corps: the Central Plain, the Northeast, the North, the East, and the Northwest. Liu was the

commander of the Central Plain corps. The Nationalist army was organized into three field army corps: the Northeast, the Northwest, and the
Central Plain.

The Nationalist Northeast corps fought the Communist Northeast corps
in Manchuria and was defeated. The Nationalist Northwest corps invaded
the Communist base but was bogged down, and the retreat route was cut
off, preventing it from joining forces with the Central Plain corps.

The stage was set for the task force of Nationalist Central Plain corps
to face the Communist Central Plain corps and the East corps. In 1948, a
battle between the two sides took place, waged around Xuzhou in Jiangsu
Province. The Nationalist army had 800,000 troops and the Communist
army 600,000 troops. For the Communists, General Liu Bocheng was the
commander in chief, General Chen Yi the deputy commander, and General Deng Xiaoping the commissar. The Communists scored a decisive
victory. The Nationalist forces were demolished and their equipment and
supplies captured. A large number of Nationalist officers and troops surrendered. This victory made it possible for the Communists to gain the
control of the country north of the Yangtze River.[24]

A division of opinion arose at the Communist headquarters as to how
to proceed after the victory. Some wanted to stop fighting and consolidate,
as the Nationalists still had about a million troops south of the Yangtze
River. But General Liu Bocheng wanted to cross the river to push south,
not giving the enemy a chance to recuperate. The decision was made to
cross the river. General Liu was made the commander in chief with General Deng Xiaoping as the commissar. The troops were trained for river
warfare, and equipment and supplies were made ready. The crossing took
place at Anqing in Anhui Province in 1948. Under the protection of some
300 pieces of heavy artillery, about 16 divisions of troops made the crossing and established a beachhead 200 miles long and some 20 miles deep.
The Nationalist troops were forced to retreat. Eventually, about a million
Communist troops crossed the river and went south. General Liu Bocheng
captured Nanjing, the capital of the Nationalists, and established a people's government in the city. From there, the Communist forces gained
control of Jiangsu, Zhejiang, Jiangxi, and Fujian provinces, thus gaining
control of southeastern China. The Nationalist task forces moved to Sichuan in southwestern China to join the regional forces. Chiang Kaishek
established his government at Chungqing. It was the military operations
of General Liu Bocheng in defeating the Nationalist army that made it
possible for the founding of the People's Republic of China.

In 1949, General Liu was called back to Beijing to participate in the
preparation for the founding of the People's Republic of China. On October 1, 1949, the People's Republic was inaugurated, and General Liu
was on the platform by the side of Chairman Mao along with the other
leading generals at the ceremony at Tiananmen Square.

A few days later, General Liu left Beijing and went to southwestern China to finish his work in waging the war against the Nationalist forces. As the battles were joined, it was apparent that the Nationalist position was hopeless and that its troops were tired of fighting. A large detachment of Nationalist forces surrendered, making a rigorous defense impossible. The forces were crushed except for a detachment that was able to flee to Indochina, south of the border, and eventually join the Nationalist forces in Taiwan. Chiang Kaishek and his leading generals fled to Taiwan. Thus, the major battles in the conflict between the Communists and the Nationalists were over, leaving only pockets in China to be mopped up.

In 1950, General Liu ordered his troops to go into Tibet and put down the resistance of local forces. The Dalai Lama and his followers fled to India. Thus, Tibet was put under the military control of China, making it possible for China to strengthen its security over the southern Chinese border. The Tibet autonomous region was organized to give the Tibetans the control of the regional government and allow the Tibetan culture and religion to be preserved.

The central government wanted to establish direct control over the provinces and not allow the regional commanders to have political powers there. The generals would retain their military control of the regions, but the army would be apolitical to avoid the revival of the warlord situation. General Liu was offered the position of the general chief of staff of the army, a position he held at the beginning of the Long March. He rejected the offer but requested to be the founder and the first commander of the new Military Academy of the Army. The request was granted. It was decided that the Military Academy was to be located in Nanjing. In 1951, the Military Academy was established, and the training of officers started for the army, the navy, and the air force. The first class of officers graduated in 1954. In 1955, General Liu was promoted as one of the 10 field marshals in the country. In 1956, General Liu took sick leave and was hospitalized for a brain operation, and in 1957 he resigned from the Military Academy.

During the Cultural Revolution, the field marshals were divided in their positions. General Lin Biao supported the Gang of Four, but five field marshals were against them. These five included Generals Chen Yi, Nye Rungchen, Xu Xiangqian, Ye Jianying, and Liu Bocheng.[25] With the support of Chairman Mao, Lin Biao gained the upper hand, and the five field marshals had to conduct self-criticism and make public confession of their mistakes. They were assigned different posts away from Beijing. In 1972, General Liu lost sight in both eyes and was hospitalized. In 1973, he suffered from Alzheimer's disease. He died in 1986 at the age of 94. His wife, Wang Ronghua, and four sons and two daughters survived him. The daughters are medical doctors and the sons military officers.[26]

THE KOREAN WAR

In 1950, the Korean War began. China was involved in international warfare, facing UN forces with their modern equipment and technology.

Since 1910, Korea had been a Japanese colony. At the end of World War II, Soviet Russian troops occupied the North and American forces the South. A government was established by each side with the 38th parallel as the dividing line.

North Korean forces crossed the 38th parallel and overran the country, pushing the South Korean forces to Pusan at the southern end of the Korean peninsula. The United States and 15 other nations came to the aid of South Korea. General Douglas MacArthur, the commander of UN forces, fought the North Koreans and regained the territory south of the 38th parallel. MacArthur sent the U.S. Air Force to land in Inchon in the rear of the North Korean forces and captured Pyongyang. The UN forces continued to move north.

China had a military alliance with North Korea and needed it for a buffer zone against military threats from the West. Zhou Enlai, through the Indian ambassador, sent a message to the United States saying that if MacArthur should cross the 38th parallel and approach the Yalu River on the Chinese–Korean border, China would intervene. MacArthur crossed the 38th parallel and advanced north.

A debate in the Chinese government ensued as to whether China should enter the war. Knowing that it was a war that China could not win and one that would cause heavy casualties, the decision was made to send troops nonetheless.

On July 28, 1953, under President Dwight Eisenhower's directive, a truce was signed to end the Korean War. The 38th parallel was again made the dividing line between North and South Korea, restoring the conditions that existed prior to the war. During three years of fighting, the American casualties reached 160,000 and the Chinese about 800,000.

INVOLVEMENT OF CIVILIANS IN THE WARS

The author graduated from Yenching University in 1941, and shortly thereafter wars became widespread. The life experiences of members of this graduating class varied greatly, from outstanding success to miserable misfortune and disappointment. An energetic classmate asked the class members to write up their life stories and then compiled these stories into a book to commemorate the class's 50th reunion. The following discussion is based on excerpts from this book.

On the first day of school, President Leighton Stuart addressed the class in Chinese. He was born in 1876 to a missionary family at Hongzhou in Zhejiang Province. Hongzhou is a scenic city, with a beautiful lake and a pagoda by its side. It is an area of silk and tea, inhabited by gentle, peace-loving people. In 1887, Stuart's parents brought him back to the United States for education. He graduated with a BA degree in 1896 and from a theological seminary three years later. He was ordained as a minister in 1902 and married in 1904. The young couple went to China that year. After a short stay in southern China as a teacher, Stuart traveled to Beijing in 1919. He was made the president of Yenching University, an institution jointly supported by a number of churches in the United States. He started to build the university from scratch. He bought 200 acres of land five miles west of Beijing, the former garden of the Shao family in high position in the Ming dynasty. He hired an architect from Yale University to draw plans for the school. Buildings on the main campus housed classrooms, administrative offices, dormitories, and a gymnasium. A South Compound contained residences for foreign faculty, and an East Compound housed the Chinese faculty. In the center of the main campus was a lake with a pagoda alongside to re-create the beautiful scenery of Stuart's hometown. All the buildings were of the Chinese palace style with red columns and tile roofs. The university complex had a power plant, a water supply with a water tower built in to the pagoda, and modern plumbing. The campus came to be known as the most beautiful in China, with facilities matching the better universities in the United States. In 1926, the university moved into the new campus from the city where it started. In 1929, the Harvard Yenching Foundation was established to research Chinese literature and history and provide scholarships for graduates from Yenching to go to Harvard for PhD training. Through the years, about half a dozen Chinese have earned their PhD degrees from Harvard and returned to join the faculty of the Department of History at Yenching. In 1933, the Princeton Yenching Foundation was established, and scholarships were provided for Yenching graduates to go to Princeton for PhD training. A couple of Chinese students, including the author, having earned their PhD degrees from Princeton and returned to join the faculties of social sciences.

From 1937 to 1941, the university was in operation while the Japanese occupied the surrounding areas. Yenching was left untouched by the Japanese, as it was an American-funded institution and the United States had not yet declared war on Japan.

Stuart hired a Japanese full professor from Imperial University in Tokyo as a resident scholar. Being a government university professor, he had the rank of a general. Whenever troubles occurred between Yenching and the Japanese military authority, the Japanese professor would be sent to the city to talk to the commanding officer, who happened to be a lieutenant general. The problems would be easily solved because the professor outranked the general, and rank mattered to the Japanese.

In 1941, after the United States declared war on Japan, Yenching was closed down. Stuart and two officials of Peking Hospital, another American-funded institution, were arrested. Stuart was interrogated. He admitted that he had helped students and faculty members who wanted to travel to the Communist or the Nationalist areas get in touch with an underground network that made arrangements for their journeys, but he refused to reveal the names of the people involved in the network. Stuart was not tortured.

Toward the end of World War II, Stuart was asked to help in the arrangement of the Japanese surrender. He refused. The Japanese wanted to release him, but he refused to leave unless the other two cell mates were released as well. The three remained in jail until the war was over. In 1946, Stuart was named the American ambassador to China. In 1949, Mao invited Stuart to travel to Beijing to talk about the normalization of relations between China and the United States. On the eve of the journey, President Truman called Stuart back to report. It was then that the United States adopted the policy to contain China to prevent China from extending its influence in Asia.[27]

In these war years, many faculty members and students had gone from Yenching to the Communist or the Nationalist areas, including Edger Snow, born in Kansas City in 1905. In 1929, he went to Yenching as an instructor. An American girl was taking courses at Yenching who later became Mrs. Helen Snow. In 1929, the Yellow River flooded south of the river's bend. Snow, as a journalist, went there to investigate. About six million people died, and many more were made homeless. He saw corpses lying by the roadside and trees stripped of leaves and bark to be used as food. He wrote a report that rated half of a column in the inside space of the *New York Times*. For years, Snow sought permission to visit the newly emerged Communist base, but his requests were to no avail.

One night, a girl student brought along two young ladies to see him, asking whether he would escort the two ladies to Tianjin by train. Snow, an adventurous soul, readily agreed. The two young ladies were disguised as his servants. On arrival in Tianjin, protective escorts met the two ladies. Beijing at that time was under Nationalist control, and many relatives of Communist leaders in the Beijing area were caught and executed. Snow probably did not know the danger to which he exposed himself.

In 1935, the Nationalists were given publicity for fighting Japan by the international media and gained international support. The Comintern sent a Lin Yuying to Yanan to take a memorandum to Mao that the Chinese Communist Party should establish connections with international media to compete with the Nationalists for international recognition and support. At this time, Liu Shaoqi had already established headquarters at Tianjin for the underground North China Bureau. Snow was informed in 1935 that he would be welcome in Yanan. This made him the first American journalist to be admitted into the Communist area. On arrival at

Yanan, Zhou Enlai met Snow, and he was later introduced to Zhou Enlai's lover. The Communists had abolished the word *taitai* (wife) and replaced it with *airen* (lover), and after marriage the wife would retain her maiden name. To his surprise, Snow recognized that Zhou Enlai's lover was one of the two ladies he had escorted to Tianjin. Zhou Enlai was forever grateful for the help Snow rendered to his wife. Through Zhou's good office, Snow interviewed many of the Communist leaders and generals and became a good friend of Mao. Snow wrote many articles about the Communists that appeared in newspapers all over the world. Eventually, his book *Red Star over China* became a classic of Chinese modern history.

In 1936, Mao told Snow, "Whoever wins the peasants will win China; whoever solves the land problems will win the peasants."[28]

On October 1, 1971, when the country was celebrating the national anniversary of the founding of the People's Republic of China, Mao invited Snow to sit beside him on the public rostrum in Beijing to honor one of the friends of China from the early years. Mao told Snow that President Richard Nixon was welcome for a visit to China, and Snow relayed the message, laying the groundwork for the normalization of relations between China and the United States. Through some negotiations by Henry Kissinger, Nixon finally made his historic trip to China in 1972. Before Snow died, he requested that his ashes be buried on the bank of the lake at Yenching. This was done.

The author had an English professor, Ralph Lapwood, who was a strong, energetic gentleman. He was soft spoken, friendly, clean shaven, and sharply dressed, wearing a Cambridge blazer and white collar. Born in 1909 in Birmingham, England, he went to King Edward VI School in 1922 on a scholarship and later to Cambridge University in 1928 on a scholarship as well. On graduation in mathematics, he chose to go to China to teach, arriving in 1931. In 1932, he went to the area around Nanjing that had been devastated by the flooding Yangtze River and saw scenes similar to what Snow had seen in the Yellow River area. He was deeply saddened by the suffering of the peasants. He taught at Medhurst High School in Shanghai for a while and then went to teach at Yenching in 1936. It was customary for a foreign professor coming to Yenching to share the president's house with Stuart until a house was ready for him. Then he could hire a cook and a maid to do the housekeeping. Professor Lapwood was from a humble background, and he opted to stay in the student dormitory, eat at the student dining hall, and wash his own clothes. In 1937, the author was in his class. He was a strict teacher, holding daily quizzes and monthly examinations. The author was interested in Christianity, and Professor Lapwood wanted to help. The two got together almost daily for discussions. One summer, the professor sent the author on a vacation trip, financed out of the professor's pocket, to Shanghai to stay with a missionary family and gain traveling experience. That was the first vacation the author ever had. One day, Professor Lapwood asked the author to join him on a bicycle trip to a nearby park, Jade Spring Hill, a few miles away. Before they started, a lady joined them. She was Miss Nancy Stuckey, born in Tianjin of an Australian missionary family. The professor was courting her, and the author was brought along as a chaperone.

As a Christian, according to Professor Lapwood, his life had as its purpose the pursuit of four virtues: honesty, love, unselfishness, and puritanical sex. None of that conflicted with the virtues of a Chinese gentleman. The author accepted those virtues but added a few others taught by his parents: *qin* (diligence), *lian* (accountability in dealing with public funds), and *wei* (not to be confrontational in case of conflicts of interest but to show generosity in accommodating others). He added one more: service, taken from the motto of Yenching University, "Service for Truth through freedom." Truth was like a myth to a 20-year-old, and freedom posed no problem. He was brought up in a family where the parents always let him make his own decisions and respected those decisions. Service made life meaningful if it benefited humankind in its perpetual evolution. The author felt that to pursue life on these virtues, he could face the world. Professor Lapwood was his mentor.

In 1939, Professor Lapwood left the campus and joined a group of four people led by a Mr. Xiao Tien, a workman at Yenching's machine shop, to sneak through the Japanese front line to go into the Communist area. The four people included Professor Lapwood, Xiao, Lord Michael Lindsay, and a Mr. Charles Chao. Xiao was a strong man who had been constantly traveling to the Communist area to bring in medical and other supplies. Professor Lapwood had, since his arrival in China, traveled for several years in China. The group drove a car going west from the campus to the foothills of the Western Hills. There they left the car with a friend to be driven back to the campus and started out on foot. Local farmers were hired to carry the luggage. For several days, the rain was heavy, but they walked in it nevertheless because the rain kept the Japanese soldiers in their barracks. Before long, their food was gone, and they had to buy whatever was available from the peasants. When they came to a shallow river, they would cross it, holding on to one another. When they came to the Hun River with its swift current, they had to wait for two days, as the water was too high because of the rain. On the third day, they found a cable anchored on the banks across the river. The bargeman used a chain to loop over the cable and tied the chain to a barge. Guided by the cable, the barge made the crossing.

At nighttime, they stayed at local inns. They were bothered by bedbugs, and their clothing was full of lice. Finally, after nine days of walking, a team of soldiers that was sent out to receive them met them. They were taken to the headquarters of General Xiao Ke, the commander of the area.

From there on, they rode horses to Xian, where they were received by Generals Zhu De, Peng Dehuai, and Nie Rongzhen. There the group separated. Lord Lindsay went back to Yenching by way of Hong Kong, Xiao went back on foot, and Chao remained. Professor Lapwood went on by himself. Three months later, after walking 1,000 miles, he arrived at Chengdu. Asked about his long walk, he said it was difficult but it was for only three months, whereas the guerrilla soldiers were doing it for life. At Chegdu, he joined his friend Rewi Alley in working for the industrial cooperatives. Earlier, when Professor Lapwood first arrived in China, he met Alley in Shanghai when Alley was working in the Fire Brigade for the International Settlement. He took Professor Lapwood along while inspecting the fire hazards in Shanghai's factories. They saw the hard life of workers and the terrible working conditions, especially the harsh ones of child labor. In Chengdu, Alley started the industrial cooperatives in the 1940s to improve the workers' lots by making them the owners of the factories so that they could reap the rewards of their hard work. Under the management of workers, the working conditions of the factories improved. Professor Lapwood worked for two years for the cooperatives. A Mr. Shi Quan, whose name was originally Liu Shi, was the author's classmate at Yenching. Shi was an underground Communist agent operating in Chengdu. He often used Professor Lapwood's house for meetings. In 1940, Nancy Stuckey went to Chengdu to join Professor Lapwood. She came from Tianjin by way of Hong Kong, Haiphong, and Kunming. They were married in 1940. In 1942, when Yenching opened a branch campus in Chengdu, Professor Lapwood joined Yenching and was the acting dean of the College of Natural Sciences and the chairman of the Department of Mathematics. In 1945 when Yenching re-opened in Beijing, Professor Lapwood and his wife returned to Yenching. In 1952, he returned to England with his family. He received his PhD degree from Cambridge and served as the chairman of the Department of Mathematics and vice proctor of Emmanuel College. He retired in 1976 and visited China four times from 1980 to 1984, although he was not well, suffering from hardening of the arteries. His doctor and his wife advised him not to go, but he insisted on making these trips. He died in China in 1984, which is probably as he wished it. He was cremated, and, as he instructed, his ashes were buried on the bank of the lake on campus.

Another of the author's tutors was Michael Lord Lindsay, who accompanied Professor Lapwood in the 1939 trip to the Communist area. He was born in 1910 in London. His father, A. D. Lord Lindsay, was the master of Baliol College of Oxford University. By an agreement between Oxford and Yenching, Oxford was to send two tutors to China, and with a Chinese tutor, a tutorial system was to be established for social studies. Eight students, including the author, were selected from the sophomore class to study with these tutors for three years to complete their BA training. The courses would follow the Oxford curriculum of logic, scientific methods, history, sociology, political science, and economics. Daily assignments and weekly papers were to be completed. Michael Lord Lindsay, the eldest son of A. D. Lord Lindsay, was sent to Yenching as one of the tutors. He graduated from Oxford in 1936, spent a year in the United States, and went to China in 1937. On the boat to China, he met Dr. Norman Bethune, a Canadian medical doctor who devoted his life to working in the Communist area in China. Lord Lindsay was the opposite of Professor Lapwood. Michael Lord Lindsay was from the upper class, had sandy hair and a small mustache, constantly smoked a pipe, and dressed sloppily in a tweed jacket. He was a very kind, resourceful person. He shared the house with President Stuart. Each semester, he would give a dinner party for his students. The dinner had several courses. For each course, a waiter in a white jacket would carry a huge tray of food and serve each guest. Second helpings were always requested, as the students were young and growing. After the dinner, coffee and chocolates would be served. For one evening, the students lived like Oxford undergraduates. Michael Lord Lindsay built a short-wave radio station and had a large supply of medicines.

Among the eight students in the tutorial system, there was a girl, Li Xiaoli, who was born in Taiyuan in Shanxi Province. She was very healthy, a track-and-field athlete, and shy. When the author came calling on Michael Lord Lindsay, Miss Li was often there. This was not unusual because the students were supposed to see their tutors frequently. Michael Lord Lindsay was the most sought-after bachelor on the campus. Many foreign female faculty and staff members had a crush on him. In 1941, after Miss Li graduated, she and Michael Lord Lindsay were married, to the surprise of many people. But looking back, Michael Lord Lindsay made the ideal choice because right after their marriage, before Yenching was closed down, the two went to the Communist area, where they traveled together for four years. It took a strong Chinese girl to endure the journey and to take care of him. When they left Yenching, they carried six suitcases full of radio equipment and medicines. They drove a car to the foothills of the Western Hills and hired horses to carry the suitcases. The medicines were for Dr. Bethune, and the radio parts were for the radio stations that Michael Lord Lindsay was to build for the Communist army at different locations. He was appointed a consultant for the army's Department of Communications. The radio stations he built at Yanan could send and receive messages from as far as San Francisco. Another assignment for the couple was to act as hosts to foreign dignitaries and serve as interpreters. Lady Lindsay also taught English. In 1945, when World War II was over, the couple returned to England. Mao gave them a farewell party, went to the airport to see them off, and gave them a check for U.S.$3,000 as a token of his appreciation. In 1949, Michael Lord Lindsay was appointed by the United Nations as the chairman of the Far East Economic Commission with headquarters in Shanghai. He could not report to work because the Nationalists still held the area and refused his entry to China. After the founding of the People's Republic of China, the couple visited China several times, and in 1992 they settled in Chevy Chase, Maryland, in the United States.[29]

Another classmate of the author was Han Yin, whose name was originally Han Zunying. He was from a poor family and went to Yenching after graduating from Baoding High School. He had no support from his family, and his scholarship was not enough to cover his living expenses. He could not afford to live in the dormitories, so he shared a room off campus. He took a part-time job working in the university library. As a student from out of town, he did not have the required English language ability, but all the reading and writing assignments were in English. After two years of study, he withdrew from the university in 1939 and returned home to join the guerrilla forces operating in the Taihang Mountains in Hebei and Shanxi provinces. He was the commissar of a regiment of the Sixth Army. In 1941, an underground agent by the name of Miss Su Shan came from the Taihang Mountain area to meet with Stuart to recruit students. She was probably sent by Mr. Han Yin. Stuart called in three students from the graduating class to meet her, including Sun Yikuan, Chen Peichang, and Fang Daci. All three were ready to go. Miss Su Shan repeatedly warned them that the conditions were harsh and that the assignment was dangerous, and she thought that the boys were too young. The three went, spending eight years in the guerrilla forces until the war ended in 1949. Their assignments were to inspect the frontline activities and make reports. In 1942, one of the three, Chen Peichang, sent an underground agent, Gou Zhiqing, to go to Beijing to buy supplies and asked Chen's classmates Yang Sishen, Zheng Wenchao, and Wang Zhiren to look after the agent. At that time, Yang stayed in a room at the back of Changan Theater in the western part of the city of Beijing. No problems arose on the first two trips. However, on the third trip, all four, including a visitor, were arrested by the Japanese military police. For days, they were tortured in an effort to obtain information on the network of underground agents in the Beijing area. Each day, they endured interrogation and torture until they passed out. Actually, they knew nothing of the underground agents in the Beijing area. Eventually, the families bribed the Japanese military police for their release.[30]

In high school, the author had a teacher of Chinese literature, Professor Dong Luan. He was a popular teacher who joked and laughed all the time. In 1935, he joined the faculty of Yenching University. After the author entered Yenching in 1937, he often visited Professor Dong at his home. In 1937, he was chairman of the Department of Chinese Literature. He was a scholar of Buddhism, and his study was filled with Buddhist classics.

One day in 1942, the author called on Professor Dong. Mrs. Dong came out crying and showed the author a note written by the professor saying that he was tired of his life and his work and had gone to a Buddhist monastery to became a monk, asking his wife for forgiveness. Years later after the war, it was found out that the professor, together with two other professors, Wang Xisheng and Cui Yuling, accepted invitations from the Union University of North China in the Communist area to work there. The professor's study of Buddhism, his collection of Buddhist classics, and Mrs. Dong's tears were just a facade. Professor Dong was a person with a great sense of humor. All three professors held high positions in the university and later in the government. Professor Dong died in 1953 and was buried in the government cemetery in Beijing.[31]

After reviewing the life stories of professors and classmates, the author felt that although their fates varied from success to sad misfortune, all had done well for themselves and their friends. They did not intentionally cause anyone any harm and were trying to be as helpful as they could. They might differ in ideology, but all were brave and patriotic, demonstrating the Christian spirit of Yenching University at a trying time in Chinese history.

NOTES

1. Agnes Smedley, *The Great Road: The Life and Times of Chu Teh* (New York: Monthly Review Press, 1956), p. 12.

2. Chungi Jin (ed.), *A Biography of Zhu De* (in Chinese, *Zhu De Zhuan*) (Beijing: People's Publishing Co., 1993), p. 4.

3. Smedley, *The Great Road*, p. 93.

4. Jin, *A Biography of Zhu De*, p. 26.

5. Smedley, *The Great Road*, p. 122.

6. Jin, *A Biography of Zhu De*, p. 53.

7. Ibid., p. 73.

8. Smedley, *The Great Road*, pp. 223–224.

9. Jin, *A Biography of Zhu De*, p. 165.

10. Smedley, *The Great Road*, pp. 2–3.

11. Ibid., p. 367.

12. Ibid., p. 130.

13. Deng Liqun (ed.), *A Biography of Peng Dehuai* (in Chinese, *Peng Dehuai Zhuan*) (Beijing: Contemporary China Publishing Co., 1993), p. 5.

14. Ibid., p. 14.

15. Ibid., p. 178.

16. Ibid., pp. 218–228.

17. Ibid., p. 286.

18. Jonathan D. Spence, *The Search for Modern China* (New York: W. W. Norton, 1990), p. 487.

19. Ibid., p. 493.

20. Ibid., p. 507.

21. Ibid., p. 508.

22. Deng Liqun (ed.), *Biography of Liu Bocheng* (in Chinese, *Liu Bocheng Zhuan*) (Beijing, Contemporary China Publishing Co., 1992), p. 43.

23. Ibid., p. 101.

24. Ibid., pp. 480–481.

25. Ibid., p. 679.

26. Ibid., p. 687.

27. Li Zhen, *The Sound of Bell at Yenching University* (in Chinese, *Yenyuan Zhong-sheng*) (Tianjin: Union University Press, 1992), p. 289.

28. Harrison E. Salisbury, *The Long March* (New York: Harper & Row, 1985), p. 69.

29. Li, *The Sound of Bell at Yenching University*, pp. 224–225; Yenching Alumni Class of 1941, *Fiftieth Reunion Memorial* (in Chinese, *Ruxue Wushi Zhounian Jinian-kan*) (Beijing: Yenching University Press, 1988), pp. 16–17.

30. Li, *The Sound of Bell at Yenching University*, pp. 245–246.

31. Ibid., pp. 228–229.

CHAPTER 3

Development under Mao

From 1950 to 1976, China was under the leadership of Mao Zedong. This period saw five major developments: security, infrastructure, agriculture, the Great Leap Forward, and the Cultural Revolution. A new society appeared in the country, but disappointments were experienced as well.

SECURITY

Because of the large territory it covers, China needs a strong central defense system to hold the country together. At the time of the weakening of the central authority, the country would repeatedly break up into warring regions that fought each other until a strongman managed to conquer them and reunite the country. The primary duty of the government is to maintain a strong central defense system to guarantee the unity and stability of the country.

China underwent 250 years of fighting: the Warring period from 471 to 221 B.C., 60 years of fighting in the Three Kingdoms period from A.D. 220 to 280, 169 years of fighting in the South and North Dynasty period from 420 to 589, 53 years of fighting in the Five Dynasty period from 907 to 960, 17 years of fighting in the Warlords period from 1911 to 1928, and 3 years of fighting in the Revolutionary War period from 1948 to 1949.

The direct consequences of these warring periods were the loss of lives and property due to military operations. The indirect consequences were the floods, droughts and diseases that would follow because of the lack of preventive measures. Famine and diseases would take a major toll on the population.

Northern tribes and foreign powers have repeatedly invaded China. Some of these invaders have managed to maintain control of the country for long periods of time.

China saw 218 years of rule by the Liao dynasty from 907 to 1125, 109 years of rule by the Jin dynasty, 134 years of rule by the Yuan dynasty, 267 years of rule by the Qing dynasty, and 14 years of rule in the coastal areas during the Japanese occupation.[1] The government must build up a strong defense system to fend off foreign invasions.

The backbone of the Chinese defense system was the People's Liberation Army, which defeated the Nationalists in conquering the country and fought in the Korean War. The army was a highly disciplined unit. It was recruited from farmers and workers and had maintained good relations with the working class. Camaraderie had developed among the army personnel. The officers and men lived the same way, wore the same uniforms, and often ate the same food.

Deng Xiaoping was quoted in praising the army: "Why is it that the officers and men of the People's Liberation Army could defeat the Nationalist army which was superior both in number and equipment? Is it not chiefly because they wanted to serve the people and had maintained a good relationship with the people?"[2]

By the 1978 Constitution, the armed forces were placed under the supervision of the Military Affairs Commission in the Central Committee of the Communist Party. The commission decided on defense policies and appointed and removed regional commanders. Its Political Department took charge of the political education of the armed forces. The commission was composed of senior military leaders who interfaced with the Politburo, which decided on government polices. The first vice chairman of the Military Affairs Commission was the minister of defense, who was under the supervision of the premier of the State Council. The chief of staff was under the supervision of the defense minister.[3]

China saw 13 military regions, 23 provincial military districts, and nine garrisons for metropolitan centers. During the Cultural Revolution, from 1966 to 1976, the army did not cooperate with the Gang of Four, who created the people's militia as a military base of their own. After the downfall of the Gang of Four, the people's militia was reorganized as auxiliary forces under the army.[4]

Fearful of an attack from the Soviet Union and from Taiwan with the backing of the United States, China since 1953 has given priority to the development of nuclear weapons.

Mao's dictum was "dig tunnels deep, store grain everywhere and never seek hegemony." Hegemony refers to the Soviet Union's expansion policy to dominate Asia.

General Li Xiannian was quoted as saying, "China would keep on developing nuclear weapons of its own, as long as the United States and the Soviet Union continued to develop theirs."[5]

From 1942 to 1944, two Chinese nuclear physicists, Hu Ning and Zhang Wenyu, went to the Advanced Institute at Princeton University to do post-doctoral studies under Professors J. Robert Oppenheimer and Albert Einstein. The author was a PhD candidate at Princeton at the time. He met them frequently in restaurants and at friends' parties. They returned to China in the late 1940s and worked on the atomic bomb.

Zhao Zhongyao, a nuclear physicist, enrolled in the California Institute of Technology and earned his PhD degree in 1926 when he was 24 years old. He remained at the institute as a senior research fellow in nuclear studies. He was appointed by Taiwan as an official observer at the American atomic bomb test at the Bikini Islands. In the 1950s, Senator Joseph McCarthy was starting a drive to rid the United States of Communists. Zhao realized that it might be difficult for him to leave the country if he stayed too long. Thus, he joined a group of Chinese scientists and boarded the SS *President Wilson* to go to China. The Federal Bureau of Investigation (FBI) found out that too late and finally caught up with the group at Yokohama, Japan. The group was detained for a few weeks but was let go, as the FBI lacked jurisdiction on foreign soil. Zhao later worked on the atomic bomb in China.[6]

Qian Xueshen, a missile expert, was born in Shanghai. After graduating from Jiaotung University, he went to the Massachusetts Institute of Technology to study on a fellowship and received a master's degree. He transferred to the California Institute of Technology and became a protégé of Professor Theodore von Karmon, who recommended Qian to serve as a member of the Scientific Advisory Group of the military and was conferred the rank of colonel. Qian was made a group supervisor of the Jet Propulsion Laboratory at the California Institute of Technology with a staff of 264 scientists. In 1945, the missile produced by the laboratory tested successfully in New Mexico. The War Department awarded Qian a meritorious civil service medal. Qian often attended discussion groups at the home of Professor Sidney Weinbaum, who came from Russia and became a naturalized American citizen. In 1950, Professor Weinbaum was arrested and accused of operating a Communist cell in Pasadena, California. Qian was also arrested, and his security clearance was withdrawn. Consequently, his career came to an end.

Qian went to Washington and requested that he be allowed to return to China. The request was denied, and he was stranded in the country for five years. In 1955, Qian was informed that he was allowed to leave. The Chinese and U.S. governments had come to an agreement for an exchange. The Chinese government was to release 11 airmen who had strayed from the border during the Korean War and were captured in China, and the U.S. government was to release 39 Chinese scientists in the United States.

Qian was among the group. In China, Qian worked on the atomic bomb and missiles.[7]

In the 1950s, a group of Chinese students and engineers were sent to the Soviet Union for training and studies. In the late 1950s, they returned to China. After about 30 years of working in the government, many have reached the first-echelon ranks, including Li Peng (the current premier) and Professor Song Jian, the minister of the State Science and Technology Commission. Many have become ministers and vice ministers in the government and presidents and vice presidents of colleges and universities.

Chinese scientists trained in the United States and in the Soviet Union combined their expertise in the development of the Chinese space and nuclear weapon systems. Of the 15 scientists working on the atomic bomb, five were trained in the United States, including Hu Ning and Zhang Wenyu from the Advanced Institute at Princeton and Zhao Zhongyao, Qian Xueshen, and Guo Yinghuai from the California Institute of Technology.[8]

In 1964, the first Chinese atomic bomb tested successfully. China eventually developed a nuclear weapons system strong enough to deter foreign invasion. In this respect, Mao has served the nation well.

INFRASTRUCTURE

By 1952, the economy had recovered from the war, and in 1953 the country started the First Five Year Plan for 1953–57. The plan put emphasis on infrastructure and industrial development following the Soviet pattern. After this, several Five Year Plans followed, but the economic performance was erratic with many interruptions, such as the Great Leap Forward from 1958 to 1960 and the Cultural Revolution from 1966 to 1976. The economy was able to maintain annual growth in the gross national product of 5 to 6 percent in real terms.[9]

The planned economy under Mao was highly centralized. All production units were given quotas of outputs to be delivered to the government, and the supplies were distributed through government stores at fixed prices. Commodities that were in short supply were rationed. The management of all units—productive, political, social, and educational—was in the hands of party cadres and the working class, and professionals and intellectuals had little share in this. At the beginning of Mao's rule, the country worked hard to develop its infrastructure as a base for economic progress.

China's major rivers, flowing from the mountains in the west to the east where they entered the oceans, provide good inland waterway transportation for the country. Railroads are built to go from the north to the south along the coast and into central China. The rivers and railroads are tied together to form a network of transportation. Bridges are built on the rivers where the railroads come to cross, such as the Changjiang Bridge at Nanjing.

Because of equipment shortages, all types of locomotives are still used for trains, from the coal-burning type to diesel engines. Trains in China run on time.

Under Mao, the transportation system in China was greatly improved. From 1949 to 1980, railroad mileage improved from 13,000 to 32,000 miles, highway mileage from 49,000 to 552,000 miles, inland waterway mileage from 45,000 to 84,000 miles, and air route mileage from 8,000 to 110,000 miles.[10] This development is essential to economic progress and improves the country's ability to mobilize the armed forces to maintain unity and stability in the country.

At the time of the founding of the People's Republic in 1949, the country's flood control projects had been long neglected because of the many years of war. Floods affected 30 to 40 percent of the country's arable land. A nationwide reconstruction of the flood control projects was required.[11]

Mao was magnificent in maneuvering the masses for this task. He initiated several projects, each of which involved hundreds of thousands of people in long periods of work lasting several years.

The Thought of Mao, a small pamphlet, was widely circulated in the country, and a personality cult developed from it. With popular support, Mao could literally tame rivers and move mountains.

An example is the Huai River project in Jiangsu Province. At one time, the Yellow River flooded and worked south. It changed its course and entered the Huai River as its route to enter the sea. The Huai River was forced to take a new route to the sea. From time to time, the Huai River would flood because it had an inadequate outlet. Mao led the farmers in a project to dig a 90-mile irrigation canal from Hungze Lake to the ocean to give the river a new outlet. Along the canal, a system of irrigation channels was constructed to supply water for the nearby farms. The project was completed after years of hard labor. Pictures show thousands of people digging with picks and shovels with mounds of earth standing 30 feet high. The original level of the land was at the tops of the mounds.[12]

Another example is the Min River dyke, called Du Jiang Yan, at Guanxian in Sichuan Province about 40 miles northwest of Chengdu. In 256 B.C., Prince Li Bing of the state of Shu started a flood control project on this river. The Min River runs directly to Mountain Yulei, at whose foothills the river had to make a sharp turn to go around the mountain. When water levels were high, the rushing current could not negotiate the sharp turn, and floods would result. The prince sent an engineer to build a dyke at the foothills to control the floods, but the rushing current could not be contained. A second engineer was sent there to build much stronger dykes, but still the flooding continued. No solution to this problem could be found during the prince's reign. The prince's son (who succeeded the prince) sent a third engineer to help solve the dilemma. Instead of building stronger dykes, however, he had a channel dug through the mountain to provide an outlet for the rushing water. In the middle of the river in front of the foothills, a dyke was constructed to divide the river into two currents—one current following the original riverbed (the outer river) and the other entering the new channel through the mountain (the inner river). As the two rivers passed through and around the mountain, they flowed into the plain. The currents slowed down, and the new river was guided so that it would merge with the original river. Along the two rivers, reservoirs with irrigation channels were constructed to regulate the water flow of the rivers. At high water levels, water gates were opened to allow water from the rivers to flow into the reservoirs for irrigation. At low water levels, water was allowed to be emptied from the reservoirs into the rivers so that the reservoirs could take in water from the rivers at the time of the next high water level. The project worked. The local people built a temple—the Temple of Two Princes—to honor the princes for their persistent leadership on this project. The project has been maintained for the past 2,000 years. In 1949, Mao enlisted the people to improve the project and enlarge the irrigation channels. When the project was completed, the system supplied water to 2,000 square miles of farmland, four times the area that existed before 1949.

AGRICULTURAL REFORM

The two aspects of agricultural development under Mao were the expansion of arable land and the collectivization of farms. To maximize the use of arable land, Mao ordered the people to cremate the dead and to level the graves that existed on arable land to make room for cultivation. No ruler in China up to that time had dared issue such an order because of the popular reverence for ancestors. But this time, people followed Mao's order. According to a survey in the 1930s, about 2 percent of arable land was occupied by graves.

While the graves were being dug up, many treasures were discovered in coffins and burial chambers. For instance, a farmer was digging for water near the tomb of the emperor Qin, the first emperor of China, in Xian, Shaanxi Province, when thousands of life-size terra-cotta warriors were discovered. Also discovered were terra-cotta horses and bronze chariots, all in good shape, having been buried for over 2,000 years. Now several buildings have been constructed to cover up the excavation site. These buildings were made into a museum, an excellent tourist attraction.

To expand the arable land, Mao ordered gently sloped mountains to be terraced for farms. An example is the Dazhai commune in Xiyang, Shanxi Province, about 60 miles southeast of Taiyuna in the Taihang Mountains, the home ground of Mao's forces in the Sino–Japanese War. It was originally a very poor area. Taking orders from Mao, thousands of farmers worked for 10 years terracing the hillside. They carried rocks and stones on their back to the terraces to reinforce the banks, used topsoil from the riverbed to spread around the terraces, and dug canals to guide the mountain streams to irrigate the land by the force of gravity. After the project was completed, the commune became a prosperous community. A slogan was coined by the government: "learn from Dazhai about farming" (in Chinese, "Nongye Xue Dazhai").

In touring the countryside, the author saw many terraced farms on gently sloped hillsides and forests of young trees of about the same height on the steeper hillsides. These trees were planted to reduce soil erosion and to produce timber.

A land reform program was carried out under Mao. First, the rent paid by tenant farmers to the landlords was reduced, and then a rent ceiling of 37.5 percent of the crop was fixed. Finally, land was taken from the landlords and distributed to the farmers. A total of about 115 million acres were distributed to some 300 million farmers, averaging about a third of an acre per farmer. However, the result was not satisfactory. Earlier, when the landlords were in charge, they financed farmers for the purchases of seeds and fertilizers, provided farmers with implements and equipment, and marketed the crops. Now the farmer had to learn the various aspects of farm management from scratch.

The government tried to help farmers in the management of their farms. In 1953, the government organized teams of mechanics to bring farmers implements and equipment to help them do heavy work. In 1955, the government organized cooperatives to help farmers buy seeds and fertilizers and to market their crops. About 30 to 40 percent of farmers received help from these teams.

From 1956 to 1958, the government took the land back from farmers and started to collectivize farms following the Soviet pattern. The biggest farms were made into state-owned and -operated farms. Farmers working on these state farms were paid wages by a point system that was based on the amount and types of work done. Medium-size farms were made into collective farms owned by the state but operated by farmers. Collective farms were assigned quotas of crops to be delivered to the government and paid government prices. The income of the collective farms was distributed to farmers by the point system.

From 1958 to 1960, the state and collective farms were converted to communes managed by farmers. By 1960, 98 percent of the farm families were part of the commune system. The country had about 24,000 communes with about 5,000 households for each. Each commune was divided into brigades with about 2,000 households for each. The brigade was again divided into teams with about 30 households for each. Each brigade and each team was given an assignment. In 1961, to encourage productivity, each household was given a private plot of land. After having finished their jobs for the commune, farmers would spend their spare time working on their plots doing whatever they wanted with them. They were allowed to sell the crops grown on their plots on the free market. This was a great improvement, as it gave farmers a chance to develop their managerial skills. This was the beginning of the free-enterprise and free-market system in China.

Key agricultural products, such as rice, wheat, meat, vegetable oil, and sugar, were placed under the control of the planned system. These crops were produced by communes and distributed by government stores at fixed prices and in some cases were rationed. This would ensure the supply of basic necessities for the people and help curb inflation. Non-key agricultural products, such as fruits, vegetables, and eggs, were not controlled but were left in the free-enterprise and free-market system. However, these products were susceptible to inflationary pressure.

THE GREAT LEAP FORWARD

Mao's rule was for the most part successful until the time came for the industrial development of China. In 1957, a group of Orthodox Marxists obtained Mao's approval to embark on a three-year program to accelerate the output of steel, coal, and electric power in the country. They advocated mass participation in the program. The underlying assumption was that if Mao could motivate hundreds of thousands of people to work in flood control projects and terracing mountainsides, they could improve industrial output in the same way.

By the fall of 1958, millions of people participated in the project, many of them from the countryside. Suddenly, some 600,000 steelmaking furnaces sprang up in people's backyards everywhere, and some 11 million tons of iron and steel were produced. The question was whether such an increase in iron and steel production was what the country needed. Because of the rush to steel, farming was neglected, and agricultural output declined. A period of famine followed in China.[13]

Steelmaking is a highly technical field requiring the supervision of engineers and technicians and the use of modern plants and equipment so that the iron and steel produced are good enough for industrial use. No provisions were made for meeting these requirements, and consequently 27 percent of the total iron and steel production was unfit for industrial use.[14]

Another project of the Orthodox Marxists was the construction of public dining halls. Instead of family members eating their meals together as a family, they were asked to eat at public dining halls and pay for their meals.

Glorious reports with falsified statistics were sent in by the cadres of the Orthodox Marxists to please the chairman and also to keep him from learning the truth of the situation. Some party leaders began to sense that the Great Leap Forward and the public dining halls were not doing well, and Mao was criticized by these leaders, the most blunt being the outspoken General Peng Dehuai, the minister of defense. Peng was the commanding general of Chinese forces during the Korean War. In fighting the American forces, the Chinese were poor in firepower but enjoyed the advantage of more manpower. The Chinese used the technique of human sea warfare to overwhelm the enemy with large numbers of soldiers, but facing the strong firepower of the Allied forces, the Chinese suffered a tremendous number of casualties. Peng learned that, in modern warfare, technology and equipment were more important than the size of the military. He realized that the modernization of the military would be an expensive project and possible only if the country were successfully prosperous. He assumed the task of leading economic and military reforms.

In 1957, Peng went to northeastern China to investigate. He followed the old tradition, coming in disguise, avoiding the officials, but talking directly to the people. He found out that the pig-iron project was a waste of resources, that the communes were not productive because of a lack of incentives for the farmers to work hard, and that the public dining halls took away people's family lives.

In 1958, Peng went back to his hometown of Xiangtan in Hunan Province to investigate. He stayed with his family instead of the official hostel. He found the same story. He then went to Shaoshan in Hunan Province, the hometown of Chairman Mao. Again he found the same story. He discussed his discoveries with his colleagues, many of whom asked him to talk directly to the chairman and show him the reality of the situation.

In 1959, Peng led a group of military officers to tour Eastern Europe and the Soviet Union for 50 days. On returning to China, he was summoned to Lu Shan, a summer resort area in Jiangxi, for a conference called by Chairman Mao. The chairman was aware of the problems of the Great Leap Forward and was taking steps to make corrections. The conference was made into a social gathering, with meetings held during the daytime and movies and dancing in the evenings. Mao was definitely on the side of the Orthodox Marxists, and his position was to strike a balance between the two factions: the reformers and the Orthodox Marxists. At this moment, Mao felt that the reformers were becoming too powerful, and he wanted to protect the Orthodox Marxists.

As the conference was nearing its end, Peng decided to have a talk with the chairman. On July 12, 1959, he went to see him. Guards told Peng that the chairman was taking a nap. Peng decided not to wake up the chairman, as he did during his home visit from the front in the Korean War. Peng had a great deal to say to the chairman, including the problems of the Great Leap Forward, the future role of China in the world, and the needed military and the economic reforms. However, he knew that he was not accomplished in oral presentation, and he did not want to forget some of the details of his plans for reforms. He wrote a long letter and had the letter delivered to Mao.[15]

On receiving this letter, Mao extended the conference for a week and summoned many other high-level officials to come to Lu Shan for a discussion. Mao had the letter reproduced and distributed at the conference. He presided over the meeting and talked for three hours, saying that although problems existed, he wanted the communes, public dining halls, and pig-iron projects to continue.

On July 30, 1959, Peng was called to a meeting with Mao that included many other high-level officials, including Zhou Enlai, Zhu De, Liu Shaoqi, and Lin Biao. Mao began to criticize Peng, saying that 70 percent of the time he disobeyed Mao's orders. Peng said that he always considered Mao his mentor and had obeyed his orders at least 50 percent of the time. Lin Biao, the hero of the war in Manchuria against the Nationalists, criticized Peng as a person with a great ambition and political motives. Mao asked Peng, "Whom do you think the army would listen to, you or me?" Peng replied that he never dreamed of contesting the chairman for power. In Mao's mind, Peng had become too powerful. If Peng were allowed to have his way, in time it would not be difficult for him to push Mao aside. In 1959, Mao was 66 years old and Peng 61. Mao had decided to make an Orthodox Marxist his successor, doing whatever reforms were necessary but keeping the power in the hands of farmers and workers so that the Communist revolution was not fought in vain. Mao considered that Peng, as the leader of the reformers, had become too powerful and must be relieved.

Lin Biao accused Peng of having political ambitions to seize power by organizing a military club (a clique among high-ranking officers) and by soliciting foreign help during his tour of Eastern Europe and the Soviet Union.

In 1959, Peng was relieved of the position of minister of defense and all other military assignments. Lin Biao succeeded him as the minister of defense. Peng and his family were removed from the Central and South Lake residence and resettled in Wu's garden, Guajiatun, west of the city near the Summer Palace. It was a joke played against Peng. *Guajiatun* means "the place for the retired general to hang up his armors," and Wu's garden was formerly the residence of a traitor, Wu Sangui, who tried to overthrow the government of the Ming dynasty by enlisting help from a border tribe in northeastern China. The residence was comfortable, being a compound surrounded by walls on four sides with 14 rooms and occupying an acre of land.

Peng's daily routine included physical exercise and gardening, reading newspapers and magazines, and writing in a diary. He was to report to the Central Party School twice a week to study Marxism with a tutor.

Peng's wife, Pu Anxiu, was the assistant party secretary at Beijing Normal University in the city and stayed at the university. She went home to join Peng on weekends. The couple had never quarreled, but they began to blame each other more frequently. Peng refused to see his colleagues for fear of being accused of plotting against the government and not wanting to implicate the visitors. Many family members frequently visited him, including the widow of one of his brothers and his two nieces.

Lin Biao, a junior officer, was on Peng's side at the Huili Conference in 1935, when Peng criticized Mao for the guerrilla warfare techniques. Now Lin was Peng's equal. Lin sided this time with Mao, defending Mao's ideas and policies. Mao welcomed this support from Lin and rewarded him.[16]

In 1959, Mao relinquished the presidency of the People's Republic of China to Liu Shaoqi. In 1961, Mao told Lord Montgomery that Liu was his successor.[17]

The Great Leap Forward was a failure, causing a three-year famine, from 1958 to 1961, and killing millions of people by starvation.

THE CULTURAL REVOLUTION

When the People's Republic of China was founded in 1949, Mao was the leader of the country and held supreme power. He had control of the Communist Party as its secretary-general, control of the military as the chairman of the Military Affairs Commission, and the support of the public through the personal cult. Terms of his office were without limit. He was to keep his office for life and pass on the rule of the country to his successor. The qualifications of the successor were that he be loyal to Mao, carry out his policies after Mao's death, and be patient and not usurp authority before Mao's death.

Living in the former Imperial Palace, Mao developed an interest in Chinese history, especially the lives of the previous emperors. He spent a great deal of time studying *The History of the Twenty Four Dynasties.* He discovered that within the past 400 years, three emperors were deposed, and this alarmed him. The last emperor of the Ming dynasty, from 1368 to 1644, lost the empire to a rebel. He fled from the palace and went to Coal Hill on the north side of the palace. He bade farewell to the country and to his ancestors and hanged himself on top of the hill. Emperor Guangxu of the Qing dynasty attempted to free the country from the emperor's absolute rule and form a constitutional monarchy, but he failed. The conservatives replaced him by making Empress Dowager the ruler. The emperor was put under house arrest and died in 1907 at the age of 37. The last emperor of the Qing dynasty, Puyi, was deposed by the revolution of

1912. In 1931, Japan invaded Manchuria and established a puppet regime, Manchukuo, with Puyi as the chief executive. When the People's Republic of China was founded, Puyi was taken prisoner. He attempted suicide by slashing his wrists, but he was discovered and saved. He was released from prison after many years of detention and became a gardener. A movie was made depicting his miserable life.

Mao developed a paranoia that he might be deposed by either ambitious generals or Communist Party leaders. To preserve his power, he cultivated popular support through the personal cult and developed a secret service, similar to the KGB of the Soviet Union, to keep a close watch on his subordinates. The secret service was placed under the charge of Kang Sheng, who had brought Jiangqing from Shanghai to Yanan and promoted her marriage to Mao. Both Kang Sheng and Jiangqing were among the leaders of the Orthodox Marxist faction of the party.

In the 1960s, the Communist Party had two factions: the Orthodox Marxists and the reformers. The former were led by Jiangqing, Mao's wife; Kang Sheng, the head of the secret service; and General Lin Biao, the defense minister. The reformers were led by Liu Shaoqi and Deng Xiaoping.

The reformers gradually gained control of the party machine. Liu Shaoqi became the first vice president of the Central Committee of the party and Deng the secretary-general of the party.

Liu Shaoqi was born in 1898 in Ningxian in Hunan Province. In 1920, he joined the Communist Youth League. In 1921, he was sent by General Zhang Guotao to the Soviet Union to study, enrolling at the East Worker's University in Moscow. There he joined the Communist Party. He returned to China as an agent for the Communist International (Comintern). He was arrested twice, in Changsha and in Shenyang, and both times he managed to escape. In 1947, he married Miss Wang Guangmei, a beautiful, talented young lady. He was chosen to be the successor of Mao in 1949.

His book *How to Be a Good Communist* sold a staggering 15 million copies between 1921 and 1966, exceeding in that period the sales of any work by Mao.[18]

Jiangqing was born in 1915 in Zhucheng in Shangdong Province. Her first husband was a young businessman. After a while, they broke up, and she went to Qingdao, a seaport. There she fell in love with a young Communist, her second husband. When this husband was arrested, she moved to Shanghai in 1933 to begin a stage and screen career. She assumed the theatrical name of Lanping. In 1936, she married Tang Na, a theater critic, her third husband. After the Japanese attack of Shanghai, she journeyed to Yanan. With Kang Sheng's help, she became Mao's secretary and later married him in 1938. Mao assured his colleagues that Jiangqing, the name given by Mao, would not get involved in politics. But she was not content to be just a housewife. Under constant pressure, Zhou

Enlai appointed her adviser on the arts to the People's Liberation Army. She staged a number of operas to present the revolutionary theme.[19]

Gradually, differences arose between the reformers and Mao on policies. While Mao insisted on the centralization patterns of the Soviet Union, Liu and Deng were supported reform that would give farming families and factory managers more freedom of management. When the Vietnam War started, Liu and Deng advocated a closer relationship with the Soviet Union to counter the growing influence of the United States in Asia; Mao was leaning toward the United States. Mao felt that Liu had become more a competitor than a successor.

For instance, when Andre Malraux, France's minister of culture, went to Beijing for a state visit in 1965, he was received in the Great Hall of the People. Liu Shaoqi and a group of ministers stood on one side, and Mao by himself stood on the other side. Malrauz presented a letter from President Charles de Gaulle to Liu, but before Liu could say anything, Mao took over. Throughout the entire meeting, Liu did not have a chance to speak. Mao remarked to Malrauz that neither the problems of industry nor those of agriculture had been solved and that many of the writers in the country were anti-Marxists, showing his dissatisfaction with the reforms of Liu and Deng.[20]

Jealousy developed between the wives of Mao and Liu. For instance, in 1964, when Madame Sukarno, wife of the Indonesian president, visited China, Liu's wife, the accomplished Wang Guangmei, was the official hostess. Wang was a beautiful young lady, well educated, and fluent in English. The next day, a photo of Madame Sukarno and Wang appeared on the front page of *The People's Daily*. Five days later, a party honoring Madame Sukarno was given by Mao and Jiangqing, and another photo, this time of all three, appeared on the front page of *The People's Daily*. In all the years since 1949, no photo of Mao and Jiangqing had ever officially been released. It seemed that Jiangqing and Wang Guangmei were vying for the role of first lady of China.[21]

To combat the growing power of the reformers, the Orthodox Marxists started a cultural revolution aiming at removing the reformers from important government and party positions. The leaders of the group were Jiangqing; Zhang Chungqiao, a political journalist; Wang Hungwen, a cotton mill worker; and Yao Wenyuan, a pamphleteer. They were later referred to as the Gang of Four. Lin Biao, the defense minister, and Kang Sheng, the head of the secret service, supported the group. They organized high school and college students into Red Guards to carry out a campaign to revive Marxism–Leninism by attacking the old Chinese ideals, customs, and culture. They began destroying temples, monuments, and museums. They stopped going to classes and taking examinations. When teachers wanted to resume classes, they turned against the teachers, many of whom were declared counterrevolutionaries and were beaten up. On many campuses, students who opposed the Red Guards rose up, fighting broke out among the two groups. The army under Lin Biao and the police under the secret service sided with the Red Guards.

Liu Shaoqi and Deng Xiaoping went to Hongzhou, Mao's summer resort, to see him. Mao was not responsive. Meanwhile, Kang Sheng of the secret service told Mao that Liu and Deng were plotting against him. In 1966, Mao returned to Beijing and accused Liu and Deng of sending teams of government agents to universities and schools to suppress the activities of the Red Guards. The Red Guards met at Tiananmen Square. Mao appeared to talk to the group with Lin Biao by his side.

In 1967, Red Guards began attacking the reformers in the government, including Zhu De, Liu Shaoqi, Deng Xiaoping, He Long, Li Xiannian, and Liu Bocheng. Besides Liu Shaoqi and Deng Xiaoping, these individuals were leading generals in China. This was Lin Biao's plot to eliminate his peers and consolidate his rule of the military. Red Guards broke into the homes of reformer leaders and beat them up. They were proclaimed counterrevolutionaries and were dismissed from their offices. Liu Shaoqi was sent to Kaifeng in Henan Province under house arrest where he died in 1969. Under Jiangqing's direction, the Red Guards accused Liu's wife, Wang Guangmei, of being a U.S. spy and sent her to prison, where she stayed for 13 years until 1979. Liu Shaoqi's son, Yunruo, studied at Moscow and fell in love with a Russian girl. Jiangqing directed Red Guards to arrest Yunruo as a Russian spy using the love letters to the Russian girl as evidence. He was released eight years later, suffering mental illness, and soon died of lung disease. This is a case of a woman driven to extreme cruelty by jealousy.[22]

Lin Biao would not leave Peng Dehuai alone. In 1966, Peng was in Chengdu, and Lin Biao had him brought to Beijing. Peng was accused by Red Guards as a counterrevolutionary and beaten up. He became ill in 1973 and died in 1974.

Many of Peng's associates were attacked by Red Guards, including He Long, the commanding general at the Nanchang uprising in 1927 and one of the founders of the Red Army. He Long was born in 1896 in Sangzhi in Hunan Province in the autonomous region of Miao minority. He was from a minority race. As a youngster he was a hoodlum. He joined the Nationalist army in 1921 and rose to division commander in 1926. In 1927, he joined the Communist Party and led the uprising in Nanchang. His units became the original Red Army. Red Guards broke into his home and beat him up. At that time, he was seriously ill, suffering from diabetes. He was moved to the hospital, where he died, probably from not being given the proper medication. Mao attended his funeral, expressing his regrets and realizing that Jiangqing and Lin Biao had gone too far. The masses could be moved to perform gigantic tasks by personal cult, but sometimes the behaviors of the mob could get out of control. Mao asked He Long's wife what he could do. The wife said, "Please clear his name."[23]

After consolidating his control of the military, Lin Biao began to extend his power in the political structure. By 1969, half the 279 members of the Central Committee of the Communist Party were military officers. Furthermore, Lin managed to have military personnel assigned to the political bureaus in factories and schools.[24]

Lin made known his wish to be appointed the president of the People's Republic of China, the post vacated by the fall of Liu Shaoqi. Mao would not comply, and criticized Lin for his wish. Mao began to feel the threat from Lin as a rival.[25]

Zhou Enlai was helping Mao in a move to initiate a rapprochement with the United States. Lin was against it. If not pro Soviet Union, Lin wanted China to be evenhanded toward the United States and the Soviet Union. In the fight over foreign policy between Zhou and Lin, Mao strongly supported Zhou.

In 1971, Mao started a campaign to undermine Lin's power. He criticized the senior military officers under Lin and required them to make public statements to criticize themselves, replaced Lin's supporters with his men in the armed forces in the Beijing region, rotated the assignments of the commanders of the military regions in the country, and made a trip to Nanjing and Guangzhou to reassure himself of the loyalty of the regional commanders.[26]

Lin could clearly see that Mao's moves were targeted at him and that his days were numbered. Lin plotted to assassinate Mao by blowing up the train on which Mao was supposed to be traveling to Shanghai. The plot was discovered, and Mao delayed his trip. Lin was at his summer home in Baidaihe, a resort in Hebei Province on the coast. On hearing the failure of the plot, he fled the country in a Chinese air force plane together with his wife and three of his senior officer followers. The plane crashed in Mongolia, some 100 miles beyond the Chinese border.[27]

In 1973, through Zhou Enlai's intervention, Deng was ordered back to Beijing and reinstated as vice premier. In the same year, Deng began to consolidate his position, and Marshal Ye Jianying came to his support. Deng was made a member of the Central Committee of the Communist Party, a member of the Central Military Committee, and the chief of staff of the armed forces. By then, the power in the party, the government, and the military were all centered in Deng's hand. It seemed that finally Deng was on his way to succeed Mao.[28] Deng reinstated to key positions in the government some 300 top civil servants who were dismissed during the cultural revolution.[29]

In 1934, Deng went to see Mao in Changsha and complained about the Gang of Four. Mao was also aware of the grievous damage the Red Guards had done to the country and began to criticize the Gang.[30]

Zhou Enlai died in January 1976. In March, the populace in Beijing, Nanjing, Hangzhou, Zhengzhou, and Taiyuan assembled to pay tribute to Zhou, and a movement was in progress to attack the Gang of Four.[31]

Alarmed at the rise of Deng, the Gang began to plot to seize power in the event of Mao's death. They set up headquarters at the Great Hall of the People. A special militia was organized in Shanghai, and at the same time they won the support of Mao's nephew, Mao Yuanxin, who had a militia of 10,000 men in Manchuria. They also won the support of Wang Dongxing, the commander of the special unit at Beijing with about 20,000 men, and the support of General Hua Guofeng.

In April 1976, the Gang of Four members still controlled the Politburo. They attacked Deng and had him relieved of all his duties.[32] This was his third fall. Field Marshal Ye Jianying, fearing that Deng's life might be endangered, secretly sent him to Guangzhou and put him under the protection of General Xu Shiyou.[33]

In July 1976, Field Marshal Zhu De died, and in September, Mao Zedong died. In 1976, the country suffered the loss of three of its top leaders—Zhou Enlai, Zu De, and Mao Zedong—who were among the founders of the People's Republic.

Mao, on his deathbed, gave General Hua Guofeng a letter of instruction making him his successor, hoping that Hua could protect his wife.

The Gang of Four planned a plot to seize power. Mao Yuanxin was to lead his troops to Beijing from Manchuria to join forces with the militia coming from Shanghai, and Wang Dongxinn was to seize Beijing with his special unit. The Gang would take control of the country and continue with the Cultural Revolution and Red Guard activities. The nation was facing a crisis, and it would require a brilliant statesman with the courage and the resources to avert this course of doom.

THE DOWNFALL OF THE GANG OF FOUR

The Gang of Four tried to enlist the support of General Chen Xilian, the commander of the Beijing region. Chen refused and informed Field Marshal Ye Jianying of the plot. Ye Jianying was from a businessman's family and learned the techniques of a persuasive negotiator.

Field Marshal Ye Jianying was born in 1897 in the Mei District of Guahgdong Province, the most westernized area in China with developed commercial connections with the outside world. His father was a businessman, and Ye had traveled with him to Singapore and Hanoi. Ye graduated from high school in 1915 and studied at the Yunnan Military Academy. In 1920, Ye joined the Guangdong army, which supported Dr. Sun Yatsen. Ye was a division commander under Chiang Kaishek during the northern expedition to unify the country. In 1924, Ye was among the founders of the Communist Party and participated in the Nanchang uprising. In 1928, he went to Moscow and studied at Sun Yatsen University and visited Germany. He had acquired a cross-cultural background. In 1933, he was the chief of staff of the First Army, and in 1934 he participated in the Long March. In 1935 at the Zunyi conference, Ye supported Mao in his fight with the Moscow-dominated faction. In 1936, in the campaign forming a united front with other military forces against Japan, he was instrumental in persuading the generals of the Manchuria army in Shaanxi to form an alliance with the Communists. This event culminated in the Xian incident, in which Chiang Kaishek was captured as he sought to gain control of the Manchurian army. This led to the agreement between the Nationalists and the Communists for a united front against Japan. Here, Ye had demonstrated his talent in the traditional role of a persuasive strategists, *Shuoke*, one of few persons in Chinese history who by talking to commanding generals or kings could persuade them to change their strategies or policies. In 1945, when the Nationalists and the Communists were holding talks to form a coalition government under the mediation of General Marshal, Mao took Ye to Chongqing, where Ye was left as a permanent representative. Ye, being an amiable person, made many friends among the top leaders of the Nationalists since many of them were his colleagues during his early service in the Nationalist army and at the Whompoa Academy. Ye helped keep the talks friendly, but such a coalition government would not be attained.

Ye had the talent of not allowing himself to be involved in any political struggles. Through all the controversies between Mao and Peng Dehuai and between Mao and Lin Biao, as well as the confrontation between the Orthodox Marxists and the reformers (not to mention the Cultural Revolution), Ye was not implicated. He maintained a nonpolitical position and made friends with all factions. He was a wise old man who kept out of all troubles. He spent a great deal of his spare time dancing with beautiful girls, assuming the posture of a playboy. No one took him seriously. Meanwhile, he was able to rise to a powerful position. He was made field marshal in 1958, the vice chairman of the Military Affairs Commission in 1966, and a member of the Politburo in 1969. He sided with the reformers of the Communist Party. As a student in Guangdong, he developed a taste for dog meat, a cheap source of protein, as many people in Guangdong did. He often played a joke on his colleagues by inviting them to a dinner of dog meat, which to many people tasted sour. As he was the senior officer, his colleagues had to force themselves to swallow the meat while pretending to enjoy it. He himself was perfectly happy enjoying himself. He was nicknamed "the dog meat field marshal."

Field Marshal Ye's house in Beijing is located at 5 Xiaoxiangfeng Lane, Liuyin Street, on the south bank of the Rear Lake in the northern part of the city not far from Jongnanhai, the seat of the government. In 1976, Deng Xiaoping was replaced by Hua Guofeng as the premier, and Ye was replaced by General Chen Xilian as the vice chairman of the Military Commission. It was announced that Ye was replaced because he was sick, but he really was not.

Field Marshal Ye moved from his house in the city to building 15 in the restricted military area in Western Hills, 10 miles west of the city, to take a rest for his alleged illness. The area is heavily guarded. The real reason for the move was that he felt unsafe in the city with the mob of Red Guards roaming around attacking the reformers. The building had dozens of rooms, including a living room, bedrooms, offices, meeting rooms, a dining room, and bathrooms. Apple and pear trees surrounded the building, as did flowers. Stone benches bordered a pond. It was a place that Ye often visited on weekends or for a few days of retreat.

Many field marshals and generals went to Western Hills to see Ye to inquire after his "illness," and Ye asked them to keep in touch with one another so that although he was out of the city, he was never isolated.

Among the visitors was a General Wang Zhen, who was very close to Ye. Ye assigned him the task of liaison among the fields marshals and generals especially those who were members of the Politburo. Ye also asked him to keep in close touch with General Wang Dongxing, the commander of the units guarding Beijing. This commander happened to be a former subordinate of General Wang Zhen. This measure was not only for self-defense to keep the military from being taken over by the Gang of Four but also a preparation for any action in the event of an open struggle against the Gang.

On July 6, Field Marshal Zhu De died. A memorial service was held on July 11. Two weeks later, Kang Keqing, Zhu's wife, went to Western Hills by car to see Ye. As they met, Ye turned on the radio and the water faucets. This startled her until she was told that this was normal procedure for fear of hidden microphones. Ye asked what Zhu De had said before he passed away. Zhu had said, as related by Mrs. Zhu, that we should not be afraid of the Gang of Four even though they were very powerful and treacherous. The public did not support them, and eventually they would fall. They wanted very much to control the military, but they would not be able to do so, as no officers above the junior ranks would want to follow them. We could rely on our old comrades. This amounted to a hint that Supreme Commander Zhu had assigned Ye to take care of the military and assume leadership in fighting the Gang of Four. Ye told Mrs. Zhu that he understood.

In the summer of 1976, many top-ranking military officers went to Western Hills for a vacation for a few days. This gave ample time to establish liaison with Ye. Ye became the unofficial commander of the military, and all the visitors pledged their allegiance to him and would go into action on his orders. The military was ready for action.

Meanwhile, the Gang of Four was also getting organized. Earlier, they had established an office in the Great Hall of the People at Tiananmen Square, but now they moved into the Diaoyutai compound in the north-western corner of Beijing, a place to house visiting foreign dignitaries. Zhang Chunqiao took building 9, Wang Hungwen building 16, and Jiangqing building 17. Yao Wenyuan did not move in but kept an office there.

After Mao's death, Field Marshal Ye moved back to his house in the city to be on hand for any possible operations. He issued an order to all military units that no troop movements would be allowed without his orders, and if there were unauthorized troop movements, he wanted to be informed.

The Gang of Four believed that the units under Generals Hua Guofeng and Wang Dondxing in the area around Beijing were on their side. Militia units were organized by the Gang in Manchuria and in Shanghai, and they could order these troops to go to Beijing. They were in the process of arming the units with equipment and supplies.

A quarrel developed between Jiangqing and Hua Guofeng. Jiangqing wanted Mao's personal file to be delivered to her. These materials were in the hands of Miss Zhang Yufeng, Mao's secretary and confidant. Hua refused to comply with Jiangqing's request. The file contained documents supplied by the secret service units on the alleged wrongdoings of many top military officers. Jiangqing wanted to use these documents to prosecute these officers and replace them with her men so as to gain control of the military.

Generals Hua Guofeng and Wang Dongxing, the commanders of the units guarding Beijing, held a strategic position. When the reformers took action to depose the Gang of Four, a war against the two generals could not be avoided if Hua and Wang were staunch supporters of the Gang of Four.

Field Marshal Ye wanted to find out how the two generals stood with the Gang of Four and wondered whether he could use his power of persuasion and his leadership position in the military to talk to them to turn them around. This was a risky undertaking, as Ye could be arrested and shot for plotting against the Gang, who at the time controlled the Politburo.

Field Marshal Ye sent General Wang Zhen to see the two generals to test the water. The reports came back, saying that the two generals were critical of some of the Gang of Four's activities persecuting reformers. Ye then went to see them separately, asking them whether they approved the Gang of Four's project arming the militia in Manchuria and Shanghai. They said they had not come to a position on this matter. When Ye said that he thought it seemed unnecessary at the moment, they both agreed. This amounted to saying that they were not staunch supporters of the Gang of Four. Ye then asked whether they would support the group to depose the Gang of Four. General Wang readily agreed to do so. General Hua said that he was a relatively junior member of the party and wondered whether he would be supported by the senior leadership. Ye asked him to talk to the most senior leaders. Hua did so and then pledged his support to Ye.[34]

On October 4, 1976, an editorial appeared in Shanghai's *Guangming Daily* saying Premier Hua Guofeng was pursuing the capitalistic road and should be replaced so that the Jiangqing group could carry out the policies of Chairman Mao. This seemed an attempt to prepare the public for some drastic action on the part of the Gang of Four against Hua. This alarmed Ye and Hua. Ye also received a report that a tank unit in a suburb of Beijing was being readied by the Gang of Four to proceed to Beijing to seize power. Ye decided that the time had come for action. He went to see Hua at his home and decided on a plan to summon the Gang of Four to a meeting at Huairen Hall in Jongnanhai at 8:00 P.M. on October 6 and had them arrested there. He then went to see General Wang Dongxing to make preparations for his plan.[35]

Field Marshal Ye asked General Hua Guofeng to dispatch troops to the Great Wall to intercept any troops or militia that might come from Manchuria. Ye alerted the regional commanders of Fuzhou and Nanjing to keep watch on the Shanghai militia and intercept them if they should go to Beijing. He ordered General Xu Shiyou of Guangzhou to have two divisions ready to be airlifted to Beijing on short notice.

On October 6, the day of action, Ye got up early. It was a crucial moment. The fate of China hung by a thread. If the plan worked, power would be restored to the reformers. With that, China could become strong and prosperous, but if the plan failed, another period of mob rule by the Gang of Four would ensue, and Ye's life, together with the lives of many of his associates, would be numbered in days.

Field Marshal Ye went through his daily routine. He read newspapers, had his lesson in English, and took a walk in the yard. He was not nervous but, rather, quiet and deep in thought.

At 4:00 P.M., a telephone call came from Premier Hua's office saying that a meeting of the Politburo would be held at 8:00 P.M. and asking Ye to come an hour early. This was a signal that the plan would be put into action. At 6:00 P.M., Ye put on his new uniform and was on his way to the meeting. He asked the driver to travel to the northwestern section of town near the residences of the Gang of Four and go through Tiananmen Square. He wanted the driver to do this because if the plan had been leaked, the Gang of Four would take drastic action against the military leaders, and the northwestern section of town would have heavy traffic and Tiananmen Square troops gathered for Ye's arrest. He felt relieved when the two areas were quiet and orderly.

Generals Hua and Wang were at the meeting place when Ye arrived.

All preparations were made, and troops were deployed nearby but hidden.

At 8:00 P.M., Zhang Chunqiao of the Gang of Four arrived first, followed by Wang Hungwen. They were immediately arrested. General Hua read a prepared statement that they were being detained for an investigation. While this was going on at the meeting place, Huairen Hall, Yao Wenyuan arrived. He was ushered into a waiting room and was arrested there. Jiangqing had not appeared, as she was usually late for meetings. For fear that she might get wind of what was happening and escape, a guard unit was sent to her house and arrested her there. The project was completed in an hour without any bloodshed, thus putting an end to the mob rule of the Gang of Four.

The reasons for the plan's success were that the plan was kept secret, known only to the three generals (Ye, Hua, and Wang), and that they carefully attended to every detail. This fully demonstrated the leadership and experience of General Ye.

Military units were sent to take over all the media facilities, including television, radio, and newspapers, hitherto controlled by the Gang of Four. The media released the news of the Gang's arrest.

A meeting of the Politburo was called at 10:00 that evening at building 9 at Jade Fountain Hill, west of the city. This was the third residence of Ye, in addition to the ones in Western Hills and in town. Ye kept three residences to conceal his whereabouts and confuse his enemies. There is a Chinese saying: *Jiaotu you sanku*, meaning "A cunning hare keeps three caves."

All the members of the Politburo who were in town, except the Gang of Four, went to the meeting. Generals Ye, Hua, and Wang made their reports. The group was very pleased. Immediately, the Politburo, in retrospect, gave its approval to the action taken. The members of the Politburo who were away from the city were informed of the event and gave their approval.

General Hua wanted Ye to take over the government. Ye declined, saying that he was content to maintain his role in the military. Hua was then made the head of the government and the head of the Military Commission. Hua revealed Mao's letter to him asking him to take charge.

The nation was overjoyed, and the only protest came from the militia in Shanghai that had been organized by the Gang of Four. The leaders of the Shanghai militia were invited to Beijing for a talk. Instead of being arrested, they were allowed to go back to their units. A delegation of top-ranking generals and admirals were sent to Shanghai from Beijing for further negotiations. Finally, the matter was resolved by incorporating the Shanghai militia into the army. A glorious moment came for Field Marshal Ye in 1977 on his 80th birthday. A big celebration held at his home in town was attended by all the top-ranking military leaders. Deng Xiaoping, who had been dismissed by the Gang of Four and was rehabilitated by then, went as well. Poems were written by guests to honor the home, as was the custom for such an occasion.

On January 25, 1981, the People's Supreme Court, in concluding the trial of the Gang of Four, sentenced Jiangqing and Zhang Chunqiao to death but delayed the execution for two years. Two years later, the death penalty sentence was reduced to life imprisonment. Wang Hungwen was given life imprisonment and Yao Wenyuan imprisonment for 20 years.

When the government urged the senior officers to retire to make room for the younger generation, Ye was the first to volunteer to retire. In 1986, he died in his hometown of Guangdong. He would be happy knowing that he played an important role in the reform of China.

On the eve of a plot by the Gang of Four to seize power, Ye rose to the occasion. The nonpolitical general with a playboy reputation, Ye revealed his true self as a political strategist able to conceive of and conduct a campaign to redirect the course of Chinese history.

In 1976, the Red Guards were dissolved, and in 1978, Deng was called back to Beijing and restored to his former positions. He was then 73 years old.[36]

In 1991, Jiangqing was allowed to leave prison to visit her daughter. She committed suicide in her daughter's home by hanging herself. In 1980, Li Ne, the surviving daughter of Mao, was married to one of Mao's guards and had a son. They lived happily together.[37] Hua Guofeng did not have the seniority in the party that Deng had, nor did he have the support of the military. Eventually, Hua bowed out, and Deng finally became the real successor of Mao.[38]

NOTES

1. Zhewen Luo (ed.), *Through the Moon Gate* (Hong Kong: Oxford University Press, 1986), p. x.

2. Robert Maxwell (ed.), *Deng Xiaoping: Speeches and Writings* (New York: Pergamon Press, 1984), p. 7.

3. Harrison E. Salisbury, *The New Emperors: China in the Era of Mao and Deng* (Boston: Little, Brown, 1992), pp. 148–149; James C. F. Wang, *Contemporary Chinese Politics: An Introduction* (Englewood Cliffs, N.J.: Prentice Hall, 1980), pp. 74–76.

4. Wang, *Contemporary Chinese Politics*, pp. 150–151.

5. Ibid., p. 75.

6. William R. Ryan and Sam Summerlin, *The China Cloud* (Boston: Little, Brown, 1967), pp. 45–46.

7. Immanuel C. Y. Hsu, *The Rise of Modern China* (New York: Oxford University Press, 1983), pp. 15, 45–46, 154.

8. Ibid., p. 154.

9. Wang, *Contemporary Chinese Politics*, pp. 196–197.

10. Immanuel C. Y. Hsu, *China without Mao: The Search for a New Order* (New

York: Oxford University Press, 1990), p. 13; Alfred K. Ho, *Developing the Economy of the People's Republic of China* (New York: Praeger, 1982), p. 18.

11. Hsu, *The Rise of Modern China*, p. 652.

12. Joint Economic Committee, *Mainland China in World Economy* (Washington, D.C.: U.S. Government Printing Office), pp. 49–52; Zhewen Luo, *Through the Moon Gate*, pp. 131–133.

13. Harrison E. Salisbury, *The New Emperors*, pp. 166–168.

14. Hsu, *The Rise of Modern China*, pp. 751–778.

15. Chenxia Huang, *Mao's Generals* (in Chinese, *Chongguo Junren Zhi*) (Hong Kong: Research Institute of Contemporary History, 1968), pp. 438–444; Hua Hu, *Biographies of Leaders of the Chinese Communist Party* (in Chinese, *Zhonggong Dangshi Renwu Zhuan*) (Xian: People's Publishing Co., 1989), vol. 30, pp. 1–115; Harrison E. Salisbury, *The Long March* (New York: Harper & Row, 1985), p. 190.

16. Hu, *Biographies of Leaders of the Chinese Communist Party*, pp. 438–444.

17. Salisbury, *The New Emperors*, p. 212.

18. Ross Terrill, *China in Our Time* (New York: Simon & Schuster, 1992), p. 60, and *The Biographical Literature* (in Chinese, *Zhuanzhi Wenxue*) (Taipei: Biographical Literature Co.), vol. 40, no. 2, pp. 134–136.

19. Terrill, *China in Our Time*, pp. 63–64, 146; Sheng Ping (ed.), *Who's Who of Chinese Communists* (in Chinese, *Zhongguo Gongdang Renming Daci Dian*) (Beijing: New China Book Store, 1991), p. 214.

20. Terrill, *China in Our Time*, p. 60.

21. Ibid., pp. 55–56.

22. Salisbury, *The New Emperors*, pp. 273–275.

23. Ibid., pp. 232–234.

24. Terrill, *China in Our Time*, pp. 126–127.

25. Ibid.

26. Jonathan D. Spence, *The Search for Modern China* (New York: W. W. Norton, 1990), p. 616.

27. Salisbury, *The New Emperors*, p. 327.

28. Ibid., p. 331.

29. Hsu, *China without Mao*, p. 13.

30. Salisbury, *The New Emperors*, p. 352.

31. Ibid., p. 355.

32. Hsu, *China without Mao*, p. 13; Shuo Fan, *Ye Jianying in 1976* (in Chinese, *Ye Jianying zai yijiuqiliu*) (Beijing: Central Party School Press, 1990), pp. 167–168.

33. Hsu, *China without Mao*, p. 17; Fan, *Ye Jianying in 1976*, p. 25.

34. Hsu, *China without Mao*, p. 17, Hua Hu, *Biographies of Leaders of Chinese Communist Party*, vol. 40, pp. 1–115, and *The Biographical Literature*, vol. 50, no. 1, pp. 102–103.

35. Salisbury, *The New Emperors*, pp. 138–139; Hua Hu, *The Biographical Literature*, vol. 50, no. 1, pp. 102–111.

36. *Beijing Review* (San Francisco: China Books and Periodicals), vol. 35, no. 1, p. 15.

37. Hsu, *China without Mao*, p. 44.

38. *The Biographical Literature*, vol. 62, no. 4, pp. 34–35.

CHAPTER 4

On the Eve of the Reforms

Let us go back to the period of Mao Zedong's rule for the 27 years from 1949 to 1976 to find out which stage of modernization China was in when Deng Xiaoping took over. Deng's policies may be easily understood if we approach them from the view that Deng was to accentuate Mao's achievements and rectify Mao's mistakes. In a sense, Deng's rule was a continuation of Mao's rule with modifications and improvements.

To describe the society that Mao had created, it is best to go to the author's personal observations. The author left China in 1941, and after some 30 years in the United States, he returned to China in 1973. What he saw of China under Mao was a completely different world from the one he left—in appearance, ideology, people's behavior, social structure, and economic system.

The author was born in China. That makes him a Chinese citizen subject to Chinese laws. Entering China, he could be detained with a job assignment and never be allowed to exit the country. This is the risk he had to take.

After taking the train from Kowloon, Hong Kong, to the Chinese border, the author got off, walked across the border, and boarded the Chinese train to Guangzhou, a metropolitan city in southern China. Hotels were modern, streets were paved with asphalt, and trees lined the sidewalks. There were no billboards and no signs of commercialism. Everyone wore a Mao suit in different colors: green for the military, blue for workers, and black for farmers. The Western-clad upper class had completely disappeared. The author was the only one wearing Western-style clothing, his Sunday best. Buses ran constantly throughout the city, and those not on a bus were riding bicycles. The author was given the privilege of using taxis because as an American professor he was thought to be unable to cope with the traffic on a bicycle. In touring the country, he went by taxi, sightseeing in style.

The author visited Mao Zedong's headquarters (now a museum) when the revolution started in Guangzhou. It was not a fancy complex but rather a modest house. The gate opens to a yard. Facing the gate was a room that was Mao's bedroom and office. The furniture in the room included a bed made of wood planks covered with a quilt, a table, a chair, and a wash basin on a stand. Three rooms on each side of the yard housed Mao's aides who later were China's generals and field marshals. The rooms had no furniture, but straw was placed on the floor on which the aides slept. Most of the time during the revolutionary wars, the People's Liberation Army operated in the poor regions of the interior of the country, where the officers' accommodations were probably not much better.

An argument the author overheard on the train from Guangzhou to Shanghai illustrated the difference between the free-market economy and the planned economy.

A lady tourist from Hong Kong asked a cigarette vendor, "How much for a package?"

Vendor: Ten cents.

Lady: How many packages do you have?

Vendor: Fifty.

Lady: I will take all.

Vendor: You can't. You can buy only one package.

Lady: Why not? I am doing you a favor.

Vendor: Others want to buy.

Lady: I don't care.

Vendor: I don't understand you.

Lady: Don't you want to sell more?

Vendor: Just because you have the money you can buy any amount you want?

Lady: Why not?

Vendor: You can only buy one.

Lady: I don't understand you.

There is no way to settle the argument. The lady comes from Hong Kong, where there is no rationing whatsoever. The vendor does not understand that. The vendor is a government employee. Whether he sells more or less, he is paid a fixed wage. He is under instruction to ration the cigarettes one package to a customer. If he is caught disobeying that instruction, he will be disciplined. The lady does not know that.

At Nanjing in Jiangsu Province, the author saw the Changjiang Bridge across the Yangtze River. The bridge is about a mile long. The Beijing–Shanghai railroad goes through here. Before the construction of this bridge, trains had to be taken off the rails, put on a ferry to cross the river, and then put back on the rails. Now trains can cross the river on the bridge without interruption. The current of the river at this point is swift, which made the work of constructing the foundation for the bridge difficult. After several attempts, the foundation finally held. The construction of this bridge was a magnificent feat of engineering and is regarded as one of the wonders of China.

At Shanghai, one of the sightseeing stops was at a hospital where, through the windows, the author saw three patients undergoing operations through acupuncture. One patient had an operation on the throat, one on the lung, and one on the stomach. All the patients were conscious with their eyes open. Because of the shortage of Western medicine, the People's Liberation Army probably depended heavily on Chinese traditional medicine, such as acupuncture and herbs. Now Chinese hospitals have two sections—a Western medicine section and a Chinese medicine section—from which patients can choose at the same cost. Chinese doctors are trained in medical schools in either Western or Chinese medicine. In his youth, the author stayed at home until he moved to the dormitory of an American missionary college. During all his years at home, he used only Chinese medicine, which did wonders for him. Either the Chinese medicine was effective, or the author never was seriously ill.

The author went to Beijing. In 1973, the city looked quite modern, totally different from his memory of the city. Around the Imperial Palace were 10 giant modern structures of the Russian style. These included a museum, an assembly hall, a library, and several government offices. Most of the inner-city walls and the outer-city wall were gone, but the Imperial City and the Forbidden City were untouched. China saw many wars and foreign invasions, but it was taboo for anyone to cause damage to the Imperial City or the Forbidden City, a symbol of China. On seeing that a battle was lost, a defending general would leave the city, avoiding any street fighting. During the Japanese invasion, when the Japanese took Nanjing, many were killed, and looting was rampant. But when they took Beijing, only the cavalry paraded into the city on horseback, quietly and without any disturbances, leaving the main body of the forces outside the city.

Beijing expanded by absorbing many of its suburbs. A new airport was built to the west of the city about a 40-minute drive away. The road to the airport was lined with trees three or four rows deep.

Finally, the author went to Tianjin, where his family resided. On arrival, a dinner was arranged at a restaurant where he saw his parents, brothers, a sister, and their children after some 30 years of separation. When he left

China, he was 22, and his parents were in their fifties. Now coming home, he was 54, and his parents were in their eighties. He was a long-lost son who had just returned. Everyone was in tears.

The author found that the living style of the people had changed. He remembered that as a boy of 10, he often roamed around the city on a bicycle. One morning, he had ventured into a new world, the Legation Quarters inside the inner-city wall just east of the Front Gate. All foreign embassies were located there. It was an entirely different world. It was like carving out Massachusetts Avenue at Dupont Circle in Washington, D.C., and transplanting it to an old Oriental city. Each embassy was housed in a compound surrounded by walls. Guards in bright uniforms stood at the gate. The yards contained green lawns, flowers, and modern office buildings. A bugle sounded at the French Legation, and the French flag was raised. Then the same happened at the British legation. A junior consular officer came out of the American legation. He stopped and took off his hat when the American flag was raised. This gave the author a chance to observe him. He was smartly dressed in a black chesterfield overcoat, blue business suit, and black shoes. His collar was white and stiff. This was the first impression the author gained of how a westerner looked.

Fourteen years later, the author went to Princeton University as a PhD candidate on a university fellowship. He immediately went to a fashionable clothing store in New York to buy a wardrobe. After putting on his new clothing, he realized that was "keeping up with the Joneses" or, rather, imitating the style of the junior consular officer he saw at the legation quarters.

After returning home to Tianjin, the author continued wearing his Western-style clothing. One day, his brothers decided to go to a Chinese opera. The elder brother asked the author, "Are you coming? You, capitalist." The author agreed to go but was puzzled by the remark because he was always called "slowpoke." That evening, he consulted his mother on what to wear for the opera. His mother said, "Maybe you want to put away your Western clothing and wear a Mao suit. You will be more comfortable." He understood that his mother was really saying, "It was time to get off your high horse." The author borrowed a Mao suit and a bicycle from a brother and went to the opera. All the brothers smiled on seeing him, apparently approving of the change. The elder brother then said, "How come you are so late? You slowpoke." The author replied, "It took a while to get used to riding a bicycle." He knew that he had come home. Now, in front of a mirror, he looked the way he dressed when he was 10 years old. In 30 or so years, the style of dress had come a full circle. In China, the sentiment was that one should put oneself on equal terms with others, neither upstaging anyone nor showing off.

One day during his stay at home in 1973, the author went to the Beijing headquarters of the International Travel Service to apply for approval to lead a group of American faculty and students on a tour of China. He arrived at the headquarters wearing a Mao suit and riding a bicycle. All the officers at the gate were taken by surprise, as they expected someone dressed like a diplomat to arrive by taxi. The author shook hands with the officers while mopping up perspiration from his forehead. When the talk on the proposal began, the author spoke in Mandarin, the dialect of Beijing, which the officers used. The author knew that he was no longer being treated as a foreign visitor but as a native son coming home. His proposal was granted, and the dates set without any red tape. These officers became the author's good friends and approved a total of eight trips that the author took in the period from 1973 to 1988. Some of the trips were tours of China, and some were lectures given at Chinese universities. There is a Chinese saying: *Ry guo wen jin, ru xiang wen su,* meaning "On coming to a country find out what the restrictions are, on coming to a village, find out the local customs."

CHAPTER 5

Deng's Economic Reforms

Following the Chinese tradition, the basic policies of the Communist Party are to fulfill the fundamental objectives of the country, which are economic development and military strength, or, in Chinese, *fuguo chiangbing.* Economic development for the country calls for the sustained growth of the gross national product (GNP), which can be promoted by the following factors: population, agricultural output, industrial output, technology, trade, foreign capital, a free market, macroeconomic control of the state, and a management system providing material incentives.

The Chinese population is large and has a tendency to grow rapidly. A policy will be needed to slow down population growth to prevent long-term unemployment and a declining standard of living.

Agricultural output, industrial output, and technological growth are basic to economic development.

China will have to be opened to the outside world to encourage trade, and foreign capital will need to be secured through a joint venture system where Chinese firms and foreign firms join hands in business endeavors.

The planned economy will have to be gradually replaced by a free-market economy. The management system will have to be modified to provide material incentives to encourage hard work and competition.

In 1975, Zhou Enlai, then the premier, proposed a two-stage plan for the economic development of the country. In the first stage, from 1975 to 1980, China should concentrate on industrialization; in the second stage, from 1980 to 2000, China should pursue a program of four modernizations: agriculture, industry, defense, and technology. It was hoped that China would be able to catch up with the advanced countries through this plan. Unfortunately, Zhou died in 1976 and did not have the chance to see his program carried out. Deng took over in 1978 and pursued the program of four modernizations.

In 1979, Deng hoped that the GNP of the country would quadruple, from U.S.$250 billion to U.S.$1 trillion by the year 2000. Then the per capita GNP would be around U.S.$800. To accomplish his ambition, the GNP needed to be 7.2 percent per year for the next 20 years.[1]

By 1980, the economic reforms began to pay off. From 1980 to 1990, the average yearly GNP growth rate was 8.9 percent; the population growth rate was 1.5 percent, and the GNP per capita growth rate was 7.4 percent.[2] The program had improved the standard of living of the people with a sharp rise of income for 80 percent of them.[3]

A transformation was occurring in the country's economic structure. The share of agriculture in the GNP declined from 30.4 percent in 1988 to 23.3 percent in 1990, while the industrial share rose from 49.0 percent in 1980 to 52.7 percent in 1990, and the tertiary share rose from 20.6 percent in 1980 to 24.1 percent in 1990. China had become industrialized.

Similarly, a transformation was occurring in the employment structure, with a steady transfer of manpower from agriculture to the other two sectors. The agricultural share of the total employment fell from 68.9 percent in 1980 to 60.0 percent in 1990, while the industrial share rose from 18.5 percent in 1980 to 21.4 percent in 1990, and the tertiary share rose from 12.6 percent in 1980 to 18.0 percent in 1990.

The country enjoyed full employment and prosperity. The ratio of employment to population rose from 42.9 percent in 1980 to 49.6 percent in 1990.[4]

Foreign trade expanded. The combined value of exports and imports reached U.S.$120 billion in 1990. By 1992, trade surpluses have enabled the country to build up foreign currency reserves of U.S.$40 billion.[5]

The country enjoyed price stability. Retail prices rose by 2.1 percent in 1990 and 2.9 percent in 1991.[6]

In 1992, the growth rate of the GNP was 12.8 percent, and the growth rates of the various sectors were 3.7 percent for the primary sector, 20.5 percent for the secondary sector, and 9.2 percent for the tertiary sector. The GNP for 1992 was 2.4 billion yuan.

How does the Chinese economy rank among other countries of the world? For comparison with other economies, the Chinese GNP figure in yuan will need to be converted to U.S. dollars. The problem will be determining the proper exchange rate to use for the conversion.

Traditionally, the Chinese official exchange rate has been used. However, the Chinese government practices a devaluation policy that gives its currency a lower value in relation to other currencies. Using the official exchange rate for the conversion, the Chinese GNP amounted to 2 percent of the world domestic product. Another exchange rate that can be used in the conversion is the purchasing power parity rate, which compares the world currencies on the basis of what they can buy. The staff of the International Monetary Fund (IMF) debated on which exchange rate to use (for a four-year period) and finally decided on reevaluating the various nations' economies by the purchasing power parity rate. The new calculation put China's GNP at 6 percent of the world domestic product, three times larger than the earlier calculation. In its report *World Economic Outlook*, the IMF ranked China's economy the third largest in the world after the United States and Japan.

The World Bank takes a similar position. In its study *Global Economic Prospects and the Developing Countries*, the Chinese economic area, which includes mainland China, Hong Kong, and Taiwan, will rank fourth in the world after the United States, Japan, and Germany.

The new calculations startled the world. However, China is by no means a rich country, considering its large population. In 1992, the per capita income for China was U.S.$1,600, compared with that of the United States at U.S.$22,204 for the same year, about 14 times larger.

A dispute exists between China and the IMF in that, if China is said to be overly concerned to save "face," one would think that China would want to overestimate its economic strength and the IMF go for a lower, more realistic estimate. Strangely, however, they seem to have taken the opposite positions. The IMF is giving the Chinese economy a high estimate, and the Chinese government prefers a lower estimate for its economy. The reason is that China has been given a large number of loans from the World Bank, such as U.S.$2.5 billion in 1992, about 40 percent of which was interest-free soft loans. Now that China is considered economically strong, total loans from the World Bank will be reduce, as will soft loans. Sources said that in 1993, soft loans from the World Bank to China would be reduced from U.S.$1 billion to U.S.$800 million. The Chinese government prefers more loans than prestige.[7]

The streets of Chinese cities are crammed with goods and consumers. Streets are lined with billboards advertising the good life. Traffic jams involving many foreign-made cars occur in large cities.

The success of his economic reforms pleases Deng. As he is quoted in saying, "The magnitude of the influence we exercise in world affairs depends on the magnitude of our success in economic construction. At present our influence in world affairs is by no means small, but if our material base and our military strength increase, our influence will be greater."[8]

Before Mao Zedong and Zhou Enlai died, Deng's persistent efforts in pushing for economic reforms had caused many confrontations between him and the dogmatists. He could rely on Mao and Zhou to bring opponents together to preserve the unity of the Communist Party. Now, with Mao and Zhou gone, the responsibility for maintaining the unity of the party fell on his shoulders. He had to come to terms with the dogmatists.

The compromise was to carry out economic reforms under the condition of the four cardinal principles:

1. The country must in its policies follow the socialist road, which means that the interests of the working class come first.
2. The leadership of the Communist Party in the country must be preserved, which means that the party of the working class must be the party in power.
3. A democratic dictatorship will be in place, which means that people other than the working class, such as intellectuals, professionals, and experts, may be represented by other political organizations, but they must not override the Communist Party.
4. The country must follow Marxism–Leninism and Mao Zedong's thought, which means that Communism must be the ideological base of the country's policies.

The dogmatists imposed these guidelines because they did not want to see China revert to the traditional society dominated by intellectuals, professionals, and experts. They feared that the economic reforms might increase the political influence of these groups and undo the socialist revolution.

Deng had no quarrel with these guidelines, as since his youth he had always wanted to work to promote the welfare of the working people. However, reform that aimed at the building of a multiparty democratic government would have to be postponed.

These guidelines gave the dogmatists an instrument by which to examine each step of the economic reforms to see whether the four cardinal principles were violated.

THE LEADER

In 1979, the people in the West had their first glimpse of the successor of Mao Zedong when Deng Xiaoping, as the vice premier of China, visited the United States. He flew to Washington, D.C., on January 28, 1979, and toured the country for eight days, covering Atlanta, Georgia; Houston, Texas; and Seattle, Washington. His visit was the first made by a senior official from the People's Republic of China. Deng ranked third on China's protocol list but wielded the real power in that country. The U.S. government gave him a lavish, regal reception. On the first day, Deng was officially welcomed on the White House lawn with a 19-gun salute and a review of the honor guard. President Jimmy Carter greeted him and said, "It is a day of reconciliation when windows too long closed have been reopened."

Deng was gracious in his reply but lost no time attacking the Soviet Union. He said, "The world is far from tranquil. There are not only threats to peace, but the factors causing war are visibly growing."

After the reception, the two leaders and their aides conferred privately for four hours.

At the White House reception, which was attended by hundreds of corporate leaders, members of Congress, and prominent citizens, Deng delivered another attack on the Soviet Union's attempt to seek hegemony over other countries.

At a party, Deng was introduced to Armand Hammer, the prominent industrialist, and Deng immediately recognized him. Deng said, "You are a good friend of Lenin and are helpful to the Soviet Union. Why don't you come to China?" Hammer responded, "I have a problem. I am too old to ride a commercial flight, and your country does not allow private planes to land." Deng said, "It is simple. Next time when you want to come, send a cable to me in advance, and I will make the necessary arrangements."

Later, Hammer did go to China in his private airplane. At a party in Beijing, Hammer thanked Deng for the special airplane landing privilege. The only other special airplane that is allowed to land in China is Air Force 1, which carries presidents of the United States.

At another party, Deng met Mrs. Helen Snow, the widow of Edger Snow. She was in Yanan in 1937. After interviewing Mao Zedong, Zhou Enlai, and Zhu De, she wanted to interview Deng Xiaoping, but Deng was stationed in Yunyang. Helen brought a letter of introduction from Mao to go to Yunyang to see Deng. When she arrived at Yunyang, Deng had already left for another post. Finally, in 1979, 42 years later, Helen caught up with Deng at the party. Helen was properly introduced to Deng when she showed him Mao's personal letter.[9]

On Capitol Hill, Deng took the senators and congressmen by storm. He hoped to bring about a reunification of China and Taiwan through peaceful means. With regard to the most-favored-nation status regarding trade with China, Deng noted the Johnson–Vanik Amendment, which denied such status to countries that did not permit free emigration. Deng said, "That is no problem for us, but do you really want 10 million Chinese to move to the United States?" This brought about an outburst of laughter from the assembly. It seemed that no one could resist Deng's humor. Deng made it clear that while China needed the capital and technology from abroad, it could offer a vast market for foreign countries.

This visit gave Deng a chance to personally observe the workings of American democracy and the operation of a capitalistic economy. These observations left their imprint on Deng's reform programs in China. His visits to the Ford assembly plant in Seattle left him with vivid impressions of the hard work of the personnel and the well-run system of operation that had made possible the high standard of living in the United States.

Surprisingly, this political giant of one of the largest countries in the world is 4 feet 11 inches tall. In the West, height has an advantage in the political arena as well as in many human endeavors. But in China, physical stature is of little importance. As the Chinese saying goes, *Zunzi da tou, xiaoren da jiao,* meaning "Gentlemen have large heads, while servants have large feet."

As we look into Deng's background, we find that he had a turbulent political life. Three times he was denounced by the government, stripped of all his positions, and banished to obscurity, but three times he bounced back to regain his power. The first time was in 1934 before the Long March, the second time was in 1966, and the third time was in 1974 during the Cultural Revolution.

Deng was referred to as the "little man who could never be put down." He weathered ordeals and disgrace that many others did not survive. It is his toughness that made him the real successor of Mao. The people called him an "acrobat with nerves of steel."

On further investigation, one finds that Deng is among the top few troop commanders in China. During the revolution, Deng fought numerous battles in central and southern China.[10] In 1949, in the Haui Hai operations in central China (in the final battle against the forces of the Nationalists, the Kuomintang), Deng shared the command of the Second Army with General Liu Bocheeng. Together with General Chen Yi, the commander of the Third Army, they destroyed in 65 days 56 divisions of the five Nationalist field armies, totaling about one million strong. That victory laid the foundation for the conquest of China.[11] Deng has the allegiance of the top-ranking generals, who consider him one of their group.

Just as Deng left a good image of himself in the United States, the United States also gave Deng a very favorable impression. The United States had demonstrated to Deng that in this large country, the rich resources, the skill of the workers, the technology of the engineers, the free-market system, free enterprise, and the developed financial system could all be put together to promote production and to improve the standard of living for the people. The capitalistic society may have some problems, but the economic system works. To Deng, the pragmatic observer, the question was how much of the system could be applied to China and how much was specific to the United States and could work only in America. This was a big puzzle in his mind. He wondered whether it was possible for China to modify the Communist system to acquire some of the features of the capitalistic economy. He was certain that the capital, technology, and managerial skills of the United States could help China modernize. The trip helped him realize that research and development would have a great role to play in China's future progress.

After returning to China, Deng was the chief architect of the economic and political reforms from 1978 to 1992. Under his guidance, China can now boast one the world's fastest-growing economies with a growth rate averaging over 9 percent per year.[12] This world giant hopes to quadruple its GNP on the 1980 basis by the year 2000 and bring a more comfortable life for the people. Deng set this as his ambition, and the goals are fulfilled. China's GNP in 1980 was U.S.-$250 billion, and its GNP in 2001 was given by the World Bank at U.S.-$1,130 billion, more than quadrupled since 1980.

Deng was born in the village of Paifang outside Guangan District in northern Sichuan on the upper reaches of the Yangtze River. His family was of the Hakka minority race originating in Jiangsu and Guangdong provinces and had migrated to Sichuan. He was born in 1904, the first son of a second wife. His father had four wives, who gave him eight children. Deng's father was the commander of the militia for three counties in Sichuan, a military force to protect the estates of rich landlords.[13]

Deng was brought up a Buddhist and had a happy boyhood. He was remembered in high school as a bright but mischievous student. He could read a story or an essay three times and recite it from memory. He went to Chongqing, the provincial capital, for further studies and there joined a work program to go to France to work and study part time.[14]

He was in France for five years, from 1921 to 1926. French society in the early 1920s was probably not idealistic enough for him. Instead, he was attracted to Communism as a reaction to the indulgent society.

In 1922, Deng stayed in Montargis for a while and then moved to Chatillon-sur-Seine. He met a number of Chinese Communists in France, among them Zhou Enlai, later the premier of China. The two became lifelong friends. In 1922, he joined the Chinese Communist Youth Group. In 1923, he worked at Hutchinsons's rubber factory in Monatargis. In 1924, at the age of 20, he joined the Chinese Communist Party.

In 1925, Deng lived in Paris and worked at Renault Works in Biliancourt. In 1926, he left France for Moscow.

Later, during the revolutionary war, he and his family were on opposite sides. The fiercest fighting in which the Communists engaged was not against the Japanese or the Nationalists (Kuomintang) but against the militia of the landlords. If Deng were Robin Hood, his father would be the Sheriff of Nottingham. The father and son did not face each other in a battle, but they were enemies.

Deng's mother died in 1927. According to the Chinese tradition, the son is supposed to leave his work to return home to personally manage the funeral, to oversee the burial, and to spend a period of mourning. Deng could not and did not return because the militia probably had put a price on his head. His father was murdered in 1940. Again he could not and did not return home.[15] These two events were the saddest moments in his life. In 1926, after a short stay in Moscow, Deng returned to China.

The cross-cultural experience in France and in Russia opened Deng's eyes and planted a seed in his mind that what China needed was a socialism that was in tune with Chinese conditions and Chinese culture.

POPULATION CONTROL

China is proud of its vast territory and huge population. The large land-mass with its abundant resources is always a blessing. Foreign invaders often have tried to conquer the land, but they failed repeatedly because the country is so large. The good earth of China has provided the people with life support for centuries.

The huge population can be both a blessing and a burden. The Han, a large proportion of the Chinese population, never have to fear for the loss of their identity; on the contrary, they have demonstrated their ability to absorb any number of aliens and minorities living among them. However, in times of economic difficulty, life can be hard for such a large number of people.

The rapid growth of the population can be partly explained by the social structure of the country, which is mainly rural. China is composed of thousands of villages, each of which has a number of families that represent the basic social and economic units. They compete with one another in business and for social prestige. Manpower is a major factor in competition. The family with the largest number of sons will be more productive, can acquire more land, and will become prosperous.

Young married couples are encouraged to have children to prolong the family lineage. There is a Chinese proverb: *Buxiao you san, wu hou wei da,* meaning "A son must not fail to fulfill the three major obligations to his parents, of which the greatest is to produce an heir."

In traditional China, only boys can carry the family name and prolong the family lineage, but under the People's Republic, girls can retain their maiden names after marriage.

The Malthusian doctrine comes to mind. According to Thomas Malthus (1766–1834), an English economist and clergyman, population tends to increase at a geometric ratio and the means of subsistence at an arithmetic ratio. That is, population increases more rapidly than the means of subsistence. Thus, the supplies of goods that support life will eventually become depleted. War, famine, or disease will help reduce the population unless sexual restraint helps slow down population growth. It takes an annual growth rate of 3 percent for the population to double in a generation, a rate that does occur in some areas of China.

Throughout the long history of China, war, disease, and natural calamities have been common; these helped control overpopulation. When people starve, they will become bandits or wage wars. When no resources are available to help prevent disease, to build dykes, or to maintain irrigation projects, disease, floods, or droughts will occur.

Dr. Ma Yinchu, a Chinese economist born in 1884, received his PhD from Columbia University in 1914. From 1928 to 1947, he was a member

of the Chinese Congress, the Legislative Yuan, in the Nationalist government. He was critical of the government's economic policies, which resulted in runaway inflation in the country. The government arrested him
and stripped him of his position.

Later, under the People's Republic, Dr. Ma was made a member of
the Political Consultation Conference, consisting of members of non-
Communist parties. In 1951, he was made the president of the prestigious
Peking University.

In 1953, the first census was taken. China's population was 583 million,
with a birthrate of 3.7 percent and a death rate of 1.7 percent resulting in
a natural growth rate of 2.0 percent. It was estimated that 12 to 13 million
new births would occur every year.

Dr. Ma was alarmed at this problem and wrote a paper on industrialization and population in 1955. In the paper, he was critical of the government's first five year plan for 1953–57, which gave priority to the
development of heavy industries following the Russian pattern. According to him, what China needed was to implement birth control to slow
down population growth and put emphasis on agricultural development
to provide the basic needs of the people and to maintain a stable economy.

Dr. Ma's observations were not well received. In 1958, 200 articles were
published in the country against Dr. Ma's position. He was said to have
followed the Malthusian pessimistic approach and based his analysis on
capitalistic ideas. He was labeled a counterrevolutionary and was relieved
of his presidency at Peking University.[16]

Mao Zedong was against population control. Marxism–Leninism makes
no mention of population control. Mao took pride in the large Chinese
army that was supported by a large population. He was fearful of atomic
attacks from the West and carried out a campaign to construct underground shelters and tunnels to protect the people and to disperse them
from the cities. Fearful of the heavy casualties of atomic warfare, Mao was
not concerned about the population being too large.

In 1964, China took a second census that indicated again the country's
alarmingly high rate of population growth. In the same year, China developed the atomic bomb, and the country no longer worried about
atomic attacks. In 1972, the government began to push a birth control
policy that would limit each family to one child.[17]

In 1974, China sent a delegation headed by Huang Shutse to attend the
UN World Population Conference in Bucharest, Hungary. Huang delivered a paper at the conference titled "China's View on Major Issues of
World Population." He said that the Malthusian doctrine does not apply
to China. In the 25 years from 1949 to 1974, China's population grew only
60 percent, while the output of grain more than doubled. However, the
Chinese government had adopted a policy of limiting each family to one

child. This was because China wanted to improve the health and education of children to enhance the quality of their lives, and China could accomplish this if the growth of the population was slower.[18]

In 1979, under Deng Xiaoping, the government adopted a program that offered rewards to families with one child. For instance, a subsidy of five yuan per month for 14 years was offered, free health care and free education for children up to the secondary school level were provided, and higher pensions for the parents were guaranteed. Parents who had undergone sterilization after the birth of their first child were given a free vacation as a reward. The program also imposed penalties on families with more than two children. For instance, penalties included a wage reduction of 10 yuan per month per family for 14 years, higher prices for grain rations, and the charging of fees for the health services for a third child.[19]

In 1982, a third census was taken. It was reported that China's population was 1,003,790,000. The birthrate was 2.11 percent, and the death rate was 0.66 percent, yielding a growth rate of 1.45 percent. It is evident that the population control policy has worked, though 14.5 million new births still occur each year.[20]

In 1991, according to the government's report, the birthrate was 1.968 percent, and the death rate was 0.667 percent, yielding a growth rate of 1.301 percent. It was hoped that the growth rate would be kept below 1.25 percent by the end of the twentieth century, at which rate the population is expected to reach 1.5 billion by 2025. It might be possible for the population to become stable at 1.6 billion in the period from 2040 to 2050.[21]

In rural areas, because of the need of manpower, if a couple's first child is a daughter, a second child is allowed. The primary means of birth control is contraceptives. Abortions are practiced for accidental conceptions. About half of pregnancies are aborted.[22]

TECHNOLOGICAL MODERNIZATION

A major difference between Mao's policy and Deng's policy is the way in which intellectuals, professionals, and experts were treated.

Mao sided with the dogmatists, according to whom, based on Marxist analysis, poverty in the country was due largely to the skewed distribution of income, with the intellectuals, professionals, and experts taking the lion's share and thus leaving the working class in poverty. The revolution was to pit the working class against the intellectuals, professionals, and experts so that the masses could gain their fair share of income.

After the founding of the People's Republic, intellectuals, professionals, and experts were not recruited into the Communist Party but were represented by other, non-Communist parties. Employment and promotion were made on the basis of how devoted a Marxist the person was or, in Chinese terms, how red the person was. Intellectuals, professionals, and experts who were nonpolitical were labeled "white experts" or bourgeois individualists. Teachers and professors were among the lowest-paid groups in the country. A storekeeper or a taxi driver had a higher income than a college professor. College students lived on a stipend of U.S.$10 per month.

Many intellectuals, professionals, and experts began to side with the reformers. This enraged the dogmatists. During the years of the Cultural Revolution, some intellectuals, professionals, and experts were labeled counterrevolutionaries and were harassed or beaten up by Red Guards.

All through Mao's rule, he did little to reduce poverty among the people. Some improvement was made in the GNP, but much of that improvement went to the expansion of heavy industry and building up the nation's defense. Mao managed to make more even the distribution of income in the sense of cutting up the pie into more even shares, but he did not increase the size of the pie. Adding more workers, resources, and capital can improve production, but Mao's government had no idea of the role that technology could play in such production.

Deng's first step in fighting the dogmatists after assuming power in 1978 was to ask the people to keep an open mind to find practical solutions to China's problems. Deng said, "What we want is to open our mind, and use our heads to find practical solutions for our problems. . . . Our mind must be set free, otherwise we will never be able to develop a system that will drastically improve the nation's production. Our solutions have to be applicable to Chinese conditions."[23]

Deng went back to the first premise of statecraft. According to Chinese tradition, the objectives of the government were to improve the wealth of the nation and the defense of the country—in Chinese terms, *Fuguo qiangbing*. It is not any different for a capitalistic country. For instance, Adam Smith (1723–90), a Scottish economist, titled his book *The Wealth of Nations*, in which he laid the foundation for capitalism.

Deng wanted to improve the welfare of the working class not only by bringing about an even distribution of income, or cutting the pie more evenly, but also by increasing the wealth of the nation, or making the pie bigger.

To improve the wealth of the nation, Deng, in contrast to Mao, believed that the production function of technology should be incorporated with labor, capital, and resources. For the advancement of technology, Deng brought about a reconciliation with the intellectuals, professionals, and experts in the country, restoring them to their proper role in society. To put it in concrete terms, Deng said, "It does not matter whether the cat is white or black, as long as it can catch mice."

Technological Development within the Country

Under Deng, the school system was rebuilt from the ruins left by the Cultural Revolution. Students returned to class, discipline was restored, and academic standards were raised. Nationwide college entrance examinations were reinstituted to select high school students who were destined for college. Model grade schools, high schools, universities were designated in the country, and selected students were sent there for better training.[24]

The pay of teachers and professors was increased. A new top pay scale was added for the best teachers to encourage them to make teaching their lifetime career. Two new top pay scales were added for professors: first-rank and second-rank professors. Regular professors became third-rank professors. Similar pay raises were instituted for professionals and experts, such as accountants and engineers.[25]

In 1978, a national plan for the development of science and technology was presented by Vice Premier Fang Yi and approved by the State Council. The plan called for the establishment of a number of laboratories and research centers and a system to coordinate research work in the country. The State Science and Technology Commission was reactivated to carry out the plan.[26]

In 1978, a National Science Conference was held by the government to gather advice and suggestions from representatives of intellectuals, professionals, and experts. This conference was the first time since the founding of the People's Republic that intellectuals, professionals, and experts were honored and marked the beginning of a new status for them. They were no longer part of the underprivileged class.

Deng stated at the opening session, "Of the four modernizations, technological modernization is the basic one, because the other modernizations, agriculture, industry and defense, depend on technology. Technology is among the inputs for production and it is most important because it makes the other inputs such as labor, capital and resources more productive. Intellectuals, professionals and experts belong to the working class, as some work with their brain and others with physical labor."[27]

The importance of technology in production was well documented in a study of the Japanese economy for the period from 1952–1971, when the country had among the fastest-growing economies in the world with an average annual GNP growth rate of 10 percent in real terms. The improvement in the four major inputs—labor, capital, resources, and technology—accounted for a large part of the GNP's growth. Edward F. Denison and William K. Chung, in analyzing the economic growth of Japan, managed to single out the shares of the contribution made by each of the four inputs using a multivariant regression procedure. The improvement of labor accounted for 2.0 percent of the growth of the GNP; that of capital 2.2

percent, the better utilization of resources by shifting resources from agriculture to industry 1.2 percent, and that of technology 2.4 percent, making technology the most important factor in the economic growth of Japan.[28] In the 1950s, Japan depended heavily on borrowed technology from abroad and, in the 1960s, would improve on that technology. From the 1970s on, Japan developed technology that in some areas was superior to that of other countries. Deng believed that what happened in Japan for the period from 1952 to 1971 could be repeated in China. In 1981, the Scientific Council, consisting of 400 of China's leading scientists, was established as a consultative body for the government to promote the technological development for the country.[29]

In 1982, 20 to 25 million intellectuals, professionals, and experts resided in China and were educated beyond the high school level. They were divided into four groups: those who completed their education before 1949, those in the period from 1949 to 1966, those during the Cultural Revolution period from 1966 to 1976, and those after 1977. Of the four groups, the group that completed their education during the Cultural Revolution were not up to par with the normal academic standard because of the political upheaval in the country during that time.[30]

Since 1978, intellectuals, professionals, and experts have been recruited into the Communist Party and given appropriate assignments in the government. However, the recruitment was light, accounting for 8.3 percent of the total recruitment for that year. The ratio gradually improved to 23.6 percent in 1982, 27.0 percent in 1983, and 40.0 percent in 1984.[31]

The move to recruit intellectuals, professionals, and experts into the Communist Party has helped in the development of technology and has political significance. It removed the dichotomy between the working class and the intellectuals, professionals, and experts. Consequently, the two groups were able to work together. It broadened the base of the party and strengthened the reformers in the government. It helped promote economic growth and efficiency in government operations. By 1983, China had begun to grant PhD degrees in some fields of study.[32] In 1985, the National Science Foundation was established to encourage and help finance scientific and technological research in the country.[33]

The State Science and Technology Commission had worked out two plans: the high-tech research-and-development program in 1985 and the Torch program in 1988. The high-tech research-and-development program, often referred to as the 863 program, focused on research into areas such as infrastructure and electronics. It was approved by the State Council in 1986. The Torch program focused on the commercialization of the research results so that technological advance could benefit the economy. It was approved by the State Council in 1988.[34] To facilitate implementation of the Torch program, the State Council appropriated 750 million yuan for the program in 1990, 1.2 billion yuan in 1991, and 1.6 billion yuan 1992.[35]

To encourage the research and production of high-tech products by Chinese and foreign firms, the State Council approved 27 high-tech industrial development zones in 1990 and added another 25 zones where preferential treatment was given to those firms in the areas of taxes, utilities, resources, and manpower.[36]

Dr. Song Jian, a Russian-trained space engineer, has been the minister for the State Science and Technology Commission and has provided outstanding leadership in the development of technology in China. On several occasions when the author went to China on lecturing trips, Dr. Song entertained him for dinner, once at the Great Hall of the People.

Importing Technology from Abroad

China does not have to reinvent the wheel; technology can be imported from abroad. One way to import technology is to purchase technical journals and literature. Beijing is home to the National Library, the leading institution in the country. University libraries and public libraries can be found in major cities throughout the country. A nationwide system to assign special fields of interest to the different libraries helps reduce duplication in the collection of materials.

Several libraries have expanded with government funds and through private donations. For instance, the library of Northwestern University at Xian has received donations from overseas Chinese.

Thousands of young scholars and engineers have been sent abroad, mostly to Japan, Europe, the Soviet Union, the United States, and Canada. More than 90,000 Chinese students are currently studying in the United States.

Chinese firms have entered into technical and licensing agreements with foreign firms to purchase machinery and equipment to be used in the country. China has learned from the bad experiences of some the Third World countries that have purchased machinery and equipment from abroad but failed to make full use of them because of the lack of training on the part of the workers, the lack of spare parts for repairs, the lack of expertise in maintaining the machinery and equipment, the lack of industrial supplies for inputs, and poor operations management. Machinery and equipment would break down and be discarded, resulting in great loss. Chinese firms would carefully work out the technical and licensing agreements with foreign firms in great detail so that the machinery and equipment that was bought could be put into efficient use for years to come. These agreements, which may take two or more years to complete, would include the patent rights for the machinery and equipment, the blueprint of the plant that would house the machinery and equipment, the specifications of the machinery and equipment, the utility and industrial material inputs, the sewage system for the disposal of waste, the spare parts for repairs, the maintenance procedures for the machinery and equipment, the research contract to substitute imported industrial supplies with available domestic supplies, and the training of the engineers, foremen, and skilled and unskilled workers to operate the machinery and equipment.

For instance, in 1974, a group of Chinese went to Houston, Texas, and worked at a Kellogg Corporation plant that produced chemical fertilizers. The Chinese government had a technical and licensing agreement with Kellogg to purchase eight fertilizer plants for a total of U.S.$200 million. The group that went to Houston included a manager, chemists, engineers, foremen, skilled workers, a repair crew, and a maintenance crew. They underwent training at the Kellogg plant. When the training was completed, they returned to China with the machinery and equipment packed in boxes. In China, a plant was constructed, and the machinery and equipment were installed. The plant was put into operation by the staff of those personnel who trained in Houston and under the supervision of American personnel sent from Houston. Eventually, all eight plants that were bought under the agreement were constructed and put into operation in China, forming the backbone of the fertilizer industry in China.

In 1976, a group of Chinese went to Seattle, Washington, and worked at a Boeing 707 airline plant. The group included engineers, technicians, pilots, copilots, navigators, maintenance crew, a repair crew, and a refueling crew. The group received training in the operation of 707s, for which the Chinese government had an agreement with Boeing to purchase 10. After the group completed their training, they flew the airplanes back to China.[37]

Chinese firms have been entering into agreements with foreign firms to establish joint ventures in China. At first, these joint ventures were in such service fields as hotels and restaurants that catered to foreign tourists visiting China. Eventually, the joint ventures have been in mining and manufacturing. This provides China with ample opportunity to learn from foreign firms the details of production and management.

AGRICULTURAL REFORM

The agricultural reform that was begun under Deng from 1979 to 1993 continued the improvement started under Mao. This reform aimed to modify the system to improve efficiency in farming by pushing through a transition from centralized planning to free enterprise by the farmers, from price control and rationing to a free market, and from income distribution based on egalitarian principles without effective materialistic incentives to a management system responsible for its profits and losses.

This transition phase was a huge undertaking. The Chinese government handled the transition with caution. At first, the reform was carried out in a few areas on a small scale. When the experiment succeeded, the reform was carried out throughout the country but not abruptly. The transition has been ongoing for the past 14 years but is still not completed. The Soviet Union and Poland were also undergoing the transition from a planned economy to a free-market economy. They plunged into the reforms hurriedly, partly because of the advice of some American professors from distinguished universities. Abrupt changes caused difficulties in the economy, including shortages of supplies and a breakdown of the distribution system.

When Deng assumed power, state farms and communes performed the farming in China. State farms were owned and operated by the state, while communes were owned by the state but operated by farmer managers. Communes were given assignments of producing specific amounts of crops to be delivered to the government. If the communes produced beyond the assignments, they could sell the surplus to the government or to the market and keep the profits after paying taxes. Communes were large, each consisting of about 5,000 households. They favored extensive farming, which uses large equipment to operate a huge area of land and requires fewer farmers. Extensive farming could be efficient in Russia because of the shortage of manpower.

Households in the communes were organized into teams of about 30 households each. Each team was given an assignment. The system did not encourage individuals to work hard. If a farmer worked harder, the benefit would be shared among the members of the team, and the farmer would probably receive a bonus but not the full benefit. In Chinese, the saying is, *Chi daguofan,* meaning "to share a common pot."

Since 1961, farmers had been given private plots that they could use to cultivate any crop they wanted and market the crops on the free market. This allowed them to make good use of their spare time (which was previously wasted) and gave them the experience of being entrepreneurs in a free-market system.

The Household Responsibility System

By the late 1970s, communes were not very efficient because little competition existed among them and material incentives were not strong enough for farmers to work hard. The system needed an overhaul.

In 1977, Zhao Ziyang was authorized to carry out experiments in agricultural reform in Sichuan Province. Subsequently, similar experiments were carried out by Wan Li in Anhui Province. A household responsibility system evolved out of these experiments and was carried out in Sichuan and eventually throughout the country. The system succeeded in improving the efficiency of farming.

Under the household responsibility system, the communes remained, but the management was transferred to farmer households. Each household signed a lease contract with the commune for a farm and was given full authority in managing the farm as to what and how much to produce. Each household was assigned an amount of crops to be produced and delivered to the commune. It could sell the crops produced beyond the assignment on the free market. The lease had terms as long as 10 to 15 years.[38]

The system produced efficiency in farming for a number of reasons. The households assumed full responsibility for profits and losses, as the communes would no longer bail them out. Therefore, the households had to work hard to stay in business. Those who failed would lose the lease, and the commune could then lease the land to others. Lifetime tenure no longer existed for farmers in the employ of the commune or, as the Chinese say, *Tie fanwan*, meaning "the iron rice bowl."

Since the households enjoyed the full benefit of their work, it was worthwhile for them to work hard and to invest in the land to improve its yield. Better seeds and more fertilizers would be used.

Farmers were becoming good entrepreneurs after their many years of experience in managing the commune collectively and in cultivating their private plots. They were able to respond to market forces and plan their production to meet market demands.

Small farms managed by households favored intensive farming where a significant number of man-hours were spent on farms without the use of large machinery. This type of farming is suitable for China because of its large labor force and the shortage of capital for large machines.

The household is the basic social and economic unit in China. In the tradition of family loyalty, each member puts forth his or her best effort and follows the direction of the head of the household to promote the welfare of the family. Great social pressure is exerted for everyone to be industrious.

When the households sold their crops on the free market, competition was common among the households. The price of the crops would be determined by the market, and the only way to improve income was by producing more and selling more.

The household responsibility system was put into force throughout the country. By 1984, the communes were abolished, and about 98 percent of the country's farms were operating under the household responsibility system.[39] In 1984, grain production reached 400 million tons, the largest output in recent years.[40]

In 1985, China started to export grains. China ranked as the world's largest producer of grains, cotton, soybeans, and tobacco.[41]

The improvement in farming efficiency made it possible for agricultural output in the period from 1981 to 1985 to maintain an annual growth rate of 3.4 percent, about the same as the rate under Mao but with many fewer farmers. Manpower could now be shifted to industries.[42]

Government Support for Agriculture

Under the household responsibility system, some farmers were successful. The government adopted a number of measures to give farmers more freedom of action. Farmers were allowed to buy the lease contracts of other farmers to enlarge their holdings and hire workers. They were allowed to form producers' cooperatives and to buy machinery for their farms. From time to time, the government would raise the prices it paid farmers to give them better profits. The government installed a power transmission system to the countryside to provide electricity for farmers so that they could use electrical equipment, such as power water pumps for irrigation. The government set up gasoline stations throughout the country to provide fuel to farmers to run their tractors. The tractors that were popular in China, the very small three-wheel types, were easy to maneuver on small farms, fuel efficient, and easy to maintain and repair. A trailer can be attached to the tractor to transport supplies.

Farmers became more enterprising once they were allowed to be their own bosses. They hired themselves out in the factories in their neighborhoods. They worked on construction jobs, bringing their tractors along. They owned trucks and engaged themselves in the shipping business. They operated machine shops, canning plants, food processing factories, and frozen food lockers. They had gone into the livestock business, raising chickens, pigs, and cattle.

Before the reform, farmers in China were among the poorest group, with a per capita income of about U.S.$63 per year, but by 1989 the per capita income rose to U.S.$600 per year. A few farm households made 10,000 yuan a year, the *wanyuanhu*. An average farm household had a television set, a washing machine, a refrigerator, and a sewing machine. About one-fourth of farm households had gas in the kitchen, using gas generated by biogas tanks from cattle manure.[43] Traveling in the countryside, the author saw many new homes being built with bricks and sometimes of two stories.

After the elimination of communes, farming was put largely in the hands of the private sector of farmer households, but in China farming is still done in the public sector, as the government operates state farms. In 1993, 2,166 state farms were still scattered throughout the country, including 551 large and medium-size ones. The state farms cover some 90 million acres of land and employ some five million farmers. On these state farms, the government operated 19 universities, 26 high schools, and 707 scientific research institutes. The state farms produced 90 percent of the country's rubber, 77 percent of its dairy products, and 70 percent of its hops. The state farms also branched out into food processing, spinning, weaving, electronics, machinery, chemicals, pharmaceuticals, metallurgy, and construction activities.[44]

Before the reform, the government used centralized planning on about 20 essential farm products. Now the government has reduced the scope of its planning to cover only grains, cotton, edible oil, and tobacco. The scope of planning will be further cut as soon as the supply and demand of some of these products can be balanced and market prices stabilize.

Before the reform, townships depending on the local shortage of supplies carried out rationing and price control for farm products. Now, with the improvement of farm output, rationing and price control became unnecessary. In 1992, more than 400 townships amounting to 20 percent of the total in the country had lifted the rationing and price control of grains. As a result, some 200 million urban residents could say good-bye to coupons with a sigh of relief. In 1993, Beijing had gone further in lifting rationing and price control to cover grains, edible oil, meat, eggs, and poultry.[45]

Before the reform, a commune usually covered several townships and assumed control of many services, such as maintaining land and waterway transportation, supplying fuels and power, providing farm equipment, assisting in the marketing of farm products, and operating schools. Now, with the communes gone, the responsibility for carrying out these services has reverted to the townships, which have become active and gained importance. The government is now conducting an experiment in a few selected cities, including Tianjin, Wuhan, Chongqing, Guangzhou, and Hangzhou, to reform townships in an effort to streamline their structure and make them more efficient.[46]

The transition from planned economy to market economy in agriculture seems to have worked out smoothly, and free enterprise and the free market seem to function well in China.

Two officials who contributed greatly to agricultural reform were Zhao Ziyang and Wan Li. Farmers were quoted in a folk song praising the two: *Yao chi liang Zhao Ziyang; Yao chi mi Zhao Wan Li*, meaning "If you want wheat, go to Zhao Ziyang; and if you want rice, go to Wan Li."[47]

Zhao Ziyang was born in 1919 in Huaxian in Henan Province to a landlord family. He joined the Communist Party in 1938 and worked in the party in Guangzhou. In the 1970s, he served as the party chief in several posts: Inner Mongolia, Guangzhou, and Sichuan. During the Cultural Revolution, he was among the reformers persecuted by the Red Guards. He was paraded through the streets wearing a dunce cap. In 1977, he was brought to Beijing and in 1979 was made a member of the Politburo. In 1979, he was sent to Sichuan to lead the experiment of the household responsibility system. The success of that experiment laid the foundation for agricultural reform throughout the country. In 1980, he was made vice premier and then premier. In 1981, he was made a member of the Standing Committee of the Politburo and in 1987 the first vice chairman of the Military Affairs Commission. He was then the apparent successor of Deng Xiaoping. During the Tiananmen Square incident in 1989, he was accused of mishandling the affair and was dismissed from office.[48]

Wan Li was born in 1916 in Dongping in Shandong Province. He studied in France and joined the Communist Party in 1936. In 1949, he worked under Deng Xiaoping in the Third Line campaign in southwestern China to build up that area for defense. In 1958, he was the deputy mayor of Beijing. He served as the head of several ministries, including railways and light industry. During the Cultural Revolution, he was arrested in 1966 and put in prison for two years by the Gang of Four. After the fall of the Gang of Four in 1977, he was brought back to Beijing and made a member of the Central Committee of the Communist Party. In 1977, he was sent to Anhui Province to carry out the experiment on the household responsibility system, similar to that carried out by Zhao Ziyang in Sichuan. In 1980, he was made a member of the Politburo and vice premier. In 1982, he was made a member of the Standing Committee of the Politburo. In 1988, he was made the chairman of the Standing Committee of the National People's Congress, equivalent to the Speaker of the House in the United States, until he retired in 1993. He plays bridge with Deng Xiaoping and played tennis with the first President George Bush when Bush was the representative of the United States in China.[49]

THE OPEN DOOR POLICY AND JOINT VENTURES

Theoretically, a rich farmer who has never ventured out of his province could fly to Beijing on a Boeing 707, stay at the Great Wall Hotel (a first-class hotel by world standards, jointly operated by an American firm and a Chinese firm), have dinner at Maxim's (a French restaurant), spend the evening dancing at a disco, and have a midnight snack at McDonald's or Kentucky Fried chicken and have a Pepsi.

This is just to show that a large number of foreign firms are operating in China. Of course, the rich farmer is probably just as happy to stay at a hotel for the local people and take a walk in the Summer Palace outside the city. Before President Richard Nixon's 1972 trip to China, practically no trade was conducted between China and the United States. Consider this: if an American firm in 1972 had begun trading with China and had kept a small fraction of China's trade, and if the firm could have maintained its share of the trade through the years, then in 1992, when the combined value of China's exports and imports reached U.S.$160 billion, that small fraction would have been a sizable fortune for the firm. China was among the most exciting places for foreign firms to make an investment.

Deng does not mind that the rich farmer enjoys the good life or that foreign firms get rich, but he brought about the policies of open door trade and joint ventures essentially to obtain two important inputs for the industrialization of China: foreign capital and foreign technology.

The Open Door Policy

From 1949 to 1960, China's foreign trade was directed primarily to the Soviet Union and Eastern European countries. From 1960 on, the relations between China and the Soviet Union deteriorated. China began to extend its trade to the West. The expansion of foreign trade due to the open door policy had helped China in its economic growth in two ways: from 1978 to 1989, imports promoted growth, and from 1990 on, exports pushed growth.

The open door policy, in lowering tariff rates and in liberalizing the control of foreign exchange transactions, encouraged many importers to go to China, bringing in capital goods such as machinery, equipment, and essential industrial supplies of materials to promote industrial development in China. Exports were supposed to grow with imports so that foreign currencies could be earned to pay for the imports, but they were too small to do the job, causing large foreign trade deficits. Borrowing from abroad financed the deficits. In 1978, China concluded a loan agreement with a British consortium of 10 banks for U.S.$1.2 billion at 7.2 percent interest. From 1979 to 1983, China borrowed from Japan U.S.$1.5 billion and again in 1984 U.S.$2.1 billion. Since then, China had borrowed from the United States and other countries and from international agencies such as the World Bank. By 1985, China's foreign debt from the world amounted to U.S.$16 billion, by 1968 U.S.$40 billion, and by 1990 U.S.$50 billion. Starting in 1992, China had to pay U.S.$10 billion per year in principal and interest.[50]

China cannot continue borrowing to pay for imports, as it would soon exhaust its credit and imports-promoted growth would eventually come to a stop. China had to promote exports to keep expanding trade.

To help solve the trade deficits problem, the government devalued the yuan from time to time. The yuan was made cheaper, and foreign currencies were made more expensive. By making the yuan cheaper, foreign currency prices for Chinese exports would be lower, so more exports could be sold. By making foreign currencies more expensive, the yuan price for imports from foreign countries would be higher, so fewer imports would be bought.

The exchange rate was adjusted to 1.68 yuan to one U.S. dollar in 1978, 2.50 in 1962, 2.94 in 1985, 4.78 in 1990, and 5.32 in 1991.[51] In 1978, China

was given the most-favored-nation status by the United States, subject to
yearly review by Congress. This meant that China's exports coming into
the United States would receive the treatment in tariff rates and customs
procedures enjoyed by other countries.[52] Since 1975, China's foreign trade
has been expanding rapidly, from U.S.$13.9 billion in 1975 to U.S.$59.2
billion in 1985 and to U.S.$165.6 billion in 1992. In 1992, China's exports
at U.S.$85.0 billion were larger than imports at U.S.$80.6 billion.[53] Since
1990, China's exports had overtaken its imports, making it possible for
the country to improve its foreign currency reserves. In 1983, China had
foreign currency reserves of U.S.$20 billion and by 1991 U.S.$40 billion.[54]

China's exports can be classified into primary products, such as agricultural and mineral products, and light manufactured products, such as
textiles, garments, handicrafts, and household appliances.

As China has become industrialized, a shift has occurred in the com-
position of its exports. The share of primary products declined from 50.2
percent of the total exports in 1980 to 22.5 percent in 1991, and the share
of light manufactured products improved from 49.8 percent in 1980 to
77.5 percent in 1991.[55] It is no surprise for a housewife in the United States
to go shopping at Penney's or Wal-Mart and find that many of the garments, toys, and household appliances are made in China.

One of China's promising exports is oil. China's oil reserves were estimated officially at 20 billion barrels offshore and 75 billion barrels on the
mainland. That would put China's oil reserves equal to those of Kuwait.
Some conservative estimates made by Western observers placed China's
reserves at 40 billion barrels.

In 1983, China signed 11 offshore contracts with 15 oil companies from
eight countries for oil exploration and production. In 1986, 13 U.S. oil
companies were working in offshore oil fields. In 1986, the Weizhou oil
field in the South China Sea started to produce oil at a volume of 10,000
barrels per day.[56]

China has oil supplies to meet its domestic needs. In 1977, China began
to export oil to the amount of 12 million tons, earning about U.S.$1 billion.
In 1985, China exported 36 million tons of oil, earning U.S.$6.7 billion.[57]
China was among the 23 founding members of the General Agreement
on Tariffs and Trade (GATT) in 1941, but its membership was suspended
in 1950. China wants to rejoin this organization, which promotes freer
world trade. Since 1986, China has applied for membership, and the matter has been discussed in Geneva frequently. China has taken measures
to improve its eligibility for membership, such as canceling export subsidies, liberalizing regulations on foreign investments, reducing customs
duties to bring them in line with the 13 to 14 percent tariff rates required
by developing countries, and cutting down import restrictions by licensing. GATT still insists on certain conditions for China to be admitted, such
as maintaining a uniform trade policy throughout the country by cancel-

ing the preferential treatment granted to foreign firms in the special economic and technology development zones, maintaining a uniform trade policy for all nations on an equal basis, reducing import controls, and reforming the country's price system.[58] China expects that these problems can be solved and that before long it can regain membership in the organization.

Joint Ventures

Joint ventures formed by foreign and Chinese firms to work together in manufacturing or trade are not recent inventions. They go back 150 years to the 1840s, when the British and the Portuguese established colonies in Hong Kong and Macao, where joint ventures were very active. Foreign firms engaged in activities on the high seas, and Chinese firms operated along the China coast and in Southeast Asia, where they had established contacts.

Deng Xiaoping revived joint ventures to attract foreign firms to go to China to engage in manufacturing and trade. Foreign firms would provide capital in foreign currencies, machinery and equipment, and technology, and Chinese firms would supply labor and resources. The Chinese government wants the joint ventures to earn good profits so that they can continue to operate in China and, by their success, encourage other foreign firms to come.

Foreign firms want to keep their capitalistic ways of operating. The problem is how to accommodate these foreign firms in a country with a planned economy like China. Deng solved the problem by designating a few port cities on the coast for the operations of joint ventures. Four of these—Shenzhen, Zhuhai, Xiamen, and Shantou in Guangdong and Fujian provinces—are called special economic zones. They function under the capitalistic system while the rest of the country maintains a planned economy. They are like four small capitalistic islands floating on the ocean of a planned economy. In approving joint ventures, the Chinese government wanted to know what goods were to be produced, where the markets were for these products, and what resources and how much domestic capital were required so that the joint ventures would not jeopardize the planned economy but rather complement it.

China preferred the products of joint ventures to be sold in the world market, not in China, to avoid competition with domestic products. This was where a misunderstanding arose. Foreign firms hoped to produce in China to take advantage of the huge Chinese market and were disappointed when they found out that they were not allowed to do so. In some cases, products of joint ventures were allowed to be sold in China when such products were not produced in China or were in short supply.

As joint ventures were carefully scrutinized, the capitalistic islands of the special economic zones coexisted with the planned economy. In doing this, Deng considered that he had created a country of two systems. This is the model for the unification of Hong Kong, Macao, and Taiwan with China. Hong Kong was returned to China in 1997, and Macao was returned in 1999. Taiwan will come later. China can allow these areas to practice capitalism the same way as is done in the special economic zones.

In these special economic zones, the Chinese government provides the infrastructure and the fixed assets, such as railroads, highways, seaports, warehouses, buildings, plants, utilities, telecommunications, and fire and police protection. Joint ventures, once approved, can move in and start operations immediately without much overhead.

A foreign firm wishing to form a joint venture in China has to submit an application providing the following information: the kind of firm it is; the major products it intends to produce; the scope of operation; the feasibility of the enterprise; a market survey for the products; the contributions of the foreign firm, such as capital, machinery, equipment, technology, and industrial supplies of materials; and the contributions of the Chinese firm, such as the infrastructure, the fixed assets in buildings and plants, the labor and resources supplies, and the probable major benefits for China.[59]

The negotiations may take a long time to conclude, perhaps over a year. It is too costly for individual firms to send representatives to China for negotiations, considering the expenses of hotel, office equipment, and local help. The practice is to hire an agent stationed in Beijing or in Guangzhou to work out the negotiations. The author had a couple of friends in that business. Dr. and Mrs. Julian Sobin of Boston kept an office in the Eastern Hotel in Guangzhou across from the Trade Fair Building, where negotiations with Chinese officials were held. The author made a point of visiting them when traveling in the area so as to keep in touch with the situation on joint ventures in China.

Foreign firms that are engaged in joint ventures are taxed the same way as public enterprises in China. Foreigners working for joint ventures are taxed the same way as Chinese are. But provisions are made for the taxes to be reduced under certain circumstances or to be totally exempted for a period of several years.[60] Profits earned by foreign firms can be reinvested in joint ventures or repatriated to their home countries under the control of the Bank of China.

The experiment of the four special economic zones was very successful. In 1984, 15 coastal cities were added for the operations of joint ventures: Dalian, Qinhuangdao, Tianjin, Yantai, Weihai, Qingdao, Lianyungang, Nantong, Shanghai, Ninbo, Wenzhou, Fuzhou, Guangzhou, Zhengjiang, and Beihai. Some of these are China's major industrial cities. By 1985, three coastal delta areas were added: Yangtze River, Pearl River, and the southern coast of Fujian. In 1992, more coastal areas were added: Bohai Bay, the

Jiaodong peninsula, and Pudong near Shanghai. Areas open to joint ventures so far have been confined to the coastal regions of China for the convenience of foreign firms. In 1992, for the first time, some cities in the interior were added: Harbin, Changchun, Shenyang, Xian, Nanjing, Wuhan, Chengdu, and Chongqing. Many of these are major industrial centers.[61]

From 1979 to 1991, a total of U.S.$56 billion in direct foreign investment through joint ventures was committed in contracts approved by the Chinese government, and of this amount, about U.S.$20 billion had been paid up by joint venture firms.[62]

It took about U.S.$2 billion in aid to Japan to help that country recover from the destruction of World War II. It took about the same amount of U.S. aid to Taiwan to start its economy on the way to prosperity. China is a much bigger country, but the amount of foreign capital attracted to China through the joint ventures is certainly ample to boost the country's industries.

When joint ventures were begun, the major participants were the overseas Chinese from Hong Kong, Macao, and Taiwan who wanted to invest in their homeland. In recent years, the major participants are firms from Japan, the United States, and Europe. At first, joint ventures operated in the service sector, such as by hotels and restaurants catering to tourists. In recent years, such ventures have expanded into manufacturing and mining. Some of the prominent joint ventures are the following:

In 1982, the Great Wall Hotel, a 1,000-room world-class hotel, was built at the cost of U.S.$72 million as a joint venture of the Beijing branch of the China International Travel Service and the American E-S Pacific Development and Construction Company.

In 1983, American Motors Company and Beijing Automobile Company, with U.S.$16 million of capital, formed a joint venture to produce Cherokee Jeeps in China.

In 1984, the Beijing Hospital was built as a Sino–Japanese joint venture with 1,000 beds and a research center for traditional Chinese medicine.

In 1984, Volkswagen and the Shanghai Tractor and Automobile Corporation, with U.S.$65 million of capital, signed a joint venture for an assembly plant for Volkswagen cars.

In 1985, a joint venture was signed between Mr. Armand Hammer of the American Occidental Petroleum Company and the China National Coal Development Corporation for an open-pit coal mine about 300 miles west of Beijing with U.S.$600 million of capital. The operation has been delayed because the price of coal on the international market has fallen steadily.

In 1985, Pepsi International signed an agreement with China to produce Pepsi and its plastic bottles in China.[63] In 1993, the American Telephone and Telegraph Corporation signed an agreement for a joint venture to produce telephone switches, microelectronic components, and Bell Laboratory research equipment in China. The agreement needs to be approved by the U.S. government, but no problems are anticipated.[64]

INDUSTRIAL DEVELOPMENT

Industrialization was the central theme of Deng's economic reform. The success or failure of Deng's policies would be judged by whether progress was being made in the country's industrialization. All the other reform measures were meant to assist in industrial development. Population control was meant to reduce the burden of too many children on the resources of the family so that savings could be made. As savings were deposited in banks, domestic capital was generated. Technological modernization was meant to develop and upgrade production techniques and to produce engineers, technicians, and skilled workers. Agricultural reforms were meant to improve the supplies of raw materials. As farming was made more efficient, agricultural output could maintain the required growth with fewer farmers so that manpower could be spared to provide for industries. The open door policy for trade and joint ventures was meant to improve imports of machinery, equipment, and industrial materials; to attract foreign capital; and to introduce techniques of management from abroad. All these measures are aimed at developing the country's industries. Industrial development was planned to reform the industrial structure so that all these improved factors of production could be efficiently utilized to promote the growth of industrial output.

Economic Responsibility System

In capitalistic countries, private corporations run the economy and are responsible for their own profits or losses. They have to compete with one another and therefore have to be efficient and productive.

In the planned economy of China, public enterprises, owned by the government, run the economy. Public enterprises under Mao's rule were not responsible for their own profits or losses. All profits went to the state. The public enterprises did not compete among themselves and did not have to work hard. They did not want to make improvements or try new ideas because the managers did not want to take risks. As bureaucrats, they routinely managed their business.

Deng reformed the system by making public enterprises responsible for their profits or losses. Accounting systems were improved to show these profits or losses. Profits should be shared by the enterprises. Poor managers, incurring losses, would be reassigned or demoted. Material incentive were provided to reward efficient workers. The pay for workers was based on their education, training, and performance. Good workers were paid more and promoted to better assignments. The industrial system was made more efficient.[65]

In 1979, Zhao Ziyang, the first secretary of the Sichuan provincial party, who had been responsible for the reform in agriculture, was assigned to conduct an experiment on the reform of public enterprises. He worked out an economic responsibility system and tried it on 100 public enterprises in Sichuan. The experiment was successful and was extended to 417 public enterprises in that province.[66]

The idea was to give public enterprises the full prerogatives of management with all the attendant freedom of action and to hold them responsible for profits and losses. Public enterprises were assigned production quotas. They delivered quota products to the government and were paid government prices. If their production exceeded the quotas, they could sell the surplus amounts to the government, and the profits would be divided between the government and the public enterprises. Later, a change was implemented that allowed the public enterprises to keep all the profits. If the government did not want to purchase the surplus amounts, public enterprises could sell them in the free market at market prices. Through this process, a free market came into existence.

Public enterprises had full discretion to use these profits. They could use the profits to revise the pay scales for employees or to give bonuses to encourage productivity among employees, or they could keep the profits as working capital for future use. Public enterprises were allowed to go into production of other, nonassigned commodities. Then they could decide what and how much to produce as entrepreneurs. Public enterprises were allowed to keep 60 percent of depreciation funds for fixed assets. They could use the working capital generated from profits, the depreciation fund, or loans from banks to finance the production of the new commodities. They could keep all the earnings from the new commodities. They had the right to discipline or dismiss employees for negligence, for causing damage to property, or for poor performance. They were allowed to conduct foreign trade abroad. They could export their products to earn foreign currency that they could keep to pay for importing machinery, equipment, or industrial materials. Because of these changes, public enterprises gained efficiency in management, and employees began to work hard.[67]

In 1979, the State Council established a Financial and Economic Commission to discuss and make plans for industrial reform, and a System Reform Office was set up to work out procedures to implement the plans throughout the country.[68] In 1981, the government began to apply the economic responsibility system to public enterprises throughout the country.[69]

Before 1987, high school graduates ready for work would report to the State Labor Bureau, to which public enterprises would go to ask for workers. In 1987, public enterprises were allowed to hire workers directly without going through the State Labor Bureau. Workers were given contracts and could be laid off at the end of the contract. Life-time tenure no longer existed.[70]

By 1988, about 50 percent of public enterprises were operating under the economic responsibility system.[71] The reform has brought about improved efficiency in industries. The average annual growth rate of industrial output for the period from 1984 to 1991 was 14.6 percent in real terms.[72]

Private Enterprise and the Free Market

In 1984, to help public enterprises buy and sell their above-quota outputs, the government established a wholesale market for industrial products at Chongqing in Sichuan Province. Later, these wholesale markets were set up in other cities, acting as permanent trade fairs of industrial products and exhibiting all kinds of items, such as machine tools, machinery, chemicals, industrial materials, household appliances, textiles, clothing, and kitchen utensils. Customers were consumers, cooperatives, farmer groups, and public enterprises.

Free markets expanded rapidly at the expense of government stores. Of the total value of the sales of agricultural products in 1978, 94.4 percent were sold through government stores at government-fixed prices and 5.6 percent in the free market; but in 1990, 25.2 percent were sold through government stores at government-fixed prices, 22.6 percent were sold to producer groups at prices under government guidelines, and 52.2 percent were sold in the free market.

Of the total value of sales of manufactured goods in 1978, 97 percent were sold by government stores at government-fixed prices and 3 percent in the free market; but in 1990, 29.7 percent were sold through government stores at government-fixed prices, 17.2 percent were sold to producer groups at prices under government guidelines, and 53.1 percent were sold in the free market.[73]

Under Mao's rule, high school graduates would report to the State Labor Bureaus for assignments. A waiting period was imposed if assignments were not immediately available. In 1978, the government allowed the people waiting for assignments to start small private businesses of their own. They operated tailor shops, repair shops, restaurants, and catering businesses. These small-business units increased rapidly from 180,000 units in 1978 to 11.6 million in 1985.[74]

China did not convert the planned economy to a market economy overnight, as some American economists thought could be done, as evidenced by their advice to some Communist countries. China allowed free enterprise and the free market to gradually emerge without any disturbances, and meanwhile the country enjoyed the stability of a planned economic system and the efficiency of management in the free-enterprise and free-market system.

In 1992, China had 105,000 state enterprises, of which 10,000 were large and medium size and about one-third of which was found to be operating in the red. In the same year, the government enacted a law encompassing 54 articles, further improving the powers of management for the state enterprises. They were given 14 basic rights of management for deciding on the product to produce and the scope of the production; managing imports and exports and the use of foreign exchange earned; signing contracts with workers, with the power to hire and fire workers; marketing the product; and distributing the income among the staff and workers.

As state enterprises started to streamline their operations, many workers were laid off—as many as 940,000 in 1992. Of these laid-off workers, about 840,000 were reassigned jobs by the government or given training.[75]

It was hoped that with the improvement of management, state enterprises that were in the red could become healthy; otherwise, they were allowed to merge, declare bankruptcy, or dissolve. The government would no longer bail them out.

The government did not interfere with the management of state enterprises, but it did maintain control of the overall economic conditions of the country by such macroeconomic measures as policies on taxation, interest rates, government expenditures, and trade.[76]

Private enterprise industries were still small, producing about 1 percent of the GNP in 1988, but it was growing. In 1992, the government approved 363 private shareholding enterprises.[77]

An industrialist who has contributed the most to the country's industrial reform is Rong Yiren, often referred to as Rong Laoban, meaning "Boss Rong." He was born in 1916 in Wuxi in Jiangsu Province. His father and an uncle started textile mills in Shanghai and later extended their activities into dyeing works, printing plants, and flour mills. The family became the leading business group in the country.

Rong graduated from St. John University in Shanghai, majoring in history. He studied in the United States for a short time and returned to manage the family business at the age of 30. When the People's Republic of China was founded, Rong did not flee the country as many businessmen in Shanghai did. Rong worked for the government. In 1957, with the support of Chen Yi, then the mayor of Shanghai, Rong was elected deputy mayor of that city. He served in several capacities in the central government, including as vice minister for the textile industry.

In 1979, when Deng Xiaoping initiated the open door and joint ventures policies, he put Rong in charge of the China International Trust and Investment Corporation to attract foreign capital to come to China and to promote foreign firms to form joint ventures with Chinese firms. In 1990, the corporation had assets of 51 billion yuan and more than 200 affiliated enterprises.

In 1993, with Deng's support, Rong was elected vice president of China, the first businessman to hold such a high position.[78]

NOTES

1. James C. F. Wang, *Contemporary Chinese Politics: An Introduction* (Englewood Cliffs, N.J.: Prentice Hall, 1980), pp. 197–198. A 1983 conference on economic development mapped out the policies under Deng emphasizing six guidelines: (1) Instead of development for development's sake, the policy was to improve the livelihood of the people by meeting their basic needs. (2) Instead of promoting the growth rate of the GNP, the emphasis should be on economic productivity. (3) Instead of growth skewed toward heavy industry, the growth of heavy industry, light industry, and agriculture should be balanced to promote mutual support among the sectors. (4) Instead of unrestrained population growth, population control should be instituted with improvement of human capital through training and education. (5) Instead of a closed economy for self-sufficiency, an open trade policy should be implemented to encourage trade and foreign investment. (6) Instead of an egalitarian principle for the distribution of income, material incentives should be used to reward and encourage hard-working and productive workers. Deng's policies demonstrated a break from the orthodox Communist policies under Mao. Liu Guoguang, *A Study of the Strategy of China's Economic Development* (in Chinese, *Zhongguo Jingji Fazhan Zhanlue Wenti Yanjiu*) (Shanghai: People's Publishing Co., 1983), pp. 21–26.

2. Immanuel C. Y. Hsu, *China without Mao: The Search for a New Order* (New York: Oxford University Press, 1990), pp. 169–170. The combined agricultural and industrial output grew on the average of 8.1 percent per year from 1953 to 1981. The average annual growth rate for the first five-year plan period, 1953 to 1957, was 10.9 percent; for the second five-year plan period, 1958 to 1962, 0.6 percent; for the period from 1963 to 1965 15.3% percent; for the third five-year plan period, 1966 to 1970, 9.6 percent; for the fourth five-year plan period, 1971 to 1975, 7.8 percent; and for the fifth five-year plan period, 1976 to 1980, 8.1 percent. The growth of the economy under Mao was strong but with wide fluctuations. Liu Guoguang, *A Study of the Strategy of China's Economic Development*, p. 105.

3. *The Economist* 325, no. 7780 (1992): 13. The seventh five-year plan called for GNP to grow at the average annual rate of 7.5 percent after adjustment for inflation for the period from 1986 to 1990. The average annual growth rates were targeted for agriculture at 4.2 percent, for industry at 7.7 percent, and for services at 11.4 percent. National People's Congress, *The Seventh Five Year Plan for Economic and Social Development* (in Chinese *Diqige Jingji he Shehuii Fazhan Wunian Jihua*) (Beijing: People's Publishing Co., 1986), pp. 23–24.

4. *The China Quarterly*, no. 131 (Special Issue on Chinese Economy 1992): 502.

5. *The Economist*, p. 13.

6. Ibid. In his report to the National People's Congress, Zhou Jiahua, vice premier and minister of the State Planning Commission, proposed an 8 percent rate of annual growth of the GNP for 1993; the planned annual growth rate for tertiary

industries was 9 percent, for agriculture 4 percent, and for industry 14 percent. *Beijing Review* 36, no. 13 (1993): 5.

7. *Beijing Review* 36, no. 24 (1993): 9–10.

8. *International Affairs*, 62, no. 3 (1986): 423–432.

9. Wang, *Contemporary Chinese Politics*, p. 258; Xiaoguo Zheng, *I Am the Son of the Chinese* (in Chinese, *Wo Shi Zhongguo Renminde Erzi*) (Tangshan: China International Broadcasting Press, 1993), pp. 89–92.

10. Harrison E. Salisbury, *The New Emperors: China in the Era of Mao and Deng* (Boston: Little, Brown, 1992), pp. 18–23.

11. Ibid., p. 140.

12. *Beijing Review* 35, no. 41 (1992): 16.

13. Salisbury, *The New Emperors*, pp. 30–33.

14. Ibid., pp. 25–28.

15. Robert Maxwell, *Deng Xiaoping: Speeches and Writings* (Oxford: Pergamon, 1984), p. xi.

16. Charles Donald Cowan, *Economic Development of China and Japan* (New York: Praeger, 1964), pp. 160–191.

17. *Beijing Review* 35, no. 52 (1992): 16–18.

18. *Peking Review* 17 (August 30, 1974): 1.

19. Alfred K. Ho, *Developing the Economy of the People's Republic of China* (New York: Praeger, 1982), p. 14.

20. Yuming Shaw (ed.), *Mainland China: Policies, Economics and Reform* (London: Westview Press), pp. 257–259.

21. *Beijing Review* 35, no. 52 (1992): 16–18.

22. Ibid.

23. Central Bureau of Documents (ed.), *Deng Xiaoping' Essays on Reforms and the Open Door Policy* (in Chinese, *Deng Xiaoping Tongzhi Lun Gaige Kaifang*) (Guangxi: People's Publishing Co., 1989), p. 1. Deng Xiaoping stated, "Out of the four modernization policies, the most important one is technology modernization. Without technology modernization there cannot be agricultural modernization, industrial modernization and military modernization. Without rapid technology progress, there cannot be rapid economic progress. The reason for this conference of the scientists of the country as convened by the Party's authority is to mobilize manpower to map out a system to promote technology progress in the country. Central Bureau of Documents, *Selected Writings of Deng Xiaoping* (in Chinese, *Deng Xiaoping Wenxuan*) (Guangxi: People's Publishing Co., 1983), p. 83.

24. Central Committee of Documents (ed.), *Selected Works of Deng Xiaoping* (in Chinese, *Deng Xiaoping Wenxuan*) (Guangxi: People's Publishing Co., 1983), p. 38.

25. Central Bureau of Documents, *Deng Xiaoping's Essays on Reforms and the Open Door Policy*, pp. 19–20.

26. Immanuel C. Y. Hsu, *The Rise of Modern China* (New York: Oxford University Press, 1983), pp. 838–839.

27. Central Committee of Documents, *Selected Works of Deng Xiaoping*, pp. 83–91.

28. Hugh Patrick and Henry Rosovsky, *Asia's New Giant* (Washington, D.C.: Brookings Institution Press, 1976), p. 94.

29. *Current History* 86, no. 521 (1987): 1.

30. Hsi-sheng Ch'i, *Politics of Disillusionment in Chinese Communist Party under Deng Xiaoping*, 1978–1989 (New York: M. E. Sharpe, 1991), p. 136.

112 China's Reforms and Reformers

31. Ibid.

32. *Asian Survey: An American Review* 15, no. 13 (1975): 155–171.

33. *Current History* 86, no. 521 (1987): 249–252.

34. Ibid.

35. *Beijing Review* 36, no. 10 (1993): 18.

36. Ibid.

37. Ho, *Developing the Economy of the People's Republic of China,* p. 35. On the subject of inviting foreign technicians and experts to China, Deng Xiaoping said, "We must make use of foreign human capital. We should invite foreign technicians and experts to help us in our industries, education and technology development and not to worry about the expenses. They can come on long term or short term basis. They can work on one specific topic or on technology development in general. So far we have entertained them well. Now we want to put them to work. I am sure they want to help." Deng Xiaoping, *Developing Socialism with Chinese Characteristics* (in Chinese, *Jianshe You Zhongguo Tese De Shehuizhuyi*) (Beijing: People's Publishing Co., 1987), p. 20.

38. Michael Ellmont, "Economic Reforms in China," *International Affairs* 62, no. 3 (1986): 423–432; *The China Quarterly,* no. 131:548. The household responsibility system is based on a three-party contract agreed on and signed by the state, the collective, and the peasant household. First, the state works out a plan for rural production, designating certain crops and products for a particular area. Acting on the state plan, the production team then contracts out tracts of land to peasant households to grow given quantities of a listed crop. Draft animals and medium-size and small farm tools are distributed to the peasant households by the collective production team. Land is owned collectively. Large farm machines and implements as well as water conservancy facilities are operated and managed by the collective. Distribution of income is organized as follows. Under the contract, peasant households pay agricultural taxes and sell a required quota of products to the state. The collective production team retains a share of earning from the sales for its own use. The remaining portion goes to the peasant households. Under the contract, the households may manage production with a much greater degree of freedom, and incentive exists for the households to work hard. Su Wenning (ed.), *Modernization the Chinese Way* (Beijing: Beijing Review, 1983), 26, pp. 50–51; Liu Guoguang, *A Study of the Strategy of China's Economic Development,* pp. 162–163.

39. Hsu, *China without Mao,* p. 172; Liu Guoguang, *A Study of the Strategy of China's Economic Development,* pp. 163–168.

40. Salisbury, *The New Emperors,* p. 406.

41. *Asian Affairs: An American Review* 15, no. 13 (1984): 155–171.

42. *Beijing Review* 35, no. 2 (1992): 7–9. From 1977 to 1981, agricultural output value increased at an average annual rate of 6.5 percent, of which the increase in forestry, animal husbandry, sideline occupations, and fishery was 9.1 percent annually. Wenning, *Modernization the Chinese Way,* p. 43. According to the State Statistics Bureau, China's agricultural output value in 1992 reached U.S.$150 billion, a 4 percent increase over the previous year. Compared with 1991, crop output value increased by 1.2 percent, forestry by 2.7 percent, food processing by 8.9 percent, and fisheries by 9.5 percent. *Beijing Review* 36, no. 6 (1993): 6.

43. Salisbury, *The New Emperors,* p. 401.

44. *Beijing Review* 36, no. 14 (1993): 18–20.

45. *Beijing Review* 36, no. 3–4 (1993): 17–21.

46. *Beijing Review* 36, no. 2 (1993): 15; 36, no. 7 (1993): 4–8, p. 20.

47. Salisbury, *The New Emperors*, p. 383.

48. Hsu, *China without Mao*, pp. 40–42; Sheng Ping (ed.), *Who's Who of Chinese Communists* (in Chinese, *Zhongguo Gongdang Renming Daci Dian*) (Beijing: New China Book Store, 1991), pp. 167–168; Ross Terrill, *China in Our Time* (New York: Simon & Schuster, 1992), pp. 167–168.

49. Sheng Ping, *Who's Who of Chinese Communists*, p. 185; K. G. Saur, *Who's Who in the People's Republic of China* (New York: Wolfgang Bartke, 1987), p. 662; Salisbury, *The New Emperors*, pp. 333–335, 385–386.

50. *Current History* 89, no. 548 (1990): 245–248.

51. *China Quarterly*, no. 131 (1992): 706.

52. *Beijing Review* 36, no. 3–4 (1993): 6–7.

53. *China Quarterly*, no. 131 (1992): 694–695.

54. Hsu, *China without Mao*, p. 190.

55. *China Quarterly*, no. 131 (1992): 696–698. According to Zou Jiahua, vice premier and minister for planning, the total volume of imports and exports was targeted at U.S.$185 billion for 1993, an increase of 11 percent over the previous year. The volume of exports was expected to grow at 11.8 percent and the volume of imports at 11.7 percent. *Beijing Review* 36, no. 16 (1993): 14,

56. *Asian Affairs: An American Review*, 15, no. 3 (1984): 155–171.

57. *China Quarterly*, no. 131 (1992): 694–695.

58. *Beijing Review* 36, no. 6 (1993): 13–15.

59. Ho, *Joint Ventures in the People's Republic of China*, p. 20., About the special economic zones, Deng Xiaoping said, "Special Economic Zones are the windows on foreign technology, management, and culture which are the necessary inputs for the determination of foreign policies. There may not be short term profits for our joint venture investments, but in the long run they should be rewarding. We should develop higher education and technical education in the special economic zones using foreign experts as teachers to develop engineers and technicians in the country." Deng Xiaoping, *Developing Socialism with Chinese Characteristics*, p. 41. Joint ventures have helped in the economic development in the country by improving the development of energy and transportation system, by expanding the construction industry, and by improving the technology in manufacturing. Liu Guoguang, *A Study of the Strategy of China's Economic Development*, pp. 554–556.

60. Joint Economic Committee, *Mainland China in World Economy* (Washington, D.C.: U.S. Government Printing Office), pp. 49–52.

61. *Asian Affairs: an American Review* 15, no. 13 (1984): 155–171; *Beijing Review* 35, no. 32 (1992): 24–25.

62. *Beijing Review* 35, no. 2 (1992): 7–9; *The Economist* 323, no. 7764 (1992): 36.

63. Ho, *Joint Ventures in the People's Republic of China*, pp. 53–66.

64. *U.S. News and World Report*, March 15, 1993, p. 57.

65. Central Document Bureau, *Selected Writings of Deng Xiaoping, 1975–1982* (in Chinese, *Zhongyang Wenhua Bianji Weiyuanhui, Deng Xiaoping Wenxuan 1975–1982*) (Guangxi: People's Publishing Co., 1983), pp. 30–31.

66. Central Document Research Office, *Deng Xiaoping's Essays on Reform and Open Door Policy* (in Chinese, *Zhongyang Wenxian Yanjiu Shi, Deng Xiaoping Tungzhi lun Gaige Kaifang*) (Guangxi: People's Publishing Co., 1989), pp. 94–95.

67. *China Quarterly*, no. 107 (1986): 405–433.

68. *Asian Survey* 25, no. 10 (1985): 998–1013.

69. *International Affairs* 62, no. 3 (1986): 423–432.

70. *China Quarterly*, no. 107 (1986): 405–433.

71. *Beijing Review* 35, no. 18 (1992): 20–21.

72. *China Quarterly*, no. 107 (1986): 405–433; Hsu, *China without Mao*, p. 179.

73. *International Affairs* 62, no. 3 (1986): pp. 423–432.

74. *Asian Survey* 15, no. 13 (1975): 155–171.

75. *Beijing Review* 36, no. 2 (1993): 13–18.

76. *Beijing Review* 35, no. 35 (1992): 7; 35, no. 43 (1992): 21–22.

77. Hsu, *China without Mao*, p. x.

78. *Beijing Review* 36, no. 14 (1993): 4–9.

CHAPTER 6

Deng's Political Reforms

Political reforms are not among the primary objectives of Deng Xiaoping's program of four modernizations. This is not because they are unimportant but rather because they do not have the urgency of economic reform and military preparation. Political reforms can be better pursued when the country's economy is sound and when the people are not starving. By 1982, with the economic reforms having made good progress, Deng began to turn his attention to political reforms. He proceeded to make changes in the structure of the government to make it more stable and efficient. He faced two challenges: the Tiananmen Square incident in 1989 and the strengthening of the rule of law in the country.

THE STRUCTURE OF THE GOVERNMENT

China's political institutions consist of two parts: the political parties and the government. The Communist Party is the party in power, and the government is an arm of the party.

The five supreme institutions in China are the National Party Congress of the Communist Party, comparable to the party conventions of the United States; the National People's Congress of the Government, similar to the Congress of the United States; the Chinese People's Political Consultative Conference, a uniquely Chinese institution representing the parties and political groups other than the Communist Party; the courts and the judicial system; and the procuratorates, another uniquely Chinese institution functioning like the grand jury of the United States to indict military and civilian services for wrongdoing.

Government in China consists of three levels: the central, the provincial, and the county. All five political institutions operate on all three of these levels.

Originally, around 20 parties and groups existed. Now, nine major parties remain in the country: the Communist Party in China, which is the party in power; the Revolutionary Committee of the Chinese Kuomintang, the group who surrendered to the Communists when their party was overthrown; the China Democratic League; the China Democratic National Construction Association; the China Association for Promoting Democracy; the Chinese Peasant and Workers Democratic Party; the China Zhi Gang Dang; the Jiu San Society; and the Taiwan Democratic Self Government League.

The Communist Party of China recruits members originally mainly from farmers, workers, and soldiers and lately also from business and intellectuals. Policies of the party are discussed and decided by party congresses at the county, provincial, and central levels. Members elect delegates to the County Party Congress, members of the County Party Congress elect members of the Provincial Party Congress, and members of the Provincial Party Congress elect members of the National Party Congress. The congresses at all levels meet briefly each year and elect committees that in turn elect standing committees. These committees conduct the daily operations of party affairs.

The National Party Congress of the Communist Party is the highest authority in the party. It is comparable to the party conventions in the United States. In consultation with other parties, it makes decisions on the important policies of the country. It elects a Central Committee, which in turn elects the Political Department, or the Politburo, which elects its Standing Committee, which handles the daily affairs of the party. The institutions under the Central Committee are the Secretariat of the Central Committee, headed by a secretary-general who is the leader of the party and the real head of the country; the Central Military Commission, headed by a chairman who is the leader of military forces in the country; the Central Commission of Discipline and Inspection, headed by a chairman who is responsible for censoring corruption or illegal activities of party members and officials; a Party School for the training of members and officials of the party in Marxist–Leninist thought and in party ethics; and the *People's Daily*, the official publication of the party. In China, the Communist Party supervises the executive.

The highest institutions in the executive are the people's congresses at three levels: the County People's Congress, the Provincial People's Congress, and the National People's Congress. The National People's Congress is comparable to the Congress of the United States. It enacts laws and appoints top officials. It elects a Standing Committee and the State Council. Several institutions are subsumed under the State Council, including the premier and several vice premiers; several ministries, commissions, bureaus, administrations, and councils; the Central Military Committee; the Chinese Academy of Sciences; the Chinese Academy of Social Sciences; the Xinhua News Agency; and the Patent Office. The premier in the State Council conducts the daily affairs of the government and takes direction from the secretary-general of the Communist Party.

The president of the People's Republic of China is the titular head of China, performing such functions as representing the country in international communities and receiving foreign diplomats. The real power is in the hands of the secretary-general of the Communist Party and the premier. The system functions smoothly on the basis of good working relations between the two, as demonstrated between Mao Zedong and Zhou Enlai.

The Chinese Political Consultative Conference is a uniquely Chinese institution. In 1948, the Communist Party wanted to create a broad-based government but leave real power in the party. This conference was created by Mao Zedong to form a united front with all the parties and groups in the country. Some 20 parties and groups participated in the conference. All were allowed to operate in the country, but the Communist Party was given the power to rule the country. This conference established the People's Republic of China. To conduct government affairs, the conference promulgated the organic laws governing the structure of the government and a common program providing guidance to government policies. In a sense, the Chinese Political Consultative Conference supervised the government of the Communist Party. The conference was so important that both Mao Zedong and Deng Xiaoping served as its chairman at different times.

The conference meets once every five years. It elects committees and officers who handle the daily affairs of the conference.

TIANANMEN SQUARE INCIDENT

As the nation pursued political reforms, different opinions arose among the various groups. Some students wanted to make radical changes and hasten the reform process. The reformers of the Communist Party were sympathetic to the students and wanted to deal with them with patience. However, the right wing of the Communist Party considered the students' demands unacceptable. Eventually, this conflict caused a bloody incident to occur in Beijing.

The student demonstration at Tiananmen Square lasted 50 days, from April 15 to June 5, 1989. The students' slogans were "freedom of speech," "freedom of the press," "oppose official profiteers," "oppose corruption," and "oppose bureaucrats." The Chinese government considered these broadcasts unlawful and sent officials to talk to the students to convince them of the government's firm stand against their activities but ordered Qiao Shi, the head of the security service, not to use force against the students.[1]

Deng thought that if the student demonstration was allowed to continue, it could undermine the party's authority and harm the economic reform program. However, Zhao Ziyang, in his talk to an audience of the Asian Development Bank, did not criticize the students' demand for freedom and said that the students were in no way opposed to the fundamental system of the government. This marked the start of a division in the government.[2]

On May 13, the students called a hunger strike to pressure the government to hold a dialogue with the students in the presence of foreign media.

Soviet President Mikhail Gorbachev's mission was scheduled to visit China on May 15–17. The government had given permission for the U.S. television networks CBS and CNN, as well as networks of other nations, to bring their satellite dishes and other equipment to cover the summit. Some 1,200 foreign journalists gathered in Beijing. When the television cameras turned on the students, giving the student movement international publicity, the students began to make bolder demands on the government.[3]

On the eve of Gorbachev's visit, Zhao Ziyang talked to the student leaders to persuade the students to leave Tiananmen Square so as not to disrupt the momentous negotiations about to take place with the Soviet Union. Student leaders Wang Dan, Shen Dong, and Wuer Kaixi favored the suggestion, but the hunger strike's leaders, Chai Ling and Li Lu, objected. The student leadership became divided.[4]

During Gorbachev's visit to Beijing, about 200,000 student demonstrators gathered at Tiananmen Square. Some carried signs reading "Remove China's Leadership" and "Down with Deng," causing great embarrassment to the government. Gorbachev's mission left for Shanghai on May 17.[5]

After Gorbachev's mission left China, the Standing Committee of the Politburo held a meeting to decide on a policy to deal with the student demonstration. The members recognized a fundamental difference between the positions of the government and those of the students. The students wanted Western ideas and the Western multiparty political system to prevail. The government, in order to preserve the unity of the party to carry out the economic reforms, was committed to the four cardinal principles, and this meant following Marxism–Leninism, carrying out socialist policies, working for the welfare of the working class, and keeping power under the party's control. This position ruled out Western ideas and the multiparty political system. Making concessions on the four cardinal principles would destroy the unity of the party and obstruct the economic reform program. Zhao Ziyang had been allowed to deal with the students in a conciliatory manner but without success. Zhao still wanted the Standing Committee to be patient. The vote came to four to one against Zhao, and Zhao therefore resigned. The four votes were from Li Peng, Qiao Shi, Hu Qili, and Yao Yilin. Deng would have supported Zhao if Zhao could win the unanimous support of the party and successfully end the student demonstration. Failing both, Deng had to let Zhao go and appointed Jiang Zemin to replace him. Li Xiannian, Chen Yun, Peng Zhen, and Yang Shangkun supported Deng. Zhao was sympathetic to the students, but he had put himself out on a limb.[6]

On May 20, Yang Shangkun declared martial law and ordered the 38th Army, the garrison unit in the Beijing area, to be on alert and the 27th Army from Shijiazhuang to move to Beijing.[7]

After a study of the Tiananmen Incident, the author discovered more than he thought he would. Three versions of the incident are given here to show the complexity of the event. It was a stage on which many groups of actors played their own parts. They were the students, the rioters, the government officials sympathetic to the students, the government officials taking the hard line, the party authority pursuing the socialist policies, the covert agents of foreign countries and their Chinese "friends" conspiring to overthrow the Chinese government and replacing it with a Western-style multiparty system, Chinese intellectual dissidents advocating political reforms, and foreign media looking for and trying to create sensational news to report in order to improve the ratings of their networks. Unfortunately, the interplay of these groups resulted in bloodshed. Each group probably insisted that it was doing the right thing. Then who was to blame? Unfortunately, Zhou Enlai had passed away. Had he lived or had someone with his experience and ability been in power, it might have been possible to find a way, with the united support of the party, to take control of the situation and bring the turmoil to an end early on.

REFORM MEASURES

No terms of office existed during Mao's rule. Once a person was appointed as an official in the government or the party, he would remain there virtually for life. No retirement system was in place. An official could serve until he died in office. As a consequence, the government and the party were overstaffed. To accommodate the large and expanding government units, new offices were being established constantly. They began to duplicate each other, and they fought each other over jurisdiction. Deng's reforms of the government were meant to solve these problems along the lines of fixing terms of office for elected officials, establishing a retirement system for officials in the government and in the party, improving the education and training of civil servants and military officers, and reducing the number of officials.

Officials in China are divided into three echelons, or generations. The first echelon joined the Communist Party in the 1920s, soon after the party was founded. Those who joined had decided to accept martyrdom, as a large majority of them were caught and executed by the Nationalists, the party in power, or killed during the Long March or during the wars. They were true patriots. The survivors were among the top leaders, and they were in their eighties by 1996. The second echelon joined the Communist Party before the founding of the People's Republic of China in 1949. The party was then still struggling, and many of the second echelon died during the wars. They were again true patriots. The third echelon joined the Communist Party after the founding of the People's Republic. They did not have to risk their lives, and joining the party was a way to fame and riches. Deng wanted to gradually retire the first- and the second-echelon officials and develop future leaders of China from the third echelon to lead the country into the twenty-first century. He wanted to promote people of the third echelon who had proven loyalty to the party, a good educational background, and expertise in their fields of endeavor. They could then improve efficiency in the government and in the party.

In 1982, to encourage senior officials to retire, the Central Advisory Commission was established. Instead of retiring to do nothing, these officials were removed from their active positions and appointed to the commission to give advice to the party when requested. This was a partial measure intended to ease the senior officials from power. After five years on the commission, they could be removed to total retirement. Only those senior officials with more than 40 years of standing membership in the party could be appointed to the commission, which a total of 172 such officials joined. Deng was elected chairman of the commission.[8]

In 1982, the National Party Congress elected a new Central Committee of 210 members, of whom more than half were new faces and two-thirds were under the age of 40. The Central Committee elected a 25-member Politburo and a five-member Standing Committee of the Politburo. The average age of the Standing Committee was 74.5.[9]

The new Constitution for the Government was adopted in 1982. It was the fourth constitution, the first constitution being adopted in 1957 and a second one in 1975. In 1976, a third constitution was adopted under the Gang of Four that incorporated the group's policies. The fourth constitution, adopted in 1982, purged the features put in by the Gang of Four and contained the policies of Deng's reform program. The top seven leaders of the country were assigned to five-year terms and a limit of two consecutive terms.[10] They no longer served life terms. Two of them—the secretary-general of the Communist Party and the chairman of the Military Affairs Commission—were elected by the Central Committee of the

National Party Congress, which was indirectly elected by party members. The other five—the president of the Republic, the premier, the chairman of the Standing Committee of the Chinese People's Political Consultative Conference, the president of the Supreme Court, and the chief procurator—were elected by the National People's Congress, which was indirectly elected by the general public. This marked a separation of the Communist Party and the government , as the party was made responsible to the party members and the government to the general public. This also indicated a reduction of the power of the secretary-general of the party, as the other six leaders were given terms of office and could no longer be dismissed by the secretary-general.[11]

In 1985, one million civil servants, military officers, and business managers retired, including a large number of the country's army and navy commanders.[12] Hu Qili added that by 1986, two million of the nation's 22 million party officials would be asked to step down.[13]

In 1992, the Central Committee of the National Party Congress met. Its 189 members decided on the goals and guidelines of the five-year economic plan for 1993–97 and the 15-year economic plan for 1993–2007. They also proposed amendments to the constitution to include the policies and the reform measures instituted by Deng. The amendments specified that the country was no longer carrying out Communism but rather Socialism with Chinese characteristics; the management of farms was put in the hands of households instead of communes, the management of public enterprises was made autonomous, and the planned economy of the country was supplemented by the free-market system.

In 1993, the National People's Congress met. Its 2,000 members proposed and adopted the five-year and 15-year plans following the guideline provided by the Central Committee of the National Party Congress. It also proposed and adopted the amendments to the constitution as proposed by the Central Committee.

Jiang Zemin was born in 1926 to a well-to-do family in the Yangzhou District of Jiangsu Province. His grandfather was a well-known physician. His sixth uncle, who did not have a son, adopted him and brought him up. This stepfather, Jiang Shangqing, joined the Communist Youth League in 1928 and the Communist Party in 1930. He participated in the Long March in 1935 and was a commissar in Anhui Province in 1938. He was killed in the fighting between the Communists and the Kuomintang in 1939, when he was 28 years old. This makes Jiang Zemin the offspring of a martyr, which is a sort of feather in his cap.[14]

In 1943, Jiang Zemin enrolled in Jiaotung University in Shanghai and in 1946 joined the Communist Party and did undercover work. In 1949, the Communists gained control of the country, and General Chen Yi was the mayor of Shanghai. Jiang was made deputy manager of a food processing plant. He was successful in removing from the plant the

Kuomintang members and secret service as well as underworld gangsters. He also improved the output of the plant. In 1949, when it was discovered that he was the child of a martyr, he was called to Beijing and made a bureau chief in the First Industry Department, producing heavy industrial equipment. In 1955, Jiang was sent to Russia to apprentice in the Stalin Automobile Factory in Moscow. At that time, he had already studied the Russian language. On returning to China in 1956, he was made the deputy chief of the Motor Department of the First Automobile Factory in Changchun. During the Cultural Revolution in 1966, he was attacked by the Red Guards, dragged thorough the streets wearing a dunce cap, and whipped. In 1971, he was called back to Beijing to work in the First Industry Department and in 1973 was promoted to the chief of the department's Bureau of External Affairs. He lived in a two-room apartment. His wife was working in Shanghai all this time and would come from Shanghai to visit him once a year.[15]

In 1982, the Fourth Industry Department was expanded into the Electronics Industry Department, and Jiang was promoted to deputy head of the department. That year, he also gained membership in the Central Committee of the Communist Party. In 1985, he was made the mayor of Shanghai and in 1988 was made the party secretary of Shanghai, the real boss of the city.

In June 1989, when the students rioted in Beijing at Tiananmen Square, similar rioting occurred in Shanghai. Student leaders in Beijing wanted the chairman of the People's Congress, Wan Li, who happened to be visiting the United States, to return and call a meeting to discuss their demands. Deng asked Jiang to come to Beijing to see him in Western Hills. Deng asked Jiang to detain Wan Li when he arrived at Shanghai for a few days and gave Jiang a personal letter to Wan Li. Jiang returned to Shanghai that night. When Wan Li arrived in Shanghai, Jiang met him, told him Deng's request, and gave him Deng's letter. Wan Li agreed and stayed for a few days in Shanghai.

Instead of calling troops to put down the riots as happened in Beijing, Jiang organized a 100,000-man peacekeeping squad of workers, each of whom was paid 30 Chinese dollars per day, equivalent to a half month's wage, to help the police put down the riots. The riots were halted without any bloodshed.

Deng deeply appreciated Jiang's performance in a time of crisis.[16]

When Zhao Ziyang resigned as the Communist Party's secretary-general, two names were considered for the position: Li Peng and Jiang Zemin. With the support of Li Xiannian and Chen Yun, Deng nominated Jiang for the position, and the nomination was approved by the Politburo.

In 1992, Jiang Zemin was reelected secretary-general of the Central Committee of the Communist Party of China, chairman of the Military Affairs Commission, and president of China. In 2002, Jiang, after having served two terms of five years each, was replaced by Hu Jintao as the president of China and secretary-general of the Communist Party, but Jiang has kept his position as the chairman of the Military Affairs Commission.

In 1992, Li Peng was reelected premier, serving his second term of five years. He was replaced by Zhu Rongji in 1998 and by Wen Jiabao in 2003.

The current system has a separation of powers among the different branches of the government: the party, the executive, the legislative, and the judicial. Personal dictatorship is no longer possible. Real power resides in the group of top-ranking leaders. The reformers are in control, and the reform policies will continue.

THE RULE OF LAW

The American concept of democracy and that of China differ in their priority of objectives. Bertrand Russell, the English philosopher and winner of the Nobel Prize for literature in 1950, classified societies by their dispositions regarding the dichotomy of societal authority versus individual rights. American democracy certainly favor individual rights over societal authority.

China is a community of villages composed of farming families. To ensure the welfare of the community, the family would have to be a well-run team, and members of the family would have to make sacrifices for the welfare of the family. The village would have to be a harmonious community, and families would have to make sacrifices for the welfare of the village. In China, everyone in the community would have to make sacrifices for the welfare of the group. In Russell's classification of societies, the Chinese system favors societal authority over individual rights.

American democracy developed along the lines of protecting individual rights, restraining the powers of the government, and making the government responsive to the people by frequent elections based on universal suffrage and the principle of one man, one vote. The goal is to provide individuals with the opportunity to realize their potential, the sky being the limit. It is a capitalistic democracy.

Chinese democracy developed along the lines of creating a harmonious community with income being distributed as evenly as possible, social welfare and government support for the working class, and decent living standards for all people. It is a socialistic democracy. Both the American and the Chinese systems work for the people but have different emphases.

Modern democracy can be traced to the French Revolution, when the monarchy was overthrown and the Republic was established. The battle cry was, Liberty, Fraternity, and Equality.

While American democracy concentrates on liberty, Chinese democracy concentrates on fraternity and equality. However, as domestic needs change, the social structures of the country change with them. During the Depression years of the 1930s in the United States, as a large number of people were unemployed and starving, the government took strong measures to improve economic conditions and put into force such socialistic programs as general welfare, social security, and unemployment compensation.

During the Cultural Revolution, from 1966 to 1976, the Red Guards, under the leadership of the Gang of Four, persecuted the reformers and intellectuals, causing bodily injury, loss of life and property for a large number of people, and leaving the judicial system in ruins. When Deng assumed power in 1978, he had to officially denounce this type of mob behavior and restore the judicial system to protect human rights. Consequently, the differences between the American and Chinese systems began to be reduced. Deng wanted to restore the judicial system to protect human rights. He said, "We must create the condition for the promotion of democracy and to do that it is essential to reaffirm the principle of the 'three don'ts': don't pick on others for their faults, don't put labels on people, and don't use a big stick, bypassing the legal system. We must use democratic means and not resort to coercion and force. The rights of citizens and party members are respectively stipulated by the constitution of the People's Republic of China and the constitution of the Party. These rights must be resolutely defended and no infringement of them may be allowed."[17]

According to the 1978 constitution, three components of the judicial system at the national, provincial, and local levels were the public security system, the procuratorate system, and the courts. The public security system is composed of the police force for the local, provincial, and national governments and was headed by the minister of public security. The public security system investigated crime suspects and, if necessary, arrested them for prosecution. The procuratorate system was a uniquely Chinese institution, a legacy from the days of the imperial dynasties. The procurators at the local, provincial, and national levels investigated the cases brought forth by the police force and made decisions on whether to present these cases to court for trial or dismiss them. The procurators also functioned like the grand jury in the West, censoring civilian and military officers, including the emperors in the imperial days, for crimes such as corruption, misconduct, and treason. The courts at the local, provincial, and national levels tried criminal cases presented through the previously mentioned procedure and civil cases brought forth by the people. The court handed down judgments.[18]

Deng wanted a rule of law not to be open to interference from the government leadership. To him, the leadership in the government may change, but the legal system must be preserved. He said, "To ensure people's democracy, we must strengthen our legal system. Democracy has to be institutionalized and written into law, so as to make sure that institutions and laws do not change when the leadership changes, or when the leaders change their views or shift the focus of their policies. The trouble now is that our legal system is incomplete with many laws yet to be enacted. Very often what leaders say is taken as law, and anyone who disagrees is called a law breaker. We must concentrate on enacting criminal and civil codes, procedural laws and other necessary laws governing factories, people's communes, forests, grasslands and environmental protection, labor laws and a law on investment by foreigners. These laws should be discussed and adopted through democratic procedures. Meanwhile, the public security, the procuratorate and the courts should be strengthened. There is much legislative work to be done."[19]

In 1978, the government reexamined the cases of the people imprisoned by the Gang of Four during the Cultural Revolution, and some 100,000 people were released from prison and vindicated.[20]

In 1979, the People's National Congress approved new legislation governing the detention of people. No persons shall be detained without the specific decisions of a court or the approval of the procuratorate. Within three days of arrest, the police must submit the evidence to the procuratorate. Interrogation of the detained persons must commence within 24 hours of the arrest. Persons arrested must be released if no evidence against them can be found.[21]

In 1980, the Provisional Act on Lawyers was enacted and went into effect in 1982. Legal services began to be made available in the country as law schools were established and lawyers' offices opened.[22]

By 1992, the country's criminal law system had been thoroughly reformed. The goal was to rehabilitate criminals to become law-abiding citizens and train them to join the labor force. Criminals were guaranteed their basic rights, such as the right to appeal, the right to defend themselves or have a lawyer defend them, the right not to have confession forced from them by torture, the right against corporal punishment, the right of not being denied the right to vote, the right to be provided with adequate food and medical treatment, the right to write letters, and the right to receive training.[23]

During the 20 or so years under Deng, the country has been moving in the direction of the rule of law for the protection of human rights.

NOTES

1. Che, Muqi, *Beijing Turmoil: More Than Meets the Eye* (Beijing: Foreign Language Press, 1990), p. 11; *Asian Survey* 30, no. 5 (1990): 512–513.

2. Ross Terrill, *China in Our Time* (New York: Simon & Schuster, 1992), pp. 246–247.

3. Ibid., p. 250.

4. Ibid., p. 252.

5. Kwan Ha Yim, *China under Deng* (New York: Facts on File, 1991), pp. 275–279.

6. Mu, Yi and Mark V. Thompson, *Crisis at Tiananmen* (San Francisco: China Books and Periodicals, 1989), pp. 54–60.

7. Jonathan D. Spence, *The Search for Modern China* (New York: W. W. Norton, 1990), pp. 741–743.

8. Kwan Ha Yim, *China under Deng*, pp. 101–102; Helmut G. Gallis, *China, Confucian and Communist* (New York: Henry Holt, 1959), pp. 323–333.

9. Yim, *China under Deng*, pp. 127–129.

10. Ibid., p. 205.

11. Ibid., pp. 205–206.

12. Robert Maxwell (ed.), *Deng Xiaoping: Speeches and Writings* (New York: Pergamon, 1984), p. 66.

13. Ibid., p. 68.

14. James C. F. Wang, *Contemporary Chinese Politics: An Introduction* (Englewood Cliffs, N.J.: Prentice Hall, 1980), p. 115.

15. Ibid., p. 116.

16. *Current History* 84, no. 503 (1985): 268–271.

17. Maxwell, *Deng Xiaoping*, p. 66.

18. *Current History* 84, no. 503 (1985): 268–271.

19. Maxwell, *Deng Xiaoping*, p. 68.

20. Wang, *Contemporary Chinese Politics*, p. 115.

21. Ibid., p. 116.

22. *Current History* 84, no. 593 (1985): 268–271.

23. *Beijing Review* 35, no. 33 (1992): 10–25.

CHAPTER 7

Military Modernization

As a military leader, Mao accomplished a great deal. He and Field Marshal Zhu De built the People's Liberation Army from scratch to four million strong in 1976. It was under Mao's leadership that China developed the atomic bomb, the hydrogen bomb, and missiles. The country, because of its strong defense system, enjoyed some 27 years of stability, unity, and peace under Mao's rule. China was able to protect its territorial integrity with only a few border clashes with its neighboring countries.

When Deng Xiaoping assumed power, he did not have to initiate major changes; rather, he would follow Mao's program and pursue it to its completion. Deng had to deal with developments in two areas: conventional armed forces and nuclear armament.

CONVENTIONAL ARMED FORCES

Deng had to reorganize the armed forces because of a change in military strategy. The strategy in the past was to let the enemy strike deep into China and keep the enemy engaged over a long period of time in an effort to exhaust it. The long supply lines that the enemy had to maintain made it vulnerable. Guerrilla forces would attack these supply lines and weaken the enemy. The final blow would destroy the enemy with a sea of soldiers, in Chinese, *renhai janshu*, meaning "human sea strategy." This strategy took advantage of China's huge territory and large manpower but limited fighting power.

The new strategy is to engage the enemy on the coast or at the border and confront it with the combined operations of the army, the navy, and the air force and, if necessary, with nuclear weapons. The outcome of the war at this time depends not on the number of soldiers but on the fighting power of equipment and technology.[1]

Deng's reform came in two stages: from 1978 to 1987, organizational reform of the armed forces, and from 1987 on, improvement of equipment and fighting power. Much debate took place regarding the appropriate size of the People's Liberation Army. Deng Xiaoping, Zhao Ziyang, and Hu Yaobang proposed a reduction in the size of the army of two million. They argued that a smaller-size army with better training and equipment would be more effective. The opposition, led by Ye Jianying and Chen Yun, wanted to limit the cut to half a million. The debate dragged on for three years, from 1983 to 1985.[2]

In 1987, a compromise was reached. The People's Liberation Army was cut by one million, from four million to three million. The laid-off officers and men were integrated into police forces.[3] Military schools were established to improve the quality of officers and the training of the men. Deng wanted to put young professionals in command positions in the armed forces. A new system of selection and promotion was put in force. Instead of seniority, selection and promotion are to be based on formal education, military training, and performance.

All along, the Communist Party managed to extend its power over the military by appointing political commissars to all units of the military and at all levels. This was to provide political education of officers and men and ensure that the officers in military operations followed the party line. Deng wanted to change this. To him, military operations should be entirely in the hands of military professionals without any interference from the party. In redefining the duties of commissars, Deng relegated their roles to peripheral ones.[4]

The country was divided into 11 regions, each with a regional command. To strengthen the control of the regions by the central government, Deng consolidated the regions into seven and regularly rotated the commanders from region to region to prevent any commander from making the region a base of his own. This was intended to reduce the danger of any regional autonomy from emerging. The navy, the air force, and the nuclear department have always been closely controlled by the central government.

The problem of age among the senior military leaders now must be confronted. Many started their career with the revolution. They have led a long life and are still active in military and government affairs. So far, a retirement system has not been worked out. Deng offered to retire—if they would retire with him. No one complied. Finally, in 1984, the Central Advisory Commission was created, in which senior military leaders were inducted as members. As they left their positions of active duty, younger officers assumed command. By 1992, 40 percent of army officers were college trained.[5]

As far back as the beginning of the revolution, party members also assumed military positions. A tradition had been established of interlocking members in the high command of the party and the military. Too much power over civilian affairs was vested in the hands of generals. Deng wanted to make a change—to let the generals take care of military matters and the civilians take care of civil affairs. In 1988, the People's Liberation Army finally agreed to stay out of politics both in the central government and in the regions.[6] The first phase of the organizational reform of the armed forces has been accomplished.

The second phase began improving the fighting power of the armed forces. From 1983 to 1988, China bought new sophisticated equipment for the army. The infantry was given more mobility with the support of tanks, artillery, and missile units. In 1988, China had the third-largest tank corps in the world, and the Chinese army is now equipped with high-tech instruments such as lasers and computers. By 1992, 60 percent of the Chinese army had modern equipment in terms of artillery, engineering, armored vehicles, signals, antichemical warfare equipment, electronic and computer equipment, and a strategic missile force.[7] The Chinese air force had improved its striking ability through the newly purchased long-range bomber and in-flight refueling equipment.[8] By 1985, the navy possessed five nuclear submarines, making it possible to extend the range of their operations.[9]

NUCLEAR ARMAMENT

In the area of nuclear armament development, Deng followed Mao's footsteps. Atomic bomb tests in 1984 and 1987 continued the research on nuclear weapons. About 300 nuclear warheads are currently in storage.

Deng wanted to improve the country's delivery system for atomic bombs. The navy and the air force had improved their range of operation. Deng had been concentrating on missiles. By 1980, China had developed long-range missiles capable of traveling 8,000 miles and an improvement in the range of its intermediate-range ballistic missiles to 1,500 to 1,750 miles and of its intercontinental ballistic missiles to 3,000 to 3,500 miles. This newly gained delivery ability provided China with an adequate deterrent to repulse foreign atomic attacks.

With this improvement in its defense system, China began to relax its military posture and deployment of forces. Since the 1980s, China has pulled back its crack troops several hundred miles from the Soviet border. Since 1984, the Soviet Union has decreased its East Asian forces. The possibility of more friendly relations between China and the Soviet Union was greater, as the fear of atomic war between them had been reduced.[10]

China's military budget at U.S.$7.3 billion in 1992 was not too large compared with those of the United States at U.S.$274.3 billion and Japan at U.S.$37.7 billion. Considering China's large population, the per capita military budget was small at U.S.$6 compared with those of the United States at U.S.$1,100 and Japan at U.S.$300. The 1992 military budget of China amounted to 1.5 percent of the gross national product.[11]

NOTES

1. *International Affairs* 64, no. 2 (1988): 217–233.

2. *Asian Survey* 28, no. 7 (1988): 257–275.

3. *Current History* 86, no. 521 (1987): 266–267.

4. *International Affairs* 64, no. 2 (1988): 217–233.

5. Central Document Research Office, *Deng Xiaoping' Essays on Reform and Open Door Policy* (in Chinese, *Deng Xiaoping Tongzhi Lun Gaige Kaifang*) (Guangxi: People's Publishing Co., 1989), p. 83.

6. *International Affairs* 64, no. 2 (1988): 217–233.

7. *Beijing Review* 35, no. 22 (1992): 7–12.

8. *International Affairs* 64, no. 2 (1988): 217–233.

9. *Far Eastern Economic Review* 139, no. 1 (1988): 18–19.

10. *International Affairs* 64, no. 2 (1988): 217–233.

11. *Beijing Review* 36, no. 14 (1993): 12.

CHAPTER 8

Reforms in Foreign Affairs

With the political and economic conditions in the country in good order, China now can concentrate on the improvement of its foreign relations. China wants to promote better relations with Russia and the United States and work out such problems as the return of Hong Kong in 1997, Macao in 1999, and the reunification with Taiwan later. China wants to formulate a basic strategy for its diplomacy.

SINO–RUSSIAN RELATIONS

After founding the People's Republic of China, Mao visited the Soviet Union and obtained U.S.$300 million worth of Soviet aid. In the 1950s, the Soviet Union played an important part in China's economic recovery. Large numbers of Russian technicians and engineers went to China, and thousands of Chinese students and engineers went to the Soviet Union to study and be trained. The Soviet experts helped China reconstruct cities, build the infrastructure in transportation and communications, work on flood control and irrigation projects, and develop coal mines and power plants.

Difficulties began to develop between the two countries, and eventually a split came in 1960, when Soviet aid ceased and thousands of Russian technicians and engineers left China. Reasons for the split were many. One was a difference in ideology. While Mao wanted to lead the Asian countries in an agrarian revolution, similar to that of China, Stalin considered Mao a "deviator." While the Soviet Union wanted to guide China in economic planning to develop resources and agriculture as a satellite country complementing the Soviet Union's industrial power, China wanted to become industrialized. Territorial disputes arose along the 4,150-mile border between the two countries. The Soviet Union gained territories from China (around Manchuria and in the Amur River valley and to the east of Ussuri River) through five treaties: the Treaty of Nerchinsk of 1689, the Treaty of Kiakha of 1727, the Treaty of Aigun of 1858, the Treaty of Peking of 1860, and the Treaty of Petersburg of 1881. China wanted to regain these territories and to have Mongolia restored to China.

From 1964 to 1969, 4,189 border clashes occurred between the two countries. In 1973, the Soviet Union marshaled a million men on the border, armed with missiles and atomic warheads. China countered the Soviet move by placing a similar-size army, also with atomic weapons, at the border. An armed stalemate ensued. China began to build air shelters in the cities. Mao's slogan for the day was "dig deep, store grains and fight the hegemony of the Soviet Union."[1]

In 1978, the Soviet Union invaded Afghanistan and supported Vietnam in its invasion of Cambodia. In 1979, China attacked Vietnam. Negotiations took place between the Soviet Union and China. China demanded that the Soviet Union withdraw its troops from the Chinese border, Mongolia, and Afghanistan and stop supporting Vietnam in its invasion of Cambodia. These demands were rejected by the Soviet Union.[2]

The icy relations between China and the Soviet Union began to thaw in the 1980s. Vietnam did not have significant success in Cambodia. The Soviet Union began to withdraw support and urged Vietnam to come to terms with China. In 1984, Deng Xiaoping announced that he was ready to meet with Soviet President Mikhail Gorbachev. Soviet Deputy Foreign Minister Ivan Arkhipoo was sent to China for preliminary talks. In 1996, Gorbachev announced the withdrawal of troops from Afghanistan and along the Chinese border and expressed a willingness to discuss the border issues with China.[3]

In 1989, the Soviet Union withdrew its troops from Afghanistan and reduced its forces along the Chinese border. Chinese Foreign Minister Qian Qichen visited the Soviet Union. Finally, Gorbachev went to China in May 1989 for a state visit.[4] Discussions centered around cooperation in science and technology and exchanges in cultural fields.

Trade between China and the Soviet Union expanded from U.S.$2.6 billion per year in 1987 to U.S.$3.1 billion in 1989.[5] In April 1990, Premier Li Peng made a return visit to the Soviet Union, where he had received his engineering training in power generation. In 1992, Secretary-General Jiang Zemin visited the Soviet Commonwealth of Independent States, formally the Soviet Union, and was able to achieve an agreement on the settlement of the disputes of the eastern section of the Sino–Soviet border.[6]

Since 1991, the world witnessed the disintegration of the Communist system in the Baltics, Eastern Europe, and the Soviet Union. At the same time, the relations between China and Russia were steadily improving.

SINO–AMERICAN RELATIONS

The relations between China and the United States have had their ups and downs. The 1950s and 1960s was a period of confrontation. While the U.S. foreign policy of Secretary of State John Foster Dulles aimed at undermining the Chinese government by diplomatic isolation and military confinement, China pursued a policy of alignment with the Soviet bloc. The confrontation resulted in the costly Korean War and Vietnam War. During the 1970s and 1980s, the relations improved somewhat, being a period of conciliation and cooperation. While the United States under Presidents Nixon and Carter wanted to develop normal relations with China, China pursued a more open policy for trade and joint ventures for business enterprises. American investments went to China, and trade grew between the two countries. The 1990s saw some uneasy moments. While the United States applied sanctions on China following the Tiananmen Square incident, it still intended to preserve normal relations with China. China wanted more trade and joint ventures. The business relations between the two countries steadily expanded.

Confrontation

After the founding of the People's Republic of China, Sino–American relations during the 20 years in the 1950s and 1960s were not friendly. The major issues of contention were over Taiwan, Korea, and Vietnam.

While a number of nations recognized China and engaged in normal diplomatic exchanges—including the Soviet Union, Great Britain, France, India, Burma, Pakistan, and Ceylon—the United States adamantly refused to recognize China. The major concern of the United States was fear of the expansion of Communist influence in Asia. The "dominoes" theory was frequently invoked; that is, with China joining the Communist bloc, soon other nations would follow. A policy was developed by Secretary of State Dulles under President Dwight Eisenhower to undermine the Communist regime in China by a combination of diplomatic isolation and military confinement. All manner of pressure was brought to bear on China in the hope that the Communist regime in China would collapse.[7] Dulles was quoted as saying,

My own feeling is that the best way to get a separation between the Soviet Union and Communist China is to keep pressure on Communist China and make its way difficult so long as it is in partnership with the Soviet Union.[8]

The United States proceeded to build up Japan and Taiwan with economic aid so that they could become partners of the United States in safeguarding the security of the Pacific. The Seventh Fleet was dispatched to the Taiwan Strait, and a number of military bases were acquired by the

United States in South Korea, Japan, Okinawa, Taiwan, South Vietnam, Burma, and Thailand to contain China.[9] From 1951 to 1971, the United States and the United Nations applied economic sanctions on China by setting up an embargo with a coordinating committee, the COCOM, in Hong Kong to intercept China's imports. Some 200 commodities were not allowed to enter China.[10] To compensate for the loss of trade with the West, China promoted its trade with Eastern Europe, Cuba, and some Asian countries, such as Malaysia, Singapore, and Ceylon. The embargo was aimed at achieving the collapse of China's economy. In 1971, the embargo was lifted by the United States because it had failed to achieve its goals. During the Vietnam War, from 1965 to 1973, the United States fought against North Vietnam, which China and the Soviet Union supported.

Conciliation and Normalization

By 1970, the American public was tired of confrontation, and a period of conciliation and friendship with China was ushered in for the 1970s and 1980s by Zhou Enlai and National Security Adviser Henry Kissinger, both having their finest years in public service. In 1917, Zhou Enlai invited the U.S. table tennis team, which was competing at the time in Japan, to visit China on a goodwill mission. This started the "ping-pong diplomacy" in the informal exchanges of athletes, musicians, and theater groups. Zhou wanted to have these person-to-person contacts before the government dialogues could start to break down the U.S. policy of isolating China.

In 1917, a message transmitted through the Pakistan government signaled that China would welcome President Nixon to visit China. Nixon sent Kissinger on a secret mission to China to lay the groundwork for the president's visit. This was done to avoid any opposition from the highly vocal "Taiwan lobby."

In 1972, Nixon traveled to China with Mrs. Nixon, Secretary of State William Rogers, and Kissinger. At the airport, he shook hands with the waiting Premier Zhou Enlai. This made Zhou very happy because in 1954 at Geneva, Dulles had refused to shake hands with Zhou when Zhou approached him with open arms—a snub that Zhou would never forget. Some years later, Mrs. Dulles explained her husband's action by saying that Dulles was pursuing a policy of diplomatic isolation of China and that the handshake could be misinterpreted as a reversal of that policy.

Nixon was taken to meet Mao, and they exchanged pleasantries with each other. Nixon and his entourage enjoyed their visits to the Great Wall and the Ming tombs outside Beijing.

A joint Shanghai communiqué of 1972 was issued that marked a major policy shift for both countries. The major issue was Taiwan. The United

States acknowledged that China was one and that Taiwan was a part of China. The Chinese should peacefully settle the Taiwan question. The United States would ultimately withdraw all its forces and military installations from Taiwan. In the meantime, it would progressively reduce its forces and military installations on Taiwan as tension in the area diminished.[11]

Following this development, the person-to-person contacts expanded between the two countries in science, technology, culture, sports, entertainment, and journalism. In addition, thousands of Americans went to China as tourists. They found that Chinese cities were relatively safe. One could walk about the streets without worrying about being robbed. Food was plentiful and reasonably priced. The Chinese had a unique way of cooking vegetables: they sautéed them in hot oil so that the vegetables were tender and crispy and retained the fresh green color they had in the field. Tourists visited temples, palaces, and tombs. Then they were taken to nurseries, where children, three or four years old, received them at the door. A child would take each tourist by the hand to be ushered to the play room and sit side by side with the tourist as his or her personal host for the day. Songs and dances were performed by a troop of children dressed in bright colors and with rosy cheeks. If anything could capture the hearts of American tourists, it was these children.

A prosperous tourist trade developed in China as millions of people from all over the world visited China. A ministry had to be established to handle the tourist trade, and several colleges had to train tour guides who spoke all languages of the world. The Chinese government encouraged this trade, as it brought in much-needed foreign currency.

Pending the exchange of ambassadors, in 1973 David Bruce was sent to China by the United States to establish a liaison office in Beijing, and Huang Zhen from China did the same in Washington, D.C.[12] In 1977, President Carter sent Cyrus Vance to China for an exploratory mission to listen to China's position regarding the normalization of the relations between China and the United States. He had long discussions with Deng and Secretary of Foreign Affairs Huang Hua.[13]

In 1978, Zbigniew Brzezinski was sent to China and was welcomed warmly by the Chinese because the visit, at a time of the inauguration of Chiang Chingkou as the president of Taiwan, was perceived by China as a snub to Taiwan by the United States. Brzezinski stressed the common interests between China and the United States in the containment of expanding Soviet influence.[14]

A joint communiqué of 1978 was signed by the two countries, reaffirming the joint communiqué of Shanghai in 1972. The United States recognized China as the sole legal government and Taiwan as part of China. Neither China nor the United States should seek hegemony in Asia and the Pacific region. The Chinese themselves would solve the Taiwan issue peacefully. The United States would sever diplomatic relations with Taiwan, repeal its mutual defense treaty with Taiwan, and eventually withdraw all its forces and military installations in Taiwan but would continue to sell arms to Taiwan and keep the cultural and commercial relations with that country. An exchange of ambassadors and consuls between China and the United States would take place on March 1, 1979.[15]

In 1979, China requested the release of its assets in the United States in the amount of U.S.$80.5 million frozen by President Truman in 1950, while Americans filed 384 claims against China to the amount of U.S.$196.9 million for properties confiscated by the Chinese government, such as churches, schools, business corporations, and personal properties. The agreement was for the United States to free the U.S.$80.5 million assets to China and for China to pay U.S.$80.5 million to settle the American claims at roughly 41 cents to the dollar. This agreement was made painless for China because what China had to pay was matched by the amount China was to receive, a way to clear the accounts without any additional payments.

In 1979, the U.S. Embassy was replaced by the American Institute in Taiwan, and the Taiwan Embassy in Washington, D.C., was replaced by the Coordination Council for North American Affairs.[16]

In 1979, Deng went to the United States and toured the country for nine days, from January 28 to February 6, to supervise the normalization of relations between China and the United States and to look for broader fields of cooperation between the two countries.[17]

China and the United States cooperated in sharing with each other intelligence on Soviet military capabilities. In 1980, two electronic monitoring stations were installed in western China to track Soviet missile tests. Thereafter, nine seismographic monitoring sites were constructed in China between 1984 to 1987 to assess Soviet underground nuclear tests, and the data obtained were shared by the two governments.[18]

Current Issues between China and the United States

As the open door policy and joint venture program of Deng were carried out to full capacity, trade between China and the United States grew from the combined volume of exports and imports of U.S.$8 billion in 1985, to U.S.$8.2 billion in 1986, to U.S.$10.4 billion in 1987, and to U.S.$13 billion in 1988.[19]

In 1989, a setback in the volume of the total trade occurred between the two countries at U.S.$7.2 billion because of the Tiananmen Square incident. The volume gradually recovered to U.S.$10 billion in 1990, to U.S.$14.2 billion in 1991, and to U.S.$33 billion in 1992.[20]

In its trade with the United States, China began to enjoy a trade surplus to the amount of U.S.$1.7 billion in 1986, U.S.$2.8 in 1987, and U.S.$3.5 billion in 1988. China's exports to the United States at that time were largely textiles and other consumer goods. The American textile industry demanded protection. The negotiations between the two countries resulted in imposing a limit of 3 percent annual growth on the volume of China's textile exports to the United States.[21]

Because of the persistent trade deficit the United States suffered with China, a threat was issued by the United States to impose a punitive tariff of U.S.$3.9 billion worth of Chinese goods entering the United States if China would not substantially reduce its import barriers on American goods by October 10, 1992. In response, China threatened to impose a prohibitive tariff on U.S.$4 billion worth of American goods. A trade war was developing. The United States sent a delegation to China for negotiation. After five days of discussion, an accord was signed. China was to phase out a variety of its licensing requirements, quotas, controls, and restrictions in the period between December 13, 1992, and December 13, 1993, and the United States would support China in regaining its membership in the General Agreement on Tariffs and Trade (GATT). Thus was the trade war avoided.[22]

Since 1978, American firms had been coming to China to form joint ventures with Chinese firms. By 1990, American firms had committed U.S.$4.4 billion in investment in China and paid U.S.$1.7 billion. By 1919, the commitment rose to U.S.$4.8 billion and by 1992 to U.S.$6.34 billion. By 1992, 3,900 American firms were operating in China in joint ventures.[23]

American joint venture investment was important to China, ranking third after Hong Kong and Japan. However, this investment was not very important to the United States, amounting to about 1 percent of American investments abroad.[24] The rapidly growing business relations between the two countries has become an important factor in the overall stable, friendly relations between the two countries.

China was among the 23 founding members of GATT, a world organization promoting free trade among its members. China's membership in GATT has been suspended, and the country is eager to regain its membership. Since 1982, China has been sending observers to GATT sessions. In 1984, China became a member of the Textile Committee of GATT. In 1986, China began applying for membership in GATT. In 1987, a China Workshop of GATT was established to look into China's application. By 1990, many members of GATT supported China's application, including the European Community, the Scandinavian countries, Canada, Japan, and the United States. In 1992, China began to reform its trade policy to meet the GATT requirements. China cancelled export subsidies and import regulatory taxes, lowered its tariff to an average of 22.5 percent, and promised to further reduce the tariffs to meet the GATT requirement of 13 to 14 percent for developing countries in the next five years and eased its trade controls, such as planning, licensing, restrictions, inspection, and foreign exchange transactions.[25]

With the rapid economic growth, China's trade has been expanding. Its combined volume of exports and imports amounted to U.S.$160 billion in 1993, ranking 11th in the world. About 85 percent of China's trade was with the members of GATT. GATT wanted China to have uniform trade practices throughout China, not to provide preferential trade practices in some special economic zones. It is expected that the difficulties can be worked out so that China can be readmitted in the near future and the huge market of China made more open to the world.[26]

China was given the most-favored nation (MFN) status, thus enjoying the lowest tariff rates for its goods coming into the United States. However, MFN status is subject to review annually, many times with conditions attached. In 1992, Congress passed a bill extending MFN to China on the condition that China showed good progress in the protection of human rights. President Bush vetoed the bill. During the presidential campaign in 1992, Bill Clinton lashed out at Bush's policy on China and declared that he would support Congress, if elected, in imposing conditions on the extension of MFN for China.[27]

In 1993, Congress was divided in its debates on the extension of MFN to China. The hard-line group wanted to attach conditions on the protection of human rights and other rights. This group included Representative Nancy Pelosi, Senator George Mitchell, Representative Stephen Solarz (chairman of the House Subcommittee on Asian and Pacific Affairs), Senator Jesse Helms, Senator Sam Nunn, and Senator Robert Dole. They were supported by such anti-Chinese groups as the Taiwan lobby, Amnesty International, and Human Rights Watch. The group wanting no attached conditions for MFN included Senator Bennett Johnston and Representative Lee H. Hamilton of the House Foreign Affairs Committee. They were supported by business groups. R. K. Morris, a trade analyst at the National Association of Manufacturers, said that China would become the world's largest economy early in the twenty-first century.[28]

On May 12, 1993, a letter was sent to President Clinton urging him not to attach conditions on the extension of MFN to China. Signing the letter were 298 large companies and 37 trade groups. It carried such names as AT&T, American Express, Boeing, General Electric, General Motors, IBM, and Xerox. Calman Cohen, a vice president of the Emergency Committee for American Trade, a Washington business-lobbying group that initiated the letter, said that American companies were working to improve human rights in China. The letter asserted that any restrictions on Chinese access to the U.S. market could backfire by hurting the market-oriented, pro-Western entrepreneurs in China.[29]

Winston Lord, assistant secretary of state for East Asia and Pacific affairs, was sent to China to explore ways through which the United States could be assured of progress in the promotion of human rights, such as forming a joint commission on human rights. The Chinese government agreed to consider the idea, but the talks were difficult, and little agreement was reached. The Chinese government must have been aware of a book attacking China written by Betty Lord, the Chinese-born wife of Winston Lord.

President Clinton granted MFN for China for 1993, but the renewal of MFN status in 1994 would depend on the progress made by China in the improvement of human rights. China lodged a protest on that condition.[30]

A number of other issues were confronting Sino–American relations: China's refusal to sign the nonproliferation treaty on nuclear weapons, China's refusal to sign the agreement on chemical weapons, China's sale of arms, China's exporting prisoner-made goods, and China's refusal to honor copyrights. To accommodate the United States, China took action to resolve these issues one by one.

On March 11, 1992, China signed the Non-Proliferation Treaty of 1968. By this treaty, all nations with nuclear weapons promised not to be the first to use nuclear weapons on others, not to use nuclear weapons to threaten nations without nuclear weapons, and to withdraw the nuclear weapons back to their own territories.[31] China promised not to help any country develop nuclear weapons.

In 1993, China signed the Convention on Chemical Weapons.[32] Since 1979, China had been selling conventional arms to the world, and by 1987, China ranked fifth in the world in the value of conventional arms sales to the world, after the Soviet Union, the United States, France, and the United Kingdom. In 1988, Secretary of State George Shultz and Secretary of Defense Frank Carlucci went to China and reached an understanding that China would not sell missiles abroad. In May 1993, Israeli Prime Minister Shimon Peres went to China worrying about China's arms sales. China assured him that China had not sold missiles to Iran or Syria and would not sell to them.[33]

In 1982, a joint communiqué issued by China and the United States allowed the United States to sell arms to Taiwan but on yearly reduced scale. During the 1992 presidential campaign, President Bush approved the sale of 150 F-16 fighter jets to Taiwan, thereby breaching the pattern of reduced scale. China lodged a protest with U.S. Ambassador J. Stapleton Roy.[34]

In 1992, in an agreement reached between China and the United States, China promised not to export products made by prisoners to the United States. On January 17, 1992, China signed an agreement with the United

States recognizing copyrights and, on July 30, 1992, joined the Universal Copyright Convention in Paris.[35]

On February 28, 1993, President Clinton sent a delegation led by Douglas Newkirk, assistant U.S. trade representative for GATT affairs, to Beijing. Minister of Foreign Economic Relations and Trade Li Lanqing met the delegation. They explored the development of trade between the two countries and China's application for membership in GATT.[36] This seems to be the beginning of a good relationship between the two countries.

On November 19, 1993, the Asian-Pacific Economic Cooperation (APEC) Conference met on a woodsy island in the Puget Sound near Seattle, Washington, where President Clinton met the heads of 17 Pacific Rim countries. As reported by Tom Raum of the Associated Press, President Clinton was dispensing favors along with implied threats to try to pry open difficult markets in Asia and to prod Europeans to end a stalemate on global trade talks. But it seemed unlikely that this remarkable trade forum would produce many tangible results on the trade front. The declaration issued by ministers of the group stopped far short of embracing a move toward an ultimate free-trade zone spanning the Pacific. In fact, the forum turned a rather cold shoulder to some of the key suggestions of a U.S.-led advisory group, including setting a 1996 deadline for charting the organization's future course and a move toward an eventual free-trade community. Hong Kong Trade Director Tony Miller said that it was neither desirable nor necessary for APEC to become a trade bloc. That remark clearly reflected the views of a majority of participants. The organization called for another year to study the issues further. The Asian-Pacific nations did pledge to lower some tariffs among themselves to prod a reluctant Europe to go along with a new set of liberalized global trading rules being negotiated in Geneva. President Clinton met individually with a number of Asian heads of government, including President Jiang Zemin of China. Clinton immediately laid on the table U.S. demands for China to comply with, including the human rights issue, in the belief that an honest presentation of issues would bring results. But this is not the usual approach among heads of governments in Asia. When two Asian heads of governments meet, the most important issue is to create a cordial personal relationship and a conciliatory atmosphere, leaving the hard issues to be worked out by the ministers. Jiang's position was that the conference should concentrate on trade issues but not on human rights, which to China was a domestic matter. Clinton offered to sell China U.S.-made equipment now banned, including an $8 million Cray supercomputer and Westinghouse and General Electric turbines for nuclear power plants, in hopes of winning trade and human rights concessions. The two countries agreed to discuss the issues further.[37]

Clinton's Trip to China

On June 26, 1998, Air Force One brought President Clinton and his family to Xian, an ancient capital, the first stop of their nine-day visit to China. This arrangement gave them a rest from the long, tiring flight and a chance for some relaxing sightseeing and time to recover from jet lag. A rigorous schedule awaited them at Beijing, the next stop.

On arrival, they were given a Disneyesque "emperor's welcome." Scholars in fur-lined robes, bannermen, and sleek maidens re-created a scene of the Tang dynasty (618–907), recalling life 1,300 years ago. The next day, June 27, the Clintons went to the suburbs of Xian to visit the Qin terra-cotta warriors and horses and a life-size model army of Emperor Qin Shi Huang, who ruled China from 246 to 210 B.C.

Clinton was visibly impressed and said that he hoped to learn as much as he could about Chinese history and to help the Chinese people understand more of American history.[38] At the village of Xiahe, near Xian, Clinton talked to students and their parents. This gave him a chance to have direct contact with the Chinese people.

Both political and economic factors led to Clinton's visit. Sino–American relations improved with the state visit of Chinese President Jiang Zemin to the United States from October 26 to November 3, 1997, the first by the head of the Chinese government in 12 years. The two sides agreed to build a constructive strategic partnership for the twenty-first century. This prompted Clinton to pay a return visit to China from June 26 to July 3, 1998.

In recent years, American business has developed an acute interest in China. By 1997, the United States had actually invested U.S.$17.5 billion of the contractual amount of U.S.$40 billion. More than 100 major American firms have invested in China, largely in coastal areas along the valleys of the Pearl River, the Yangtze River, and the Bohai Sea. The investment covered a large number of fields: oil, electronics, chemicals, medicine, cars, and daily necessities. To protect their interests, businesses wanted a good relationship between the two countries.

On the eve of Clinton's visit, public opinion in the United States was divided. Many groups opposed the trip: the religious right, human right groups, the Tibet and Taiwan supporters, and some of the union leadership who opposed goods produced by cheap labor coming into the United States from China. Some Republicans in Congress were also critical of Clinton's China policy.

American foreign policy grows out of the consensus of the National Security Council, the Central Intelligence Agency (CIA), the State Department, and the military. The CIA is concerned about the growth of Communism, the State Department wants to promote the spread of democracy and the observance of human rights, and the military does not want other countries to become so powerful that they rival the United States. China is not always considered a friend of the United States, but that the containment policy has not worked cannot be ignored. The administration's decision was for the president to take the trip to engage China in negotiation on a number of issues concerning the security of the region and to avoid a possible cold war between the two countries.

President Clinton went to Beijing on June 27. A summit meeting took place between him and Jiang Zemin, the president of China. They exchanged views regarding their mutual interests and the need for cooperation between the two countries. Jiang pointed out that the Taiwan issue was the most important concern of China, and he hoped that the United States would adhere to the three Sino–American joint communiqués and related statements. China recently put forward a proposal for its entry to the World Trade Organization, and the United States agreed to work with China on the issue. While the summit was proceeding, the two countries signed commercial and trade contracts worth U.S.$3.12 billion.

A number of agreements were signed between the two countries for cooperation in the fields of environment and energy, the protection of rare and endangered species, and the exchange of students and scholars. They pledged to retarget their ballistic missiles quickly so that neither side was aiming nuclear weapons at the other.[39] They agreed to continue dialogue on a number of issues, such as the nonproliferation of nuclear weapons, the control of biological weapons, and the control of arms sales.

Two significant developments came out of the summit meeting. First, the United States treated China on an equal footing with mutual respect and pledged not to interfere with China's domestic affairs. To be treated as an equal by a superpower was among the most basic objectives in China's foreign policy. It had been a long struggle for China to end the Western domination of the country in modern history. Second, an agreement was reached for the United States to help China develop its judicial system by exchanging and training personnel in the legal profession. The fundamental solution of the human rights problem in China rests not on sporadic pressure from the outside but on building up a sound judicial system whereby lawyers in court can argue grievances and judges can render their judgments to protect human rights. For the rule of law to form a basis of daily human relations, a multitude of lawyers and judges of high quality must be prepared to work unceasingly.

Following the summit, the two presidents held a joint press conference. After long deliberation, Jiang Zemin decided to give the conference nationwide television coverage. This pleased the American delegation, as it allowed the president of the United States to speak directly to the masses of Chinese people for the first time. At the press conference, pleasant remarks were exchanged. Clinton said, "A stable, open and prosperous China is good for the United States."

Clinton brought up the human rights issue, saying, "The Chinese Government had been wrong to use force to end the peaceful demonstration of the Spring of 1989. . . . I believe and the American people believe that freedom of speech, association and religion are, as recognized by the U.N. Charter, the right of the people everywhere and should be protected by their government."[40]

Jiang defended the use of army tanks and rifles to end what he called the disturbances of 1989 as essential to maintaining order. He said that the United States and China had different social systems, ideologies, histories, and cultures, so it is nothing strange that the two countries may have some differences of views regarding some issues. These were sharp exchanges. However, the close, friendly relationship between the two men seemed not to have been affected.

On June 29, Clinton addressed the students of Beijing University, which has been an incubator for political protests since its founding 100 years ago. One young woman told Clinton that democracy, human rights, and freedom were of great interest to both the Chinese and American people. She said that both should undergo criticism and self-criticism. Then she asked Clinton whether he thought the United States also had problems. This put Clinton on the defensive. He said that the United States did have problems, including racial discrimination, a legacy of slavery, and high crime rates, that prevented some people from feeling free. He said Americans are not perfect.[41]

On June 29, Clinton went to Shanghai, where he reiterated the "three no's" on Taiwan: no independence for Taiwan, no two Chinas, and no notion of one China and one Taiwan. By this, he supported China's position that Taiwan was a part of China but wished that China and Taiwan would work out the problem peacefully.

On July 2, Clinton flew to Guilin, a picturesque city on the Li River, where he delivered an address on the environment. He continued on to Hong Kong, where he gave a speech to business leaders on the turmoil in the Asian economy and conducted a news conference.

On July 1, a day before Clinton's arrival, Hong Kong celebrated the first anniversary of the return of Hong Kong to China. Chinese President Jiang Zemin was in Hong Kong on this occasion. He considered the first year of China's rule successful, even though Hong Kong was suffering from a downturn in the economy, as were many other Asian countries, in the regional recession.

On July 3, Clinton and his party left for the United States.

Many Republicans did not approve Clinton's trip to China. But when the trip was over, some of them had a change of heart, considering that, on the whole, the trip was not too bad. Before Clinton's trip, House

Speaker Newt Gingrich called on Clinton to postpone the trip. But on July 1, he admitted that the president did a pretty good job on Chinese radio and television and acknowledged that it is less expensive to be friends than to be enemies.[42] To the Chinese, the trip definitely improved relations between the two countries and especially the personal relations between the two presidents.

Now the time has come for China and the United States to put an end to the period of confrontation and begin a friendly, cooperative relationship. American businessmen have done well in China, pushing the trade between the two countries to U.S.$33 billion per year, and have signed joint ventures contracts pledging investment of U.S.$6.34 billion. The promotion of business relations between the two countries should be the major concern of the policies of both.

The U.S.–China Trade Bill

On September 19, 2000, the U.S. Senate, by a huge margin of 83 to 15, passed the China Trade Bill. During the past four years alone, it looked like the effort to normalize trade relations could be derailed by the allegations of Chinese meddling in American elections, by accusations that Chinese spies had stolen American nuclear secrets, by considerable evidence that China shipped missiles to Pakistan, by Chinese threats against Taiwan, and by the State Department's assertion that China's human rights violations had grown. The bill eventually was passed, giving President Clinton what he considered one of his crowning foreign policy goals.

In 2002, China joined the 135-member World Trade Organization. However, before joining, without the China Trade Bill, China could withhold some trade benefits from the United States that it could extend to other members of the group.

Since the signing of Trade Bill between the United States and China in November 1999, China's market has been made more open to American goods. American orange exports to China from Florida and California rose 100-fold. China would be a dynamic market for electronics, from semiconductors to circuit boards and from personal computers to cell phones.

Overall, the United States bought $82 billion worth of Chinese-made goods in 1999, $69 billion more than the value it sold to China. Such a trade deficit was a serious problem. Fierce lobbying that would pit corporate business interests against organized labor and religious groups before the House's approval of the measure in May, by a vote of 237 to 197, never materialized in the Senate because all sides knew that the Senate had been pro-trade. Labor had no heart for a second round in the Senate, so it shifted its focus to the November elections. Both the United Auto Workers and the Teamsters Union made peace with presidential candidate Vice President Al Gore. This made it possible for the labor's strongest Senate supporters to back the measure.

Governor George W. Bush of Texas, the Republican presidential nominee, supported the legislation. Gore voiced qualified support for the bill but stressed that rights of American workers must be protected.

Of the 83 senators supporting the bill, 46 were Republicans and 37 Democrats. Of the 15 who opposed the bill, 8 were Republicans and 7 Democrats. The opposition to the bill adopted the strategy of first delaying the vote of the bill and then introducing numerous amendments to the bill to force a second vote in the House. The voting of the bill was delayed, but one after another, 20 different amendments to improve human rights, religious freedom, and labor standards in China fell by lopsided votes. This showed that President Clinton's philosophy—free trade leads to free markets and freer markets could lead to more open societies—had gained support of the senators. President Clinton came to this position after he had entered the White House and had face-to-face negotiations with the Chinese leaders. Eight years earlier, he had been on the opposite side, criticizing the first President Bush's foreign policy friendly to China. The passing of the bill gave Clinton the legacy he had been craving: a foreign policy victory on par with Nixon's historic trip to reopen relations with China.

For China's reformist leaders, the passing of the bill paves the way for the long-sought entry into the World Trade Organization, the ultimate capitalist club. Beijing already had completed construction of a spacious compound to house the diplomats as well as trade negotiators who would haggle over tariff rates, export subsidies, and investment.

In 2002, China was admitted into the World Trade Organization. Low tariff rates began to be applied to Sino–American trade by both governments. The China Trade Bill would no longer be necessary.

RELATIONS WITH ASIAN COUNTRIES

China wanted to improve its relations with Asian countries, such as Japan and Korea, and to have Hong Kong, Macao and Taiwan restored to China. China wanted to improve the security of the region and promote cooperation among these countries.

Sino–Japanese Relations

From the end of World War II to 1954, both China and Japan were undergoing a period of recovery from the war's devastation. Little trade occurred between them until 1954, when they began to regain their prewar economic conditions. Trade between the two countries expanded from

U.S.$19 million in 1955 to U.S.$550 million in 1968. Japan was among the fastest-growing countries in the 1950s and 1960s.[43]

No diplomatic relations took place between China and Japan after World War II until 1972, when a joint statement for diplomatic exchange was announced. The major issue confronting the countries was the treatment of Taiwan. While Japan wanted to maintain its trade and cultural relations with Taiwan, China insisted that only one China existed and that Taiwan was a part of China. A model to solve the problem was worked out. Japan recognized China as the sole legal government, and diplomatic exchanges would be established between them. Taiwan was a part of China, so the diplomatic exchange between Japan and Taiwan should be withdrawn and replaced with informal private offices. Japan maintained its commercial and cultural relations with Taiwan without the need of approval from China. The problem between China and Taiwan would be solved by themselves peacefully. This model was used by China in its establishing a normalization of relations with the United States.[44]

In 1978, the Sino–Japanese Peace and Friendship Treaty was signed, and in 1979, a loan of U.S.$20 million was granted by Japan to China. Under this arrangement, joint ventures between the two countries were established for the construction of a transportation system to ship coal from Manchuria to Japan, resulting in three railroad lines, two seaports, and a hydroelectric power plant in northern China.[45]

Under this treaty arrangement, China began to increase its export of oil to Japan from 7.6 million tons in 1979 to 8.0 million tons in 1980, to 9.5 million tons in 1981, and to 15 million tons in 1982. China became an important supplier of resources and energy for Japan.[46]

In 1981, the trade between China and Japan rose to U.S.$10 billion, in 1989 to U.S.$20.2 billion, and in 1992 to U.S.$28 billion. Japan engaged in joint ventures in China with a scheduled investment of U.S.$4 billion, of which U.S.$3 billion had been paid up. Japan was the second-largest investor in joint ventures in China after Hong Kong and Macao.[47]

A close person-to-person relationship had been formed between the two countries. Provinces, cities, and districts of the two countries formed sister relationships, and citizens of these regularly visit one another. In 1991, 125 such relationships had been formed.[48]

The Japanese are among the largest tourist groups in China. They find the trip to China interesting because they have a common cultural background and are familiar with China's history, folklore, and literature. They find that traveling in China is cheaper than staying home because of the lower prices in China. They went to China by ship and airplane. After the Tiananmen Square incident in 1989, while many Western countries applied sanctions on China, Japan refrained from doing so.

In October 1992, Emperor Akihito visited China, the first time the emperor traveled abroad. He made remarks deploring Japanese activities in

China during World War II.[49] The emperor said, "In the long history of the relationship between the two countries, there was an unfortunate period in which my country inflicted great sufferings on the people of China. I deeply deplored this. When the war came to an end, the Japanese people, believing with a sense of deep reproach that such a war should never be repeated, firmly resolve to tread the road of a peaceful nation and address themselves to national reconstruction."[50]

Japan is now a member of the G-7 and GATT, and China needs Japan's help in regaining its membership in GATT. China is a permanent member of the UN Security Council, and Japan needs China's help gaining a permanent seat on the council. The two could help each other in these matters.

Hong Kong

The territory of Hong Kong consists of Hong Kong Island and Stone-cutters Island off the southeastern coast of China, the Kowloon peninsula on the mainland, and the New Territories located on the mainland.

Hong Kong is an island off the shore of southern China. It is 32 square miles in size and had a population of 5.7 million in 1990. The island is conveniently connected to the mainland by a ferry and a tunnel under the ocean. Hong Kong came under Chinese suzerainty between 221 B.C. and 214 B.C. Great Britain occupied Hong Kong Island in 1839, and China ceded the island to Britain under the 1842 Treaty of Nanking at the end of the 1839–42 Opium Wars.

Under the 1860 Treaty of Beijing, the Kowloon peninsula and Stone-cutters Island were ceded to Britain in perpetuity. In 1898, the New Territories were leased to Britain for 99 years and were scheduled to be returned to China on July 1, 1997.

Since the founding of the People's Republic of China in 1949, China has insisted that the treaties giving Hong Kong to Britain were invalid. China pressed its claim to sovereignty over the whole territory.

Prime Minister Margaret Thatcher visited China on September 22, 1982, and had a long talk with Deng Xiaoping. While China wanted the return of Hong Kong, Thatcher wanted a guarantee on the stability and prosperity of Hong Kong. China had no objection to Hong Kong's retention of the flourishing capitalistic system and its prosperity, as China derived 30 to 40 percent of its annual foreign exchange earnings from Hong Kong.

Britain realized that it could not hold on to Hong Kong without China's consent. Hong Kong's prosperity depended on trade with China. If China should redirect its foreign trade to Shanghai, bypassing Hong Kong, Hong Kong's economy would collapse. Chinese account for 99 percent of the population of Hong Kong. Hong Kong does not produce food but depends on the food supplies from the New Territories and the mainland.

Once the New Territories are returned to China, China could turn off the food supplies to Hong Kong, causing it to starve.

The experience of the past 40 years shows that capitalistic Hong Kong and socialist China have coexisted successfully, providing benefits for both sides. Hong Kong takes 80 percent of China's exports and reexports them worldwide.[51]

To bring about a compromise, Deng proposed a model of one country, two systems, guaranteeing the preservation of the existing political and economic systems of Hong Kong for 50 years after its return to China.

No income tax was enforced in Hong Kong, and the corporate tax was about 15 percent, among the lowest in the world. Hong Kong is a member of GATT and the International Monetary Fund.

After two years of negotiation, the agreement for the returning Hong Kong to China was signed in 1984.[52] Hong Kong, according to the treaty, will be allowed to maintain its political and economic systems and its lifestyle for 50 years after 1997, when China takes over the territory.

Ever since China started its open door policy and joint ventures, many Hong Kong businessmen have gone to China to invest and start business. Eventually, Hong Kong and Macao will rank first in the volume of investment in joint ventures in China, ahead of Japan and the United States. About two-thirds of the foreign investment in joint ventures came from Hong Kong, creating three million jobs in Guangdong Province in the past few years.[53]

When the agreement returning Hong Kong to China was announced, reactions among Hong Kong businessmen were divided. Many decided to leave Hong Kong and subsequently moved to Australia, Canada, and the United States. But a large majority chose to stay and continue their business dealings with China. The Chinese government encouraged this by giving them favorable terms, such as tax concessions. Over the years, Shenzhen, the town adjacent to Hong Kong, was transformed into a prosperous metropolitan city.

In July 1992, Christopher F. Patten was sent to Hong Kong as its governor. Patten had an interesting background. He was born May 12, 1944, in Blackpool of an Irish immigrant family. He was brought up in a lower-middle-class suburb on the west side of London. He studied at Balliol College, Oxford University, on scholarship and graduated in 1965. He went to the United States on a traveling scholarship and worked in John Lindsay's campaign for the mayor of New York. He returned to London and worked as the private secretary to Lord Peter Carrington, the chairman of the Conservative Party. Patten later became the Conservative Party chairman and helped John Major become elected prime minister but lost his own seat in Parliament. He was appointed the governor of Hong Kong at the age of 48. The post, the fourth most important after the prime minister, the foreign secretary, and the chancellor of the Exchequer, has a salary of 150,000 pounds per year, tax free. Patten was to preside over six million people of a prosperous community with 6 percent annual growth of the gross national product and a 1.5 percent unemployment rate.[54]

Patten caused a dispute with the Chinese government in October 1992, when he unilaterally changed the Hong Kong constitution by allowing more representatives from the local people in the local government. The local business community did not support Patten. They felt that if Britain were sincere about improving local representation in the local government, they could have done so during their 50 years of rule. Now, this sudden move, on the eve of the British departure, was intended merely to frustrate the Chinese government. The Hong Kong businessmen did not want to upset the apple cart in their dealings with China.[55]

The Chinese government strongly objected to this move by Patten. In April 1993, Premier Li Peng stated that Patten's action was unacceptable and, if not rescinded, would hurt British economic interests in China.[56] British Foreign Secretary Douglas Hurd wanted to meet with Chinese Foreign Minister Qian to discuss the matter. Qian refused to meet with him, saying that the quarrel started locally and could be settled at that level. Finally, the negotiations resumed when Patten went to Beijing to talk with the Chinese officials.[57]

Another dispute occurred between China and Hong Kong. During the last days of British rule, a new airport project was started at the cost of U.S.$14.5 billion. To the Chinese, this was an attempt to use up the funds in the treasury so that none would be turned over to China. After some negotiation, the dispute was settled. Great Britain accepted a ceiling on the total expenditure of the project suggested by China, and China agreed for the project to proceed.

The handover of Hong Kong was scheduled at 11:30 P.M. on June 30, 1997, in the Hong Kong Convention and Exhibition Center. At that time, China formally received the territory from Great Britain. A government of the Hong Kong Special Administration Region (HKSAR) would be established to assume the authority of the territory. To prepare for the establishment of HKSAR, the National People's Congress of China promulgated the Basic Law of HKSAR in 1990, which was accepted by Great Britain. In accordance with the Basic Law, a Government Selection Committee was established, composed of 400 permanent residents of Hong Kong. The committee was to accept applications for the chief executive position, interview the candidates, and appoint the chief executive. In 1996, three candidates applied, and by secret ballot, Tung Chee Hwa, at the age of 59, was appointed.[58]

Tung is among the pro-Chinese businessmen in Hong Kong. They invested in China and provided services in trade and shipping. From time to time, the Bank of China provided loans to them. Tung's father founded the Orient Overseas Shipping Company. Tung spent six years in England

and a decade in the United States working in the family's company. At one time, the Bank of China made a loan to the company to bail it out of a financial crisis.

For the transitional period, a Provisional Legislative Council was appointed by the Selection Committee to replace the elected Legislative Council put in place by Governor Patten. The term of the council was to last from July 1, 1997, to June 30, 1998, when an election was held for a new council. For the ceremony of the handover, the Hong Kong Convention and Exhibition Center was enlarged to a capacity of over 4,000.

On April 11, the British Royal Navy base was closed down. On the morning of July 1, the advance contingent of 509 Chinese soldiers moved across the border on buses and trucks to take over the base. At 6:00 P.M., 4,000 Chinese troops entered Hong Kong.

On June 30, 1997, the Chinese delegation went to Hong Kong, led by President Jiang Zemin and including Zhuo Lin, the widow of Deng Xiaoping. At 11:30 P.M. on the same day, the handover ceremony began on the sixth floor of the newly extended hall, which was packed with guests, including officials of 40 countries, secretaries-general of over 30 international organizations, and some 400 reporters from all over the world.

Leaders of China and the United Kingdom entered the hall at the same time and were seated on the front row on both sides of the rostrum. The Chinese leaders included President Jiang Zemin, Premier Li Peng, Vice Premier and Foreign Minister Qian Qishen, Central Military Commission Vice Chairman Zhang Wannien and HKSAR Chief Executive Tung Chee Hwa. Prince Charles, Prime Minister Tony Blair, Foreign Secretary Robin Cook, Military Representative Charles Guthrie, and Chris Patten represented the British.

In his speech, Prince Charles said, "China will tonight take responsibility for a place and a people which matter greatly to us all. . . . We shall not forget you and we shall watch with the closest interest as you embark on this new era of your remarkable history."[59]

The British national flag and the old Hong Kong flag were brought down to the playing of the British national anthem. The Chinese national flag and the new Hong Kong flag were hoisted as a band played the Chinese national anthem. President Jiang Zemin announced that from now on, China would resume the exercise of sovereignty over Hong Kong. The Chinese army's Hong Kong garrison marched in for the military handover from the British army garrison.

Following the handover ceremony was an inauguration ceremony for the government of the Hong Kong Special Administrative Region. The British delegation left the center after the handover ceremony and did not attend the inauguration. Secretary of State Madeleine Albright left with the British delegation, but the senior American diplomat, Consul General Richard Boucher, remained for the inauguration.

Tung Chee Hwa was sworn in by Premier Li Peng as the first chief executive of Hong Kong, and then the high officials of Hong Kong were sworn in by Tung. Tung took the floor and said, "As part of China, we will move forward as one inseparable nation with two distinctive systems."

In Beijing, 100,000 people gathered at Tiananmen Square, decorated with thousands of Chinese lanterns to celebrate the occasion. The night sky was lit up with dazzling fireworks.

In Shanghai, about 2,500 people gathered to cheer the handover at Bund Park, set up by the British during the rule of the Nationalist government, where at the gate a notice board was once posted, saying, "No Chinese and dogs allowed." Celebrations were likewise held in the major cities of the country, including Nanjing, Guangzhou, Shenzhen, Fuzhou, and Xiamen.

On the whole, the handover proceeded smoothly according to plan. The only protest that occurred was allowed by the government and organized by the Hong Kong Alliance at midnight on June 30. About 23,000 participated in the protest, including members of the Legislative Council who were elected with Governor Patten's support. The group went to the Legislative Council building. Martin Lee, the leader of the Democratic Party, spoke against the dissolution of the council by the Chinese government. The protest lasted a few hours, then quietly subsided.[60]

It was a sad occasion for the British government to lose the colony. However, the New Territories and some 235 adjacent islands, accounting for 92 percent of the land area of Greater Hong Kong, were on a lease for 99 years, and when the lease was up and not renewed, the British had to withdraw as a matter of normal business practice. The British could be proud of developing Hong Kong into one of the most prosperous ports in Asia. The per capita income of Hong Kong in 1996 was U.S.$23,500, just a little short of that for the United States at U.S.$26,434 and long ago outstripping the British at U.S.$18,700.[61] Hong Kong's prosperity was due to its excellent location for trade and the enterprising ability and energy of the Chinese people, but the British provided the environment and infrastructure for the development to happen.

The British people in Hong Kong fall into two large groups: the businessmen and the civil servants. Most of the businessmen would stay to protect their interests and try to continue with their business activities under the new Chinese regime. Most of the civil servants would go back to England, except those who had been asked by the Chinese authorities to stay.

The Chinese in Hong Kong mostly welcome the end of the colonial rule and the return to the motherland. Some considered the British arrogant but not oppressive, and some are even thankful to the British for their help in bringing Hong Kong to what it is today yet worry that China might not keep its promise to allow Hong Kong to remain as it is. The Chinese people, however, are adaptable. If they adjusted to colonial rule under the British, they can live under the Chinese. After the handover, life likely will remain the same for most people.

China most likely will keep its promise to leave Hong Kong as it is for these reasons: the world's attention is on Hong Kong, the Chinese government wants to make the people in Hong Kong happy, and the successful handover of Hong Kong could set a precedent for the return of Macao and possibly of Taiwan.

The experiment of one country, two systems could have difficulties, but it may succeed because it is not new. For the past 156 years, Hong Kong, a capitalistic community under British rule, has developed a good relationship with China, a Communist country, and the two economies have worked together for mutual benefit.

In the future, Hong Kong under China could have problems but may also start playing a greater role in Asia. Some speculate that Hong Kong may exert great influence on China in pushing the country to a higher level of technology and in moving the country closer to the capitalist system.

Macao

Macao is a port city on the southern China coast, across the Pearl River from Hong Kong. In 1535, Portugal occupied the area, and following a war in 1862, China ceded the port to Portugal. It has become a popular tourist resort with a flourishing gambling and nightclub business.

In 1987, China and Portugal signed an agreement for Portugal to turn over Macao to China in 1999, and the two countries had worked out a Basic Law on the Macao Special Administration Region under China. The agreement and the Basic Law were ratified by the two governments. After the return of Macao to China, the local community would maintain control of its domestic matters. The rights and freedom of the citizens would be guaranteed, and the capitalistic system would remain for 50 years.[62]

Taiwan

Taiwan was named Formosa, "the beautiful island," by Portuguese explorers who came to the island in the sixteenth century. Emperor Qianlong of the Manchu dynasty sent an expeditionary force to Taiwan and established control in 1787–88. China and Japan fought in a war over Korea, Manchuria, and Taiwan in 1894. China lost the naval battle, and by the Treaty of Shimonoseki of 1895, the Korean peninsula was made independent of China, Taiwan, the Pescadores, and the Liaodong peninsula and were ceded to Japan.

Taiwan was under Japanese rule until the end of World War II. China recovered Taiwan, Manchuria, and the Pescadores in accordance with the Cairo Declaration.

Taiwan is about 100 miles from mainland China and 695 miles south of Japan. The island is 240 miles long from north to south and 98 miles wide at the broadest points from east to west.

After the defeat by the Communists on the mainland, Chiang Kaishek managed to retreat to Taiwan with some troops. He dispatched one-fifth of the forces to the offshore islands of Quemoy and Matsu, a few miles from the China coast.

In 1954 and 1958, artillery fire was exchanged between China and Taiwan across the narrow strait. The Nationalists vowed to invade China and regain control of the mainland, but as the years went by, the Nationalist forces grew old, and the ambition to wage a war in China had to be given up. Meanwhile, Taiwan had developed, with U.S. aid, into a prosperous economy. In 1996, the per capita income was in U.S.$12,500.

China developed a policy for regaining Taiwan through peaceful means by a process of starting person-to-person relations through private visits, building up trade and investment connections, and then entering into formal negotiations based on the proposal of one country, two systems.

In 1987, China considered Taiwan as a province, and Taiwan was not allowed to attend the Olympic Games in Los Angeles as an independent country. However, China allowed Taiwan to compete under the name "Chinese Taipei" as part of China. In 1988, China invited sport teams from Taiwan to visit China.

China allowed Taiwan to enter into indirect trade with China through business firms in Hong Kong. This indirect trade grew from U.S.$320 million in 1980, to U.S.$1.1 billion in 1985, and to U.S.$2.7 billion in 1988.[63]

China also encouraged Taiwan to invest in joint ventures through business firms in Hong Kong. Taiwan businessmen could readily see the higher returns to their investments in China than at home. Taiwan businessmen wanted to do more trade and investment in China, and furthermore they wanted to do business directly in China so that they did not have to share the profits with the middlemen in Hong Kong.

In 1990, China announced that if Taiwan should return to China, the one country, two systems policy would apply. China would represent Taiwan in the international community, conduct its foreign relations, and guarantee its security, while Taiwan would maintain its capitalistic economy, manage its domestic affairs, handle its domestic security, and keep its judiciary system.[64]

Based on this assumption, negotiations started in Singapore in 1993. The representative from China was Wang Daohan, the chairman of Mainland's Association for Relations Across the Taiwan Strait. The representative from Taiwan was Koo Chenfu, the chairman of Taiwan's Foundation for Exchanges Across the Strait. They were engaged in business matters, such as trade, shipping, postal service, insurance, notary procedures, repatriation of mainland emigrants to Taiwan, prevention of smuggling, copyrights, youth exchanges, and the protection of Taiwan's business interests in China.[65] When Premier Li Peng was asked about the meeting between Wang and Koo, Li said it was unofficial but could lead to official contacts.[66]

In 1995, a crisis developed over an incident when the United States issued a visa for President Lee Denghui of Taiwan to visit the United States as a private person. Lee was on a trip to Cornell University for a reunion. Lee grew up on a farm, and his father was a tea farmer. He went to the United States to study and earned a PhD in agricultural economics from Cornell.

China lodged a protest against the issuing of the visa to Lee by the United States. As Lee was openly advocating for a prominent role for Taiwan in the international community, the visa amounted to an encouragement for Lee's position. To China, this is a departure from the U.S. agreement with China that only one China exists and that Taiwan is a province of China and should have no role in the international community. Lee, a native of Taiwan, rose rapidly in the Kuomintang government. At age 48, he was a minister of state, at age 55 he was the mayor of Taipei, at age 58 he was the governor of Taiwan, and at age 16 he was the vice president of the Republic of China under Chiang Ching-guo, the son of Chiang Kaishek. Chiang Ching-guo succeeded his father as the president of Taiwan when his father died. In 1988, Lee succeeded Chiang Ching-guo as the president of Taiwan.

On March 23, 1996, Lee ran for the presidency in a direct election by the people. This happened to be the first time that the president was to be elected directly by the people. As the election date approached, China launched a war game in the Formosa Strait involving the army, the navy, and the air force in an amphibious operation within 11 miles off the shore of Taiwan. Two missiles launched from the mainland splashed down perilously close to the island, with one to the northeast of the island and one to the southwest. Premier Li Peng reinstated that only one China existed and that Taiwan had no role in the international community. The war game was to give notice to Taiwan; if Taiwan should go the way of seeking independence, China would have to take drastic measures. The United States alerted its fleet in the area. The carrier *Independence* task force was cruising the area, and the carrier *Nimitz* task force was sailing toward the island. The ships were there to watch the situation and were cautioned not to interfere. In the midst of the turmoil, many Taiwan businessmen took their investments out of the island and reinvested in Australia, Canada, and the United States. The people rushed to use the local currency to buy U.S. dollars. The United States promised favorable treatment for any Taiwanese coming in with a million dollars to invest in a project creating 10 or more jobs, and the Canadian government did the same for any Taiwanese coming in with U.S.$200,000. The crisis was not over, however, and fortunately both China and Taiwan were cautious in their handling of the situation.

Korea

After the Korean War, Chinese troops withdrew. China treated North Korea as its most important ally. The author was in South Korea in May–June 1982 on a lecture trip and was staying on the campus of Chungnam University at Yueseong about two hours by bus from Seoul. One day, the minister of education, a former professor of philosophy, invited him to a meeting. He requested the author to make an inquiry of the Chinese authorities whether he could be invited to China either as an official or as a visiting scholar. The request was transmitted but was refused by China. At that time, North and South Korea were still hostile to each other, and China would not want to get involved in their disputes.

Both South and North Korea are now members of the United Nations. Gradually, their relations became relaxed. People were allowed to travel from one side to the other for home visits. Scholars of the two sides held conferences. Informal exchanges of opinion took place on the unification of Korea. On August 24, 1992, China and South Korea established diplomatic relations, and China supported the unification of the two Koreas.[67] President Roh Tae-woo of South Korea went to China on September 27, 1992, for a four-day state tour. He met President Yang Shangkun, Secretary-General Jiang Zemin, and Premier Li Peng.[68]

Both North and South Korea declared Korea free of nuclear weapons. China also maintains that no nuclear weapons should reside on the Korean peninsula.

On the whole, China's international position improved in the 1990s. This was an opportune time for Deng Xiaoping to retire, and he did.

BASIC PRINCIPLES ON FOREIGN AFFAIRS

In 1992, President Jiang Zemin and Foreign Minister Qian Qichen announced five basic principles on foreign affairs. By the following basic principles, China assumes a new posture in world politics:

1. China and other nations will exhibit mutual respect for sovereignty and territorial integrity. China wants to deal with other countries with respect and does not want to be a world leader or the policeman for the world. The world community is envisioned as a group of nations all treated as equals, whether large or small, strong or weak. It is on this basis of mutual respect that good relations can be formed.

2. China and other nations will exhibit mutual nonaggression. China does not want to invade any country, nor will it allow any aggression against itself by others. Nations can live together without any military threats. With the development of nuclear weapons and high-tech warfare, wars are becoming too costly. The killing of masses of people in wars should be avoided by all means.

3. China and other nations will exhibit noninterference in each other's internal affairs. The colonial days are over. Nations should be left free to manage their own internal affairs as they see fit. No nations or group of nations can force its views, priorities, or values on others, nor can they impose policies or measures to achieve these goals. Nations should be allowed to live their own lives. China would not want to intrude into the affairs of other nations, nor would it allow others to interfere with its own domestic matters.

4. The relations between China and other nations will be conducted on the basis of equality and mutual benefits. China does not want to be treated as a junior partner or a satellite country.

5. China and other nations will coexist peacefully. Nations may differ in values, religion, ideology, institutions, and ways of life, but they could live with one another in peace. Nations need not be uniform in ideology, institutions, religion, ways of life, or types of government. Countries should be left alone to preserve their own ideologies and institutions or make changes on their own initiative.[69]

China wants to make known to the world its stand on these principles and expects other countries to deal with China on a new level.

China has now come to the world scene with a new stance, just as a boy with a different lifestyle has moved into a new neighborhood. It is up to the world to embrace China as an equal, or else put it through a series of trials and tribulations.

NOTES

1. Immanuel C. Y. Hsu, *The Rise of Modern China* (New York: Oxford University Press, 1975), pp. 85–88, 676–688.

2. Harry Harding, *A Fragile Relationship: The United States and China since 1972* (Washington, D.C.: Brookings Institution Press, 1992), p. 64.

3. *Far Eastern Economic Review* 39, no. 12 (1988): 56–57.

4. *Far Eastern Economic Review* 43, no. 3 (1992): 32–34.

5. *Far Eastern Economic Review* 43, no. 13 (1992): 30–31.

6. *Beijing Review* 35, no. 9 (1992): 12.

7. Harding, *A Fragile Relationship*, p. 235.

8. Ibid., p. 29.

9. Hsu, *The Rise of Modern China*, p. 732.

10. Alfred K. Ho, *Developing the Economy of the People's Republic of China* (New York: Praeger, 1982), p. 31.

11. Jonathan D. Spence, *The Search for Modern China* (New York: W. W. Norton, 1990), p. 632.

12. Hsu, *The Rise of Modern China*, p. 743.

13. Immanuel C. Y. Hsu, *China without Mao: The Search for a New Order* (New York: Oxford University Press, 1990), pp. 59–60.

14. Hsu, *The Rise of Modern China*, pp. 811–814.

15. James C. F. Wang, *Contemporary Chinese Politics: An Introduction* (Englewood Cliffs, N.J.: Prentice Hall, 1980), pp. 261–262.

16. Harding, *A Fragile Relationship*, p. 81.

17. Kwan Ha Yim, *China under Deng* (New York: Facts on File, 991), p. 18.

18. Harding, *A Fragile Relationship*, p. 166.

19. *Current History* 87, no. 530 (1988): 241; 89, no. 546 (1990): 244.

20. *Beijing Review* 35, no. 52 (1992): 5–6; *Current History* 89, no. 546 (1990): 241–244; *Kalamazoo Gazette*, May 30, 1993, p. E11.

21. Harding, *A Fragile Relationship*, pp. 190–191; Hsu, *China without Mao*, p. 81.

22. *Beijing Review* 35, no. 43 (1992): 8.

23. *Beijing Review* 36, no. 7 (1993): 12–13.

24. Ibid.

25. *Beijing Review* 36, no. 3 (1993): 12; 36, no. 6 (1993): 3–5; 36, no. 3 (1993): 5.

26. *Beijing Review* 36, no. 6 (1993): 3–5.

27. *Beijing Review* 35, no. 52 (1992): 5.

28. *Kalamazoo Gazette*, April 2, 1993, p. A9.

29. Nicholas D. Kristof, Special to *New York Times*, March 2, 1993, p. 1.

30. *Kalamazoo Gazette*, March 30, 1993, p. E11; Harding, *A Fragile Relationship*, p. 234.

31. *Beijing Review* 36, no. 22 (1993): 5.

32. *Beijing Review* 36, no. 8 (1993): 8–9.

33. *Beijing Review* 36, no. 22 (1993): 6; *Asian Survey* 29, no. 6 (1989): 603.

34. *Beijing Review* 35, no. 37 (1992): 7–15.

35. *Beijing Review* 35, no. 5 (1992): 32; 5, no. 32 (1989): 12.

36. *Beijing Review* 36, no. 11 (1993): 7.

37. *Kalamazoo Gazette*, November 20, 1993, p. A3.

38. *Beijing Review* 41, no. 29 (1998): 8.

39. *New York Times*, June 28, 1998, p. Y1.

40. Ibid., p. Y6.

41. *Kalamazoo Gazette*, June 29, 1998, pp. A1–A2.

42. *New York Times*, July 3, 1998, International edition, p. A9.

43. *Beijing Review* 34, no. 4 (1991): 15–17; Alfred K. Ho, *Developing the Economy of the People's Republic of China* (New York: Praeger, 1982), p. 34.

44. *Beijing Review* 35, no. 41 (1992): 23.

45. Ho, *Developing the Economy of the People's Republic of China*, p. 34.

46. Ibid., p. 35.

47. *Beijing Review* 35, no. 44 (1992): 7–9.

48. *Beijing Review* 35, no. 4 (1992): 7–9.

49. *Beijing Review* 35, no. 14 (1992): 16.

50. *Beijing Review* 35, no. 44 (1992): 7–9.

51. *The New Yorker*, March 5, 1993, p. 94.

52. Kwan, *China under Deng*, p. 187.

53. *The New Yorker*, March 5, 1993, p. 94.

54. Ibid.

55. Ibid., p. 99.

56. *Beijing Review* 36, no. 15 (1993): 10–11.
57. Ibid., pp. 11–12.
58. *Beijing Review* 40, no. 25 (1997): 4–12.
59. *Kalamazoo Gazette,* June 30, 1997, p. 1.
60. *New York Times,* June 30, 1997, International edition, p. A6.
61. *Beijing Review* 36, no. 18 (1993): 1–16.
62. Harding, *A Fragile Relationship*, p. 158.
63. Ibid.
64. Ibid., p. 56.
65. *Beijing Review* 36, no. 17 (1993): 6–7; 36, no. 9 (1993): 4–5.
66. *Beijing Review* 36, no. 15 (1993): 9.
67. *Beijing Review* 35, no. 52 (1992): 9.
68. *Beijing Review* 35, no. 41 (1992): 7.
69. *Beijing Review* 36, no. 14 (1993): 13; 34, no. 14 (1991): 15–17.

CHAPTER 9

Loss of the Leader

On February 19, 1997, Deng Xiaoping died of Parkinson's disease and lung ailments. He was 92 years of age, nearly blind, and deaf. Unlike Mao Zedong, who asked that his body be embalmed and displayed in his mausoleum in Tiananmen Square, Deng asked that his ashes be cast into the sea and that no monuments be built for him.

The public took the news of his death calmly, as it was believed unlikely that major changes in policies would ensue. Everyone was a beneficiary of Deng's policies, and none expected turmoil in the country regarding the succession of leadership, as a system for the transition of power had been put in place.

Jiang Zemin, the state president, head of the Communist Party, and chief of the Military Committee, together with the core of the new collective leadership, had been ordained by Deng eight years earlier and running the government ever since.

The country held a six-day mourning period, and Jiang, at the age of 70, headed the mourning committee. On February 24, more than 100,000 people lined the two-and-a-half-kilometer route from the General Hospital of the People's Liberation Army to the Babaoshan Revolutionary Cemetery watching the hearse carrying Deng's body on the way to its cremation and burial. A grand memorial service was held for Deng at the Great Hall of the People in Beijing on February 25. At 10:00 A.M., whistles on train, ships, warships, and factories throughout China were blown for three minutes while the people everywhere stood in grief and paid their final respects to the great man. Jiang Zemin delivered the eulogy at the memorial service, which was attended by family members and relatives of Deng and the leaders of the country.

Kofi Annan, secretary-general of the United Nations, and heads of governments that had diplomatic relations with China all offered their condolences.

On March 3, 1997, a special report was issued by *Time* magazine on the death of Deng Xiaoping, the paramount leader, with his portrait on the cover. This was the third time he appeared on *Time*'s cover. Earlier he had been twice named Man of the Year by *Time*, the first time in 1979 when he visited the United States and the second time in 1985 for his policies of economic reform.[1]

NOTE

1. *Beijing Review* 36, no. 15 (1993): 8.

Conclusion

Mao Zedong, Zhou Enlai, and Deng Xiaoping, together with other reform leaders, did well in leading China out of difficult times and providing answers to the country's various problems. Their programs were successful.

They owed their success to their knowledge of the Chinese people and Chinese culture. They were keen observers and could benefit by their wide travels in the world, including trips to France, the Soviet Union, the United States, and Japan. They could incorporate the superior ideas and systems of these countries into their programs to modernize China.

Many of them personally suffered great setbacks, and it took strength of will and endurance to survive these dark times.

Usually, they worked hard to push their ideas and programs, but sometimes they had to take a detour and support the consensus of the country. They were not only advocates of ideas and programs but also leaders who shouldered the responsibility of preserving the unity of the country.

It is expected that their programs will be followed in the next few decades.

The reformers as individuals differ in personality, family background, and the degree of success gained or failure suffered. All were motivated by loyalty to the country and a devotion to their fellow men.

They were willing to take on hardship and ready to make the unavoidable sacrifices.

In ideology, they may have borrowed from Marxism, but they were basically Chinese, conducting their lives on the basis of the moral standards of the country and the code of chivalry of the swordsmen.

They worked hard, and together they launched the ship of China on a voyage toward better times.

Glossary of Names

Braun, Otto: Li De (Chinese alias), a representative of the Communist International (Comintern) in China during the 1930s

Chai, Ling: a woman student leader at the Tiananmen Square demonstration

Chen, Yi: a field marshal and an economic planner

Chiang, Kaishek: a leader of the Nationalist Republic of China and the commander-in-chief in the war against Japan and the civil war

Deng, Pufang: Deng Xiaoping's eldest son

Deng, Xiaoping: a leader of the People's Republic of China, a leader of the Communist Party, and the leader of the economic and political reforms

Deng, Yingchao: Zhou Enlai's wife

Fang, Lizhi: a dissent intellectual who found asylum in the American Embassy in Beijing

Gorbachev, Mikhail: the head of the Soviet Union who visited China during the Tiananmen Square incident

He, Long: a field marshal and a founder of the Red Army

He, Zizhen: Mao Zedong's wife during the Long March, since divorced

Hu, Yaobang: a secretary-general of the Communist Party and a successor to Deng Xiaoping, who was deposed

Hua, Guofeng: an army general who succeeded Mao but was replaced by Deng Xiaoping

Jiagqing: Mao Zedong's last wife and a leader of the Gang of Four who was responsible for the Cultural Revolution

Kang, Keqing: Zhu De's wife

Kang, Sheng: the secret service head under Mao Zedong

Lapwood, Ralph: a professor of mathematics at Yenching University at Beijing in the 1940s

Li, Peng: a Soviet trained engineer in electric power and the premier of China

Li, Ruihuan: a carpenter, a mayor of Tianjiin, and the chairman of the National Committee of the Chinese People's Political Consultative Conference

Lin, Biao: a field marshal in the civil war and a successor to Mao; plotted against Mao and failed

Lindsay, Michael: a professor of economics at Yenching University at Beijing in the 1940s and a member of the House of Lords, Great Britain

Liu, Bocheng: a co-commander with Deng Xiaoping during the civil war; known as the one-eyed dragon

Liu, Shaoqi: a secretary-general of the Communist Party, a reformer, and a successor to Mao who was deposed during the Cultural Revolution

Ma, Yinchu: an American-trained economist and advocate for population control

Mao, Zedong: the chairman of the Communist Party and a founder of the People's Republic of China

Peng, Dehuai: a field marshal during the civil war, the commander in the Korean War, and a defense minister who once was critical of Mao

Pu, Zhuolin: Deng Xiaoping's wife

Puyi: the last emperor of China

Qian, Xueshen: an American-trained missiles expert who worked on the atomic bomb in China

Qiao, Shi: the chairman of the Standing Committee of the National People's Congress

Rong, Yiren: an industrialist in charge of foreign investment and joint ventures and the vice president of China

Song, Jian: a Soviet-trained space engineer and the chairman of the Science and Technology Commission

Stuart, John Leighton: the president of Yenching University at Beijing and the American ambassador to China during the coalition talks between the Nationalists and the Communists

Sun, Yatsen: the founder of the Nationalist Republic of China

Wan, Li: a reformer and a chairman of the Standing Committee of the National People's Congress

Wang, Hungwen: a cotton mill worker and a member of the Gang of Four

Wuer, Kaixi: a student leader at the Tiananmen Square demonstration

Yang, Shangkun: a field marshal during the civil war and the president of China

Yao, Wenyuan: a pamphleteer and a member of the Gang of Four

Ye, Jianying: a field marshal and the leader who brought down the Gang of Four

Zhang, Chunqiao: a political journalist and a member of the Gang of Four

Zhang, Guotao: a general at the Long March and a rival of Mao Zedong

Zhao, Ziyang: a reformer, the premier, and the secretary-general of the Communist Party who was deposed following the Tiananmen Square incident.

Zhou, Enlai: a leader of the Communist Party, the premier of China, and a well-respected diplomat

Zhu, De: a field marshal and the commander-in-chief of the Red Army during the Long March and the civil war

Selected Bibliography

Periodicals in Chinese

Biographical Literature (*Zhanzhi Wensue*), Taipei.
People's Daily, Overseas edition (*Renmin Ribao*, Haiwai Ban), Beijing.

Books in Chinese

Central Bureau of Documents. *Selected Works of Deng Xiaoping* (in Chinese, *Deng Xiaoping Wenxuan*). Guangxi: People's Publishing Co., 1983.

Central Literature Editorial Committee. *Selected Essays of Zhou Enlai* (in Chinese, *Zhou Enlai Xuanji*). Beijing: People's Publishing Co., 1983.

Chen Minzhi. *A Study of the Economic Development Strategy of Shanghai* (in Chinese, *Shanghai Jingji Fazhan Zhanlue Yanjiu*). Shanghai: People's Publishing Co., 1985.

Cheng Xiaguo and Nan Dongfeng, eds. *I Am the Son of Chinese People: Life of Deng Xiaoping, 1977–1992* (in Chinese, *Wo Shi Zhongguo Renminde Erzi*). Beijing: China Broadcasting Press, 1993.

Deng Xiaoping. *Essays on Reform and Open Door Policy* (in Chinese, *Lun Gaige Kaifang*). Guangxi: People's Publishing Co., 1989.

Deng Xiaoping. *Developing Socialism with Chinese Characteristics* (in Chinese, *Jianshe You Zhongguo Teshede Shehui Zhuyi*). Beijing: People's Publishing Co., 1987.

Deng Xiaoping. *Essays on Upholding the Four Basic Principles and Opposing Capitalistic Liberalism* (in Chinese, *Lun Jianchi Sixiang JibanYuanze Fandui Zichan Jieji Ziyouhua*). Guangxi: People's Publishing Co., 1989.

Duan Zhenkun, ed. *Tianjin Economic Yearbook, 1989* (in Chinese, *Tianjin Jingji Nienjian, 1989*). Tianjin: Social Science Publishing Co.

Editor of Chinese Periodicals. *Inside Story of Deng Xiaoping's Restoration to Power* (in Chinese, *Deng Xiaoping Fuchu Neimu*). Taipei: Chinese Periodicals Publishers, 1977.

He Lu, Lapwood. *A Good Friend of China* (in Chinese, *Lai Puwu Zhongguode Hao Pengyou*). Beijing: Beijing University Press, 1986.

Hou Houji. *History of Contemporary Chinese Economic Thought* (in Chinese, *Zhongguo Jindai Jingji Sixiang Shigao*). Harbin: People's Publishing Co., 1983.

Hu Hua, ed. *Biographies of Leaders of the Chinese Communist Party* (in Chinese, *Zhonggong Dangshi Renwu Zhuan*). Xian: People's Publishing Co., 1989.

Hu Zhiwei. *Biographies of One Hundred Writers in Communist China* (in Chinese, *Zhongong Wenhua Bairen Zhi*). Taipei: Biographical Literature, 1989.

Hu Zhiwei. *Biography of Jiang Zemin* (in Chinese, *Jiang Zemin Chuanqi*). Taipei: Biographical Literature, 1990.

Huang Chenxia. *Mao's Generals* (in Chinese, *Zhongguo Junren Zhi*). Hong Kong: Research Institute of Contemporary History, 1968.

Li Guanglang. *Mao Zedong and Zhou Enlai* (in Chinese, *Mao Zedong Yu Zhou Enlai*). Hong Kong: Jingu Publishing Co., 1972.

Li Zhen. *The Sound of Bell at Yenching University* (in Chinese, *Yenyuan Zhongsheng*). Tianjin: Union University Press, 1992.

Liu Guoguang. *A Study of the Strategy of China's Economic Development* (in Chinese, *Zhongguo Jingji Fajan Zhanlue Wenti Yanjiu*). Shanghai: People's Publishing Co., 1983.

Ma Hong. *Modern China's Economic Chronology* (in Chinese, *Xiandai Zhongguo Jingji Shidian*). Beijing: Chinese Social Science Publishing Co., 1982.

Sheng Ping. ed. *Who's Who in Communist China* (in Chinese, *Zhongguo Gongdang Renwu Dacidian*). Beijing: New China Book Store, 1991.

Sima Changfeng. *The Story of Deng Xiaoping's Restoration to Power* (in Chinese, *Deng Xiaoping Fuchu Shime*). Hong Kong: Powen Book Co., 1980.

State Statistics Bureau. *Statistical Yearbook of China, 1988* (in Chinese, *Zhongguo Tongji Nienjian*). Beijing: China Statistics Publishing Co., 1988.

State Statistics Bureau. *Statistics on the Prices of China's Trade Commodities* (in Chinese, *Zhongguo Maoyi Wujia Tongji Ziliao*). Beijing: China Statistics Publishing Co., 1984.

Yi Monghong. *History of Modern Chinese Economic Thought* (in Chinese, *Zhongguo Jindai Jingji Sixiang Shi*). Beijing: New China Book Store, 1980.

Zhang Shangzhu, ed. *Introduction to the Criminal Code of the People's Republic of China* (in Chinese, *Zhonghua Renmin Gongheguo Xingha Gailun*). Beijing: Law Publishing Co., 1983.

Zhao Qing, ed. *Sources on China's Modern Economic Thought* (in Chinese, *Zhongguo Jindai Jingji Sixiang Ziliao Xuanji*). Beijing: New China Book Store, 1982.

Periodicals in English

Asian Affairs. London: Royal Society for Asian Affairs.
Asian Affairs: An American View. Washington, D.C.: Heldref Publications.
Asian Outlook. Taipei: Media Enterprise Co.
Asian Survey. Berkeley: University of California Press.
China Quarterly. Abingdon: Bergess Thames.
China Today. Beijing.

Current History. Philadelphia.

The Economist. London.

Editorial Committee of Nankai Institute of Economics. *Journal of Nankai Institute of Economics.* Tianjin: Nankai University Press.

Far Eastern Economic Review. Hong Kong.

Foreign Affairs. New York: Council on Foreign Relations.

Harvard Journal of Asiatic Studies. Cambridge, Mass.: Harvard Yenching Institute.

International Affairs. London: Royal Institute of International Affairs, Cambridge University Press.

Journal of American Oriental Society. Ann Arbor: University of Michigan Press.

Journal of Asian Studies. Ann Arbor, Mich.: Association of Asian Studies, Inc.

Journal of Contemporary Asia. Manila: Russell Press Ltd.

Modern China, An International Quarterly of History and Social Science. Newbury Park, Calif.: Sage Periodical Press.

The Nation. New York: National Enterprise.

The New Leader. New York: American Labor Conference on International Affairs.

The New Pacific. Washington, D.C.

The New Statesman. London: Statesman and Nation Publishing Co.

Political Science Quarterly. New York: Academy of Political Science.

The Society. New Brunswick, N.J.: The State University Press.

World Outlook. Taipei: China Art Printing Work.

World Press Review. New York: Stanley Foundation.

Books in English

Barnett, A. Doak. *China and the Major Powers in East Asia.* Washington, D.C.: Brookings Institution Press, 1977.

Barnett, A. Doak, and Ralph N. Clough. *Modernizing China: Post-Mao Reform and Development.* Boulder, Colo.: Westview Press, 1986.

Berkov, Robert. *Strong Man of China: The Story of Chiang Kaishek.* Boston: Houghton Mifflin, 1938.

Cameron, Nigel, and Brian Brake. *Peking: A Tale of Three Cities.* New York: Harper & Row, 1965.

Camileri, Joseph. *Chinese Foreign Policy: The Maoist Era and Its Aftermath.* Seattle: University of Washington Press, 1980.

Chao, Kang. *Agricultural Production in Communist China 1945–1965.* Milwaukee: University of Wisconsin Press, 1970.

Che, Nuqi. *Beijing Turmoil: More Than Meets the Eye.* Beijing: Foreign Languages Press, 1990.

Chi, Hsisheng. *Politics of Disillusionment in Chinese Communist Party under Deng Xiaoping, 1978–1989.* New York: M. E. Sharpe, 1991.

Chow, Gregory. *The Chinese Economy.* New York: Harper & Row, 1985.

Harding, Harry. *A Fragile Relationship: The United States and China since 1972.* Washington, D.C.: Brookings Institution Press, 1992.

Ho, Alfred K. *Developing the Economy of the People's Republic of China.* New York: Praeger, 1982.

Ho, Alfred K. *Joint Ventures in the People's Republic of China.* New York: Praeger, 1990.

Hsu, Immanuel, C. Y. *China without Mao: The Search for a New Order.* New York: Oxford University Press, 1990.

Hsu, Immanuel, C. Y. *The Rise of Modern China.* New York: Oxford University Press, 1983.

Luo, Shewen, ed. *Through the Moon Gate.* Hong Kong: Oxford University Press, 1986.

Maxwell, Robert, ed. *Deng Xiaoping Speeches and Writings.* New York: Pergamon, 1984.

Party History Research Center. *History of the Chinese Communist Party.* Beijing: Foreign Languages Press, 1991.

Patrich, Hugh, and Henry Rosovsky. *Asian's New Giant.* Washington, D.C.: Brookings Institution Press, 1976.

Perry, Mark. *Eclipse: The Last Days of CIA.* New York: William Morrow, 1992.

Pye, Lucian. *The Dynamics of Chinese Politics.* Cambridge: Oelgeschlager, Gunn & Hain Publishers, 1981.

Quan, Yanchi. *Mao Zedong: Man, Not God.* Beijing: Foreign Languages Press, 1992.

Ryan, William R., and Sam Summerlin. *The China Cloud.* Boston: Little, Brown, 1967.

Salisbury, Harrison E. *The Long March.* New York: Harper & Row, 1985.

Salisbury, Harrison E. *The New Emperors: China in the Era of Mao and Deng.* Boston: Little, Brown, 1992.

Salisbury, Harrison E. *Tiananmen Square Diary: Thirteen Days in June.* Boston: Little, Brown, 1989.

Saur, K. G. *Who's Who in the People's Republic of China.* New York: Wolfgang Barke, 1987.

Schram, Stuart. *Mao Tsetung.* Baltimore: Penguin, 1966.

Shaw, Yuming, ed. *Mainland China: Politics, Economics and Reform.* Boulder, Colo.: Westview Press, 1986.

Simme, Scott, and Bob Nixon. *Tiananmen Square.* Seattle: University of Washington Press, 1989.

Spence, Jonathan D. *The Search for Modern China.* New York: W. W. Norton, 1990.

Su, Wenming. *Economic Readjustment and Reform.* Beijing: Beijing Review, 1982.

Su, Wenming, ed. *Modernization the Chinese Way.* Beijing: Beijing Review, 1983.

Terill, Ross. *China in Our Time.* New York: Simon & Schuster, 1992.

Terill, Ross. *Mao: A Biography.* New York: Harper & Row, 1980.

Uhalley, Stephen, Jr. *Mao Tstung.* New York: New Viewpoints, a Division of Franklin Watts Inc., 1975.

Wang, James C. F. *Contemporary Chinese Politics: An Introduction.* Englewood Cliffs, N.J.: Prentice Hall, 1908.

Weber, Max. *The Religions of China.* New York: Macmillan, 1951.

Xue, Muchiao. *A Study of the Economic Problems of Socialism in China.* Beijing: People's Publishing Co., 1982.

Yi Mu and Mark V. Thompson. *Crisis at Tiananmen Square.* San Francisco: China Books and Periodicals, 1989.

Yim, Kwan Ha, ed. *China under Deng.* New York: Facts on File, 1991.

Yu, Guangyuan. *China's Socialist Modernization.* Beijing: Foreign Languages Press, 1984.

Index

About the Author

ALFRED K. HO is Professor Emeritus in the Economic Department of Western Michigan University, Kalamazoo, Michigan. He is also the author of *Joint Ventures in the People's Republic of China* (Praeger, 1990), *Developing the Economy of the People's Republic of China* (Praeger, 1982), and *The Far East In World Trade* (Praeger, 1967).